THE
GUERRILLAS

By the same author

THE CENTURIANS
THE PRETORIANS
YELLOW FEVER
THE BRONZE DRUMS
SAUVETERRE

Jean Lartéguy THE GUERRILLAS

translated by Stanley Hochman

An NAL Book

The World Publishing Company

NEW YORK / CLEVELAND

WORLD PUBLISHING
TIMES MIRROR

Table
of Contents

Preface / ix

1 / Che Guevara or the Myth / 3

2 / Bolívar or the Flag / 59

3 / "Saint Camilo Torres" / 122

4 / Green Berets, Guerrillas and *Caudillos* / 180

5 / A Sepulcher for Che Guevara / 237

Of course, to avoid unsettling our dried up and pretentious parrots, to avoid upsetting their snobbism, he will have to use their jargon. But I know that he will look for the true theme of his revolutionary action in the great works of Hispanic literature, in Cervantes and maybe in Miguel de Unamuno, who wrote:

You ask me, my good friend, if I know how to incite delirium, vertigo, any madness whatsoever, among these orderly and placid masses that are born, eat, sleep, reproduce themselves, and die. . . . With what collective madness might we imbue these poor masses? With what delirium? . . .

All right then, I do. I believe we might attempt the holy crusade of going to rescue the Sepulcher of Don Quixote from the hands of the university graduates, curates, barbers, dukes, and canons who occupy it. I believe we might undertake a holy crusade to redeem the Sepulcher of the Knight of Madness from the power of the champions of Reason. . . .

Once—do you remember it?—we saw nine or ten young men gather behind a youth who was saying: "Let's commit an outrage!" That is what you and I want: for the people to gather and cry out: "Let's commit an outrage!". . .

Do you not believe, my friend, that there are many solitary souls whose hearts demand some outrage, something to make them burst? Go out and see, then, if you can bring them together and form a squadron, so that we may all set out—for I shall go with them behind you—to redeem the Sepulcher of Don Quixote, whose location, thanks be to God, we do not know. The clear and resplendent star will tell us in good time. . . .

Forward then. And watch out that no graduates, barbers, curates, canons, or dukes disguised as Sanchos gain admittance to the ranks of the holy squadron. No matter if they ask you for islands; what you must do is to expel them as soon as they ask for the itinerary of the march, as soon as they talk to you of a program, as soon as they whisper in your ear, maliciously, asking for the Sepulcher's whereabouts. . . .

Set forth, then! And expel from the sacred squadron those who set themselves to studying the cadence to be followed in the march, its beat and its rhythm. . . .

Those who would convert your squadron into a dance quadrille call themselves and each other poets. They are nothing of the sort. They are anything but poets. They set out for the Sepulcher only through curiosity over what it is like, in search of a new sensation perhaps, or to amuse themselves on the way. Throw them out!

These are the ones who, with their bohemian indulgence, help to perpetuate the cowardice and falsehood and wretchedness that destroy us. When they preach liberty, they have only one kind in mind: the right to dispose of their neighbor's wife. With them everything is a matter of sensuality: they are enamored sensually even of ideas, the great ideas. They are incapable of marrying a great and pure idea and raising a family with it. The most they can do with ideas is to cohabit with them. They take them as mistresses— even for just a night. Throw them out!

Oust from the squadron all the dancers. . . . Oust them before they desert you for a plate of beans. They are cynical philosophers, indulgent, good chaps who understand everything and pardon everything. For whoever understands everything pardons nothing. Such a person has no scruple about selling himself. Since they live in two worlds they can preserve liberty in the other world and enslave themselves in this one. They are at one and the same time aesthetes, and followers of Pérez or López, of Peter or Paul, or whoever.

It is some time since it was said that hunger and love were the two wellsprings of human life. Of low life, they mean, of terrestrial life. The dancers dance only for hunger or for love; hunger of the flesh, and love of the flesh also. . . .

Try to live in a constant vertigo of passion, dominated by any passion whatsoever. Only passionate men create works that are truly enduring and fertile. . . .

You are consumed, my poor friend, by an incessant fever, a thirst for unsoundable and shoreless seas, a hunger for universes, a longing for eternity. . . .

Start out, alone. All other solitary men will walk at your side, even though you do not see them. Each one will think he is alone, but together you will form a holy battalion, the battalion of the sacred, endless crusade.*

---

*Miguel de Unamuno, *The Life of Don Quixote and Sancho,* tr. Anthony Kerrigan, in *Selected Works of Unamuno,* vol. 3 (Princeton, N.J., and London, Princeton University Press, 1967; copyright © 1967 by Bollingen Foundation), pp. 9-16.

Acknowledgments

This book was written in collaboration with my friend Louis Sapin, who with some difficulty tore me from my old Asia—an Asia logical to the point of absurdity, dynamic, swarming with life, heavy with the history of the world—to drag me off to the Latin-American continent—barren though it possesses incredible wealth, exhausted without having tried anything great, intoxicated by liberty but under the heel of several anachronistic and intolerable oligarchies. The ghost of that old madman, Don Quixote, wanders in its deserts and its jungles, its *altiplanos* and its mountain ranges, accompanied only by his Sancho Panza, a toothless, drunken, taciturn Indian—who hates him.

J.L.

Paris, October, 1967

THE
GUERRILLAS

Che Guevara or the Myth 1

This is the story of a seven-month journalistic tour of the Latin American continent and of a search—the search for the Argentine doctor Ernesto Guevara de la Serna, known as "Che," who mysteriously disappeared in Cuba on March 14, 1965. I had chosen him as the clue to this continent on which I was setting foot for the first time. Above all, I had chosen him because he was becoming a myth and I have always been more beguiled by myths than by ideas. These days, when we overfat, overreasonable men of the West are being suffocated by comfort and boredom, myths seem to me even more important than men.

I never found this small man who was both delicate and robust, ironic and naïve, courageous, obstinate, ambitious—but easily subject to despair—this doctor who from childhood on had been floored by terrible attacks of asthma and, who, unable to treat himself, had decided to use violence and disorder to cure the world of its misery. I never met up with this "vagabond of the revolution" who was made of flesh and blood, who was shaken by fits of coughing, and who may no longer exist in human form. Somehow I cannot convince myself that it was really he who was displayed—preserved in formaldehyde and stretched on a plank— in a laundry room in Vallegrande, Bolivia. On the other hand, everywhere I went I sensed, close by and inevitable, a type of revolution that resembled him. Like him it was naïve and cruel, more romantic and generous than realistic, more anarchist than Marxist, and, above all, more Hispanic.

At times it was difficult for me, a Latin of non-Hispanic origin, to understand what could make twenty-year-olds born within the Latin American oligarchy join the guerrillas in order to destroy that oligarchy—sometimes with the secret complicity of their parents—or to understand what could lead a priest like Camilo Torres to join a guerrilla front and die there with the scarcely disguised authorization of his bishop.

At the same time, everything here brought me back to that hard reality, the continuing war in Vietnam, more than six thousand miles away across the Pacific.

In a Vietnam training camp several years ago, with his colonel present, a lieutenant of the Green Berets, part of the U.S. Special Forces, was talking to me in a French restaurant in Danang: "After Vietnam, we, too, will have our Algeria. It will be Latin America. We often think about it." The lieutenant had the close-cropped haircut, lean face, ready manner, and camouflage uniform of a French parachutist. He was involved in the same war they had been in, a new kind of war imposed by the enemy: a war of hand-to-hand combat, of jungle fighting, and of the containment of minorities hostile to the Vietnamese.

Perhaps it was the Algerian wine we were served, wine from

the slopes of Harrach, that kept reminding me how useless it is to try to stem certain currents of history when they have swelled like deep-sea waves to their utmost strength. Each wave and each revolution ends by rolling gently onto a beach and licking at the feet of those they wanted to drown. One had only to wait, to be able to wait.

Nevertheless, a few days after these reflections, I came across the following statement by Robert Kennedy, who believed that a revolution in Latin America was inevitable and that all the United States could do was to make it as painless as possible. A year later President Johnson seemed to be replying to him when in the course of a visit to a camp of GIs stationed in Korea, he declared, "Don't forget that there are only two hundred million of us in a world of three billion. They want what we've got and we're not going to give it to them."

That was when I decided on this trip and this investigation. I did not actually leave until two years later. Then in seven months I touched every fever spot in the hemisphere, from Watts in Los Angeles, where there had just been violent racial outbreaks, to the Bolivian *altiplano*. In the Mexican states of Sonora and Chihuahua the population was offering armed resistance to the *pistoleros* hired by political chieftains of the Institutional Revolutionary Party who were stealing their land. In Chihuahua, the regional capital, I was told about the handful of students who had attempted to capture the Madero police station in emulation of Fidel Castro's attack on the Moncada barracks. They, too, had failed. By refusing them a public trial, the Mexican government had robbed them of a platform from which they would have been able to address the entire nation. But the people would not have listened to them. Radio, television, and the press were too carefully controlled, and, given the fact that a million people had died in the Revolution, nobody wanted a civil war.

In Mexico City other rebellious students with whom I spoke accused the current regime, which still calls itself revolutionary, of being nothing more than a juicy plum for the enrichment of professional politicians. "Behind them," they told me, "swarm the shady businessmen and the representatives of the big American banks." But these students were forgetting that the Mexico of Zapata and Pancho Villa was finally enjoying peace and stability. Compared with the other countries of Latin America, it was still the best thing going. Though the revolution there may be dead, the regime still lives off its memory and is forced to respect a certain number of taboos. Mexico refuses to have a real army, is opposed to all foreign intervention in the national affairs of a country, and, even though it is quite close to the United States, recognizes Fidel Castro's government.

In Guatemala, the country of the six hundred colonels, there was fighting in the streets. Assassination attempts and kidnappings were everyday affairs. As in almost all countries on this continent, the university was a rebel citadel. The children of the large landholders, of the colonels, of the politicians, were the ones directing the fight against the abusive and anachronistic privileges enjoyed by their families. But the guerrilla fronts of La Sierra de las Minas were in complete turmoil. The pro-Chinese Trotskyites of Yon Sosa and the orthodox communists and Castroites of César Montes—all operating in an atmosphere of mad courage, provocation, romanticism, and disorder—had wasted their time and energy fighting one another. Finally, the White Hand, a terrorist organization close to the army and supported by the parties of the extreme right, was born. It ended strife between them by liquidating rebels in areas where they created a danger—not those in bands operating in deserted regions where they had no support from the *campesinos*, but those in the cities, where they were aided by an entire segment of the population. While the whites and the mestizos slaughtered one another, the Indians from the mountains looked on indifferently and drank themselves into a stupor as they dreamed of their dead gods. At the university, the Christian-Socialists clearly carried the day against the Marxists, but their theories were every bit as revolutionary.

In Nicaragua, the Somoza clan—with the support of their private militias, their straw men, and their American advisers— were organizing the election of one of their own, General "Tachito" Somoza, to the presidency of the republic. I was to be present during these elections—the most fraudulent I have ever witnessed—and would be able to count both the votes and the corpses of the opposition. The Communists and the Castroites had not participated in the struggle. It was the Christian-Socialists who had borne the brunt of it all.

But, a few months later, the National Guard fell into an ambush in the Matagalpa region and lost twenty-eight men. This time the guerrillas belonged to a Sandinoist Front, which Havana claimed as its own.

In Costa Rica revolutionaries made little headway, for that country was then a haven of peace, with a policy of no dictators, whether of the left or of the right. Well before the advent of Fidel Castro barracks had been converted into schools and museums.

In Cuba, of course, the one country in which guerrillas had successfully made and won their war, Fidel Castro's army is considerably larger than Batista's had been—two hundred thousand men out of a total population of seven million. It is by far the strongest in Latin America. The Russians not only furnish arms and instructors, but also pay for its upkeep. Its official purpose: to defend Cuba against any attack originating abroad. Because a serious attack could come only from the United States, this army would appear to be of small use, since the United States, in return for the missile withdrawal, has committed itself not to attempt any military action against Cuba. In point of fact, however, the Cuban army is the main support of the revolution. It is in charge of the training of all Latin-American guerrillas and of the Cuban commandos, who may one day be called upon to back them up.

In Panama I met Green Berets from Vietnam solidly installed in the Southern Command and in La Escuela de las Américas. They too were busy training—training the cadres of all the Latin-

American armies. They had instructed twenty-two thousand officers. But above all they were ready to intervene at any point on the continent in small "sticks" of seven men apiece whenever insurgency suddenly turned serious. They all spoke Spanish fluently and they knew how to give instruction in the most up-to-date techniques of guerrilla and counterinsurgency warfare. They had gotten their first lessons in Vietnam.

The Latin-American guerrillas were making every effort to equal the accomplishments of the Vietcong on the Plain of Joncs or the High Plateaus, but their lack of discipline, their Hispanic self-importance, their rejection of all authority over them, made them an easy mark for the Panamanian specialists. Nevertheless, the guerrillas were beginning to learn how to keep their mouths shut—and how to fight.

Vietnam remains an example for all these Latin-American countries, but which of them would agree to become another Vietnam? For so Che Guevara had urged in one of his mysterious messages that came from nowhere and, as always, just in time to reinforce one of Fidel Castro's speeches:

We cannot imagine, we have no right to imagine, that liberty will be won without a fight. These battles will not be simple street encounters in which stones are used against tear gas, nor peaceful general strikes. Nor will they be the struggle of an enraged people destroying the repressive structure of the ruling oligarchies in a matter of two or three days. The struggle will be long and hard, and the battle lines will spring up in the guerrilla retreats, in the cities, in the homes of the combatants—where the forces of repression will look for easy victims in their families—in the massacred rural populations, in the villages and cities destroyed by enemy bombardments. . . . We must carry the war wherever the enemy is to be found—in his home, his places of entertainment. It will be a total war. The enemy must not have a moment of respite, a moment of calm, either outside or inside his encampments. We must attack him wherever he is, make him feel like a hunted beast wherever he goes. When this happens his morale will begin to deteriorate. He will become even more monstrous and the signs of his decadence will appear. . . .

A vast and ambitious program!

To fight such a war requires absolute discipline and also great humility in the leader as well as in his men. In Vietnam, children are trained for weeks, sometimes for months, to walk with equally spaced steps. Then one day they are sent to an American base to shine shoes. They walk and count the distances between each shed, each store of weapons, and each sandbag embankment.

The women who wash the GIs' laundry also walk with an equal step and count the steps that separate a command post from the guard defending it. The information is sent to the city, where other people meticulously collate it and eventually draw up a complete plan of the base. This plan is constantly being updated. It is sent off into the jungle, where it is turned into an exact model in which commandos in their turn will train for weeks or months. Everything is worked out to the last second. And then one day there will be an attack in which nothing is left to chance.

We are far from this sort of thing in Latin America. We are actually in another world—a less efficient world, but one considerably more reassuring because it is closer to our own. There is no lack of courage on this continent; but egoism, love of the fine gesture, quixotism, the appeal of lofty language, a taste for disorder, and a certain humanity all paralyze this courage. And above all the notion of self-importance. All the revolutionaries dream of being *libertadores* of their continent—from Fidel Castro, chained to his island, to Che Guevara, to the twenty-year-old student who adorns himself with the title of *comandante* and parades around the University of Caracas in full uniform. I remember a conversation with a former guerrilla who had been captured by the army but who had nevertheless been able to escape and flee to Mexico, thanks to his family's powerful connections.

"We don't want our revolt to be only national," he said. "We want it to spread to every country. We want to revive Bolívar's dream and set up a United States of Latin America within a new socialist structure. But we don't want anything to do with Marx, or Mao, or the Vietnamese. The truth of the matter is that we are the only real revolutionaries, the only ones able to think out in a new way the kind of revolution our countries need. We are the only ones who can bring the United States to its knees. When we have finished here we will come to liberate you Europeans, you Frenchmen too. You have become too materialistic, too skeptical, too disillusioned. You live in the moldy ruins of your old 1789 revolution. We will bring you fresh blood and new ideas. Yes, the new world revolution will come from us."

Like his Spanish ancestors, the conquistadores, this young man believed that everything was possible, that Mexico could be conquered by three hundred students and Peru by a hundred guerrillas. He wasn't at all concerned with realities, the complex economics, the general feelings of either the people in the cities or those in the country. These people would most often prefer even a slow evolutionary process to a revolution that they would bear the brunt of and which, as in Mexico, would only replace an old oligarchy, growing tolerant out of lassitude, with one that was more dynamic and thus more greedy. He merely ignored the fact that Yankee imperialism was considerably more solid than the kingdoms of the Aztecs or the Incas had been. Though Americans were not bringing new ideas, they were contaminating the peoples of the world with a certain way of life that was rapidly gaining ground everywhere and threatening to win this race with revolution.

I talked to him about Marx, about Mao Tse-tung, about Vietnam. It all bored him, but he tried not to let me see. When I mentioned Unamuno, his face lit up.

In Panama—in this state that is no state, that has for currency the American dollar, that has been patched together from bits and pieces by the United States, that lives off the canal and the troops that guard it—there is more and more irritation with those who only yesterday were "good allies." Today they are openly called the troops of a foreign occupation army. The capital, Panama City, or even the city of Colón at the other end of the canal, is nothing but a string of stores in which cameras and transistors are sold cheaply. Every bank in the world has set up there. Every kind of traffic is current—arms, women, drugs. On some islands that have been turned into penitentiaries, marihuana is raised—perhaps to improve the salaries of the police. I remember a narrow street of wooden houses where for five dollars a twelve-year-old boy offered me his sister, who was barely two years older than he was, while from every window on the street heavy-bosomed matrons and dark-complexioned gentlemen followed the negotiation indifferently. A few hundred yards away from all this colorful filth that smelled of spices and sweat are the fences, the green lawns, the white houses, the barbecue clubs, and the shining automobiles of the American soldiers who guard the canal—and keep an eye on all Central and South America. With them live the officials who administer the canal, as well as those other officials—those who belong to information agencies that weave their webs and arrange for the overthrow of governments.

But in the *fincas* of the David region and in the surrounding sierras men practice with pistols, carbines, Lewis guns, and grenade launchers—sometimes as their *alcades* and priests look on. For the most part they are not communists but nationalists. The Panamanians have already rebelled in 1959 and 1964 over a question of flags. These remarkable merchants will do so again, in spite of their taste for commerce and their distaste for losing all that money. They can no longer bear the idea that their territory is split in two by the U.S. Canal Zone.

At the foot of the statue of Ferdinand de Lesseps and his friends on the Plaza de Francia, which has conserved all its colonial charm, I spoke with Father Herrera, who was for a long time the priest of the city's most important parish. His face was square, his skin copper-colored, and his shoulders broad. There must certainly have been Indian blood in his veins. He was not wearing a soutane, but was dressed as a government employee. A cross gleamed on his black tie.

"The canal has turned us and our country into an American colony, and all the countries in Latin America look on us as a colony even if they too have been fairly well colonized. The trouble is that we have no currency, no economic independence. We got $250,000 for the canal when it was dug. Today its annual rental is $1,900,000. But that in no way makes up for our discomfort at having the Americans on our soil. Their presence has led to an increase in prostitution, smuggling, and traffic in drugs. We cannot rely on American good will. Violence is the only thing that will free us of this evil. But Panama has no military tradition, and it is extremely difficult to form a guerrilla front because our country is very small and the Americans occupy all of it. There are fifty thousand Americans here. They know the whole country like the palm of their hand, and the National Guard—the only force here, Panama's only army—is completely under their control. They have created enormous confusion in Panama, making the people believe that all those who are nationalists are also communists because they oppose the Americans. I have several times been accused of being a communist, not only by the Americans but also by the authorities who work for them. My ecclesiastical superiors sent me to Canada to study the social sciences because they know that I am motivated not by Communism but by true Christianity."

Father Herrera was only saying out loud what many Panamanians were repeating under their breath.

Some of them, such as former President Arnulfo Arias, who was elected with a great majority and twice thrown out of office by the Americans, told me the same thing in different terms. This thoroughly unusual man of action, this cynical popular orator with a truly magnetic power over the crowds, begins his speeches with "Quiet down, you foolish people!" It's hard to see him as a communist. During the war he was even accused of being a fascist, a not entirely unjustified charge. But he was mainly anti-Yankee.

The Spanish writer Salvador de Madariaga, spokesman and defender of Hispanism, used the following terms to define the Monroe Doctrine, which under new interpretations still tends to make Latin America into a private hunting preserve for the United States:

I only know two things about the Monroe Doctrine: the first is that no American I have met knows what it is; the second is that no American I have met will allow anybody to lay a finger on it. This being the case, I conclude that the Monroe Doctrine is not a doctrine but a dogma, since it has the two characteristics by which dogma is recognized. But when I inspect the matter more closely, I become aware that we are dealing with not one dogma but two: the dogma of the infallibility of the President of the United States, and the dogma of the immaculate conception of United States foreign policy.

On visiting a number of Latin-American countries in 1960, Madariaga observed that violent anti-Americanism had already won over all the elites, especially the university elites.

Now though the Latin-American continent may be the scene of a proliferation of colonels and armies whose special function is to originate coups d'etat or to prevent those not of their making, it is first and foremost the chosen land of the *licenciado*, of the professor and the doctor. University men are often heads of state. While the military men often allow themselves to be impressed by the force, the organization, and the efficiency of the United States, the *licenciado*, in the name of his culture, his Hispanic past, and the language he speaks, cannot prevent himself from detesting the *gringos* even when his interests coincide with theirs. The reaction is almost visceral. Madariaga sees this anti-Americanism as being born of a "feeling of wounded pride and injustice suffered." However, the Spanish writer also notes that it is extremely convenient to throw the blame for one's own faults on the United States, to make it responsible for a laziness, a changeability, an egoism that marks not only the ruling classes but the common people as well.

Seven years later I was able to see that this feeling had merely deepened. The *gringos* are hated even by those who serve them. More than ever, North Americans are identified with all forms of exploitation and oppression. They are considered the mainstay of all the most unpopular *caudillos*—in the past, of Trujillo and Batista; now, of the Somozas and "Papa" Duvalier. Indeed, it is this anti-American sentiment which has persuaded many that revolution is the only course that will preserve any national identity. In my search for a definition of this revolutionary response, I was led again and again to Cuba. The man most talked about, sometimes as a kind of Robin Hood, sometimes as a cynical killer, was the little Argentine doctor Ernesto Guevara. He had been nicknamed Che because like many Argentines he had the habit of sowing his sentences with that interjection.

Che Guevara—after having been one of the twelve survivors of the expedition of the *Granma*, the yacht fitted out by Castro to transport his small troop from Mexico to the Cuban coast, after having been one of the historic leaders of the Sierra Maestra and one of Cuba's most controversial ministers—had disappeared from the scene under mysterious circumstances. He was said to be dead. Suddenly he was reborn everywhere—the new omnipresent Lazarus, the human symbol of violent revolution against American imperialism and the governments that either collaborated or came to terms with it.

In order to determine the exact state of the Latin-American revolution I searched everywhere for Che. In Latin America, a continent where there's no such thing as a secret, anybody can be got in touch with. Everything happens in an atmosphere of fraternal indiscretion, of complete negligence of the most elementary precautions necessary for an underground struggle.

Che was not in Colombia, into which, according to certain

newspapers, he was said to have slipped disguised as a priest and then gone on to take over command of the guerrilla fronts in Santander and Huila. Nor was he in Peru—neither in Lima, nor in the Valle de la Concepción, where an old, destroyed guerrilla stronghold was being reborn from its ashes. Neither was he in the guerrilla bases in Guatemala, nor in the Sierra de las Minas, where friends of his were said to be searching for his grave. A Guatemalan newspaper reported:

> Between forty and fifty graves were desecrated in the northwest of Guatemala within a few days. The peasants of the region say this macabre task was the work of guerrillas in the Rebel Armed Forces (FAR), who are said to be searching for the body of Che. . . .
> The story is that Che had recently come to Guatemala to prepare for the return of ex-president Jacobo Arbenz, who has taken refuge in Cuba. He is said to have been killed during the course of an encounter between the army and his guards. The latter then hid his body to prevent the government from learning of this death and using the information for propaganda purposes. But the corpse had been so well hidden that the guerrillas could not manage to find it again, and hence their search.

In the above instance the account gave evidence of wild flights of fantasy. César Montes, the young leader of the "Castroite" guerrillas, had never so much as seen Che. He would, however, have had great need of his advice, for things were going badly in his guerrilla front since the discreet arrival of the Green Berets. On his part, the political leader of the rebellion told us that Che never set foot in Guatemala after the overthrow of Arbenz.

"Besides," he told us, "we may admire Fidel Castro, but we have no need of either his or his lieutenant's advice."

The Rio de Janeiro newspaper *The Globe* affirmed that the Brazilian deputy Altino Machado had been informed by a Catholic priest, Father Pelegrini, that Che Guevara was in the Amazon *selva* near the frontier between Brazil and Bolivia. Father Pelegrini administered a parish that straddled the border. He affirmed that he had seen Che with a group of twenty men who were transporting arms into Bolivia.

According to this newspaper, Che Guevara had already been in the zone when as a doctor he studied local cases of leprosy during a period that coincided with the 1952 Bolivian revolution.

I talked then to a man named Rojo del Río, an Argentine who, like his fellow countryman Che, was one of the combatants of the Sierra Maestra. He agreed that Che might well be in Bolivia.

Rojo del Río, with his sun-baked face, looks like an Estremadura peasant. Once the Cuban revolution was over, this former pilot withdrew to San José, the capital of Costa Rica, where he works at the airport, refueling the planes.

Like Che, Rojo del Río had also been a sort of vagabond of the revolution. He had set himself the goal of "destroying the oligarchy and overthrowing the tyrants." With his old crate, he flew in arms for the small group of combatants in the Sierra Maestra. During a difficult landing early in 1958 his plane crashed. He shared the hard life of Castro's guerrillas and went everywhere with his fifty-millimeter machine gun and gave instruction on its use. It was with this weapon that Castro and his men confronted the Batista troops in their first pitched battles.

When asked why he had left Cuba, Rojo del Río replied, "I didn't fight the revolution for Fidel Castro. I have never fought any revolution for any man, for any *caudillo*. I've always fought against tyranny, whether it comes from the right or the left. . . . When I no longer liked how things were going in Cuba after Fidel's victory, I asked for permission to leave and came to Costa Rica. The revolution can only be carried out by the will of the people, and when the people give a man their confidence, he has no right to deceive them. I didn't leave Cuba as a traitor. The comrades from the Sierra and I said good-bye like good friends. But we no longer saw eye to eye."

Rojo del Río told us how he had met Che. "I saw him for the first time in Naranjo. He was dirty and exhausted after a long retreat following a skirmish with the men under Comandante Mosquera, one of the rare tough nuts in Batista's army.

"The Cubans who were with him told me that he was a good fellow, somebody you could count on. As for me, I found the man very calculating, very deliberate, the kind who can plan way ahead. . . . He had a very strong personality and many people followed him. He was already known as a communist—not a run-of-the-mill communist, but somebody who really knows his doctrine. Those around him were also more or less communists. . . .

"Everybody used to boast and talk about the big things he did as a guerrilla. Not Che. He never talked about himself. He just smiled his little contemptuous smile. People thought he was conceited.

"As soon as possible I returned to Costa Rica to get myself some other weapons. But in the meantime the revolution had triumphed and I was called back to Cuba to join the general staff, which was in La Cabaña at the time. Che was in charge of things there. That was on January 8, 1959.

"In La Cabaña they were shooting all the important people who had been with Batista and the leaders of his army. Che was watching from a balcony. The *comandante* who had just been executed was taking his time about dying because the job had been badly done. One of them in the squad asked Che:

" 'Shall we give him the coup de grace?'

" 'No,' he answered, 'the *pobrecito*, he's already lost enough blood.'

"And he was left to die there writhing on the ground. Che wasn't the sentimental type.

"Camilo Cienfuegos* and his plane had just been lost. Later

---

* The son of Spanish civil war refugees, who were themselves communists, Camilo Cienfuegos was as popular as Castro in Cuba—in fact, the military preferred Cienfuegos. He was given the responsibility for the formation of army political commissars at the artillery school around the time of his disappearance, a mystery never fully explained.

they said he'd been done away with. That's not true; it was an accident. I was in the air force then, and I looked for him up and down the coast. Sick of all this talk of Camilo, Che said to me, 'Look, let me know when you've found him, but only *when* you've found him.' Then he went off to bed. No, he really didn't seem terribly wrought up about finding his comrade. There had always been a certain amount of rivalry between the two *comandantes*. Each was jealous of the fame of the other. Che didn't exactly turn up his nose at fame.

"One time, the two of us had been talking and we realized that though each of us had always done what he could for democracy, afterwards democracy had always been prostituted.

"That day there was a television broadcast showing Fidel Castro talking to an enormous crowd. The three of us—Che, who was smoking a big cigar; his fiancée, Aleida March (who later became his wife); and I—were watching. Suddenly he said, '*Los coños!* How did that man ever manage to get that crowd into his pocket, a crowd that under other circumstances would be applauding Batista?'

"The next time we met, Ernesto was president of the national bank. Imagine a man like him, a doctor, becoming a banker! There's quite a difference between handling millions of pesos and practicing medicine. The whole thing was completely nuts. It's true that when it came to nuts, Che knew his way around. People said that he'd studied psychiatry. He didn't do too well as a minister. Luckily he had adjutants, and these adjutants were capable people. The last time I saw him was in August, 1959, when we were getting up an expedition to overthrow Trujillo in Santo Domingo. I was part of the general staff. But the landing that was supposed to be made at Constanza fell through. Then I left.

"Just like everybody else, you ask me if Che is dead. Personally, I don't think so. There were often disagreements between Fidel and him. Maybe Che took pro-Chinese and anti-Soviet stands, maybe he deviated from the revolutionary plan, but Fidel would never have killed him—or had him killed—just for that kind of disagreement. True enough, he was just like Ernesto in never giving a damn about what anybody would think. But. . . .

"Myself, I think that Che began to see the revolution in a different way than Fidel did and that he left Cuba to carry out his revolution the way he saw it.

"You know, Che was just as thirsty for fame as Fidel was. Even though they liked each other well enough, they were jealous of each other. But Fidel knew how to get along with the crowds better. There was something about him. Che was a more deliberate type, more intelligent. I remember how in the Sierra we used to talk with Che about how we could continue the revolution on the continent and get rid of the oligarchies. Ernesto used to tell me:

" 'I've got a plan. If someday I have to carry the revolution to the continent, I'll set myself up in the *selva*, at the frontier between Bolivia and Brazil. I know the spot pretty well because I was there as a doctor. From there it's possible to put pressure on three or four countries [Argentina, Bolivia, Paraguay, and Brazil], and by taking advantage of the frontiers and the forest you can work things so as never to be caught.'

"If Che is anywhere, he's there."

This statement by Rojo del Río was made to us in February, 1967, three months before the guerrillas went into action in Bolivia and before Régis Debray was arrested.

It was also said that in October, 1966, Che had been seen in Buenos Aires and in Misiones, where he was raised. According to this story he had been hidden by members of Peronist unions who afterward wrote a report on his stay and his activities. This report was sent to General Perón in Madrid. In April, 1966, shortly after Che's disappearance, Perón had also received a copy of his last book, *Socialism and Man in Cuba*. In the signed dedication Guevara made honorable amends. He admitted to having been mistaken about the personality and goals of the former leader of the *justicialistas* and begged him to accept both his apologies and this token of his admiration.

Was Che sincere or was he already preparing for his return to Argentina? If he wanted to go into hiding in an Argentine city, he could only do it with the help of the Peronists. Fidel Castro had also understood the importance of Perón and his movement. On several occasions he had asked the former Argentine to come to Cuba, where in accordance with his own choice he would be treated either as an honored guest or as a head of state. Perón had refused. He was in no way eager to become a hostage and a guarantor of the Castroite revolution just when the communists in Argentina were trying to set up cells within the Peronist unions.

It was also said that Che had died in Santo Domingo. Driven from Cuba, repudiated by Castro, the story went, he had looked for a heroic death by fighting against the U.S. Marines. He was killed the second day of the uprising. A Cuban officer said he had seen his body before it was thrown into a common grave that was afterward covered with quicklime.

"No, he wasn't killed in Santo Domingo," I was told in certain exile circles, "but the Castroites want everybody to think so. Actually, Che was liquidated by Castro to please the Russians, or because the Russians demanded it. You only have to remember all his statements against the Soviets during the course of his trip around the world. He accused Moscow of falling in with American imperialists by picking a quarrel with Peking, and he said that Soviet communism was becoming self-serving and bourgeois and was using only the phraseology of socialism."

Even at the time it was difficult to accept this hypothesis. It seemed unlikely that Fidel Castro would liquidate one of his old comrades to please the Russians when he was trying, on the contrary, to free himself of their influence as much as possible. This crime would have made him their hostage forever. He would never have afterwards had the gall to get up on a platform on May 1, 1967, and have himself filmed and photographed patting the head of his victim's daughter while thousands of demonstrators waved large photos of Che Guevara. To prove that Che was alive he would not have distributed to the reporters present other photos showing the Argentine doctor shaving, or beardless, wearing a shirt and tie, and smoking a big cigar—the veritable robot-portrait of a South American plutocrat. (However, this photograph would seem to be a counterfeit. I was given the name of the man in Cuba who posed in Che's place.) He would never himself have read Che's farewell letter or his last message in which he asked all Latin-American revolutionists to create two, three Vietnams to help the Vietnamese people in their struggle.

Since we are dealing with politics, I am not going to talk about honor or sentiment, but only of evidence. It would have been too dangerous for Fidel Castro to play games with Che's body if one day the world was to learn that he had stooped to assassination. The special services of the East would have been able to uncover the secret if they had decided to get rid of this much too undocile leader of the Cuban revolution, and the United States would scarcely have held off—at least in the beginning, when Che's alleged apparitions were still bothersome for it.

I was also told that Che was in one of the East bloc countries—Poland, among others. Hadn't he left all his personal belongings with the Polish ambassador before disappearing? He was also said to be in Russia or in Vietnam—he was everywhere, he was nowhere.

For their part, the *gusanos*—the earthworms, as the opponents of the regime are called by the Castroites—sang a paraphrase of an old French tune: "I'm looking for my Titine, Titine, my Titine, I'm looking for my Titine and I can't find it." Titine was the nickname given to Che.

In Havana, on August 1, the Organization of Latin-American Solidarity, the OLAS, elected as its honorary president "Comandante Ernesto Che Guevara, who is carrying on the revolutionary struggle in Latin America." Another brick contributed to the construction of the myth of the wandering revolutionary. At the time of his disappearance, Che was not very well liked in Cuba. He was contemptuously known as "the Argentine." He had been rejected by the country; by Fidel's inner circle, the *pandilla*, where everything of consequence is decided; and by that revolution which he wanted to be even more absolute and which seemed to be settling down and gently sinking into plans for increasing the production of sugar, the planting of citrus groves, the raising of livestock.

"I'll never be one of those revolutionaries sagely seated behind a desk," Che used to say.

His father, Ernesto Guevara Lynch, also used to repeat, "Before I sit down behind a desk, I'll blow my brains out."

But two years later, Castro reared up in harness, shipped the bearded Marx-Lenin-Engels trio off to the prop room—and replaced their pictures by the more attractive one of Bolívar—no longer hesitated to tell the Russians off, and with great difficulty set up an organism to direct the Latin-American revolution. Not able to name himself leader, he pushed Che to the fore. Che or his ghost? But except for some Cuban officials who spread through the corridors of the Habana Libre promising that Che would reappear, nobody believed in it. The mystery grew thick enough to become embarrassing to Cuba. It was to become even more so when the U.S. services began in their turn to make use of Ernesto Guevara's ghost.

I went to Cuba, but I only stayed there a week. I was not able to see Fidel Castro, who was busy with the sugarcane harvest, the *zafra*, the planting of tomatoes in the Oriente province, the artificial insemination of cows, the raising of rabbits, goats, or crocodiles, the preparation of a speech, his troubles with the Russians, and his guerrilla training camps. Wasn't he simultaneously President of the Cabinet, Supreme Commander of the Army, Secretary General of the Communist Party, Minister of the Institute of Agrarian Reform, *líder máximo*, and *orientador de la revolución*! Having confidence in no one but himself, having lost the greater part of his technicians and cadres, he more and more resembled an overworked large landowner who wants to do everything himself.

The situation is hardly designed to bring order to a country already disordered by nature. The Russian, Czech, and Polish technicians had all been thrown into a state of complete confusion by their confrontation with this communism *à la* Caribbean, this tropical Marxism. However, they did not quite dare to reproach the regime too openly for its cult of personality. Hadn't they put up with Stalin for so long? To top it all off, they were sometimes treated as bunglers and bumblers by men who had known American efficiency, and there were even some remarks about the poor quality of the products they supplied without charge. They weren't loved and they knew it. They did not feel quite comfortable, and they were unable to shake the notion that since a revolution was a serious and important thing, it was, by definition, morose.

At the same time, Fidel Castro was making every effort to show himself to an entire continent as a new Bolívar who was simultaneously a liberator, a reunifier, and a prophet. It was a difficult job, for he had to be careful not to irritate the touchy national sensibilities that exist even in parties claiming to be international. He too often pointed out his own adventure in the Sierra Maestra as an example to be followed, and he wanted all the other countries to make the same kind of revolution he had made. Therefore, given the hesitations he felt, he pushed the image of Che to the fore.

It was too much, much too much for one man, even when he has the overflowing vitality and the cast-iron strength of Castro. I could very well understand that he would be unable to receive me and answer my embarrassing questions. It was known that unlike hundreds of reporters invited to Havana each year I had not come to participate in the general adulation which the *líder máximo* finds somewhat too much to his taste. Too bad, since there was a vacancy to be filled in his court circle—the vacancy left by Che, who mocked at Fidel and often deflated his self-complacency.

And so I was only a tourist in Cuba. I went swimming at the beaches, I watched parades of the militia and the *becadas* (scholarship holders) in gray skirts and white middies singing something or other about sugarcane or about agriculture. There were far too many armed men, and especially women, in uniform to suit me. At some times I seemed to be in the middle of an entrenched camp, and at others I felt as though I were surrounded by the cast of a musical comedy. It wasn't at all unpleasant.

I was simultaneously surprised, seduced, and irritated by the Cuban revolution. I was surprised because it was the first socialist country that did not reek of sadness and boredom. I was seduced by that marvelous insouciance of Fidel and his followers, who at the expense of the hypnotized Russians were treating themselves to a deluxe revolution considerably above their own means. For example, they were building (but only for a few members of the agricultural cooperatives) some lovely five-room villas for which they imported from the other end of the world the beams and metal girders lacking in Cuba. When they ran out of credit, they just forgot about the other *campesinos* in their shacks. The country children living in the villas of the rich Cubans who had gone into exile were veritable kings who happily bounced on the couches and ripped into the paintings. They were just uninteresting daubs; the government itself had sold the good paintings to American antique dealers for sums far below their actual worth. That was during the time when they had to get their hands on dollars, the Russians not having as yet taken over from the Americans the upkeep of Cuba—that fascinating, spendthrift, seductive, and ungrateful lady of the Caribbean. But the children were happy and learning to read. The fight against illiteracy, the enthusiasm, the disorder, and the joy with which it was carried on—as well as its results—are all to Fidel Castro's credit.

Everything was gently going to rack and ruin in this tropical heat. The movie houses were showing good European films and they were filled to the rafters. They had been empty when attempts had been made to have the Cubans ingest some Russian footage. There were some good painters in Cuba who were free to be as abstract as they wanted, and there were also novelists and poets capable of writing without constant reference to Marxism-Leninism. The girls were beautiful and wore cosmetics. Nobody was dying of hunger, provided he was not a foreigner exchanging one dollar for one peso (actually, the dollar was worth between six and seven pesos); life was quite tolerable in this Cuban festival, in spite of the fact that the gears creaked perceptibly.

One day I was riding along in an old Ford taxi that had been patched together like something in a Rube Goldberg cartoon. After having first made sure that I was neither a Russian, Czech or Polish guest of the government, the driver asked me:

"Do you know what Martí* would do if he came back to life in today's Cuba?"

"No, what?"

"He'd drop dead all over again."

"Why?"

"Because of all the *tonterías* committed by Fidel. You know, of course, that he's mad?"

I was afterward told that all the taxi drivers were reactionaries because they longed for the days of the American tourists. For

---

* José Martí, 1853–1895. National hero of Cuba, fervent patriot, good poet, philosopher, journalist, and professor. This son of a Spanish sergeant-major died bravely in the battle of Boca de dos Rios, where with saber drawn, he charged the army in which his father had so long served. It was said to have been his first time on horseback.

that matter, all city people, especially those in Havana, were suspected of being reactionaries and extremely critical of the regime, whereas on the other hand the people in rural areas followed Castro.

Castro did not like the cities and stayed in them for as short a time as possible. Because of this it was difficult to get to see him if you weren't a member of the *pandilla*. You had to beaver after him up and down the island.

I was irritated too. The little world surrounding Castro behaved as though it were the center of the universe and knew everything better than anybody else did—Marxism, economics, agriculture, or guerrilla warfare. You had to do as Fidel did: flatter those he liked, denigrate those he no longer liked, listen without yawning to his interminable speeches, and pretend to seriously believe him when he promised that by 1970 Cuba would be growing more citrus fruits than the United States, that sugar production would reach ten million tons, that there would be no more taxes, no more money, etc.—that Cuba would become the terrestrial socialist paradise all men dream about soulfully but in which very few manage to believe, especially those who already live in a socialist country. Even though they were on *tú* terms with him and seemed to treat him familiarly, these men behaved toward Castro as courtiers would toward a monarch. He was a free-and-easy monarch, but very thin-skinned and subject to frequent attacks of bad humor. It is hard to imagine Che in his company.

Fidel Castro managed his country as though it was his personal property, the *finca* Castro, and with the insouciance of a Spanish grandee he often preferred the sumptuous to the useful. He also settled old scores. He confided to one professor of agronomy that he hated the thorny acacia that had ripped at his flesh and his clothes when he was with the guerrillas. As a result, he had it torn up everywhere, thereby adding to the already catastrophic problem of soil erosion. The great King Xerxes had the sea beaten with iron rods when a storm carried off his bridge of boats over the Hellespont.

It's not that I reproach him for it, but except for the red flags, the slogans replacing the advertising, and the sixty-one thousand political prisoners rotting in jail, all this just doesn't seem very Leninist. I was told that if I really wanted to understand Fidel's thinking about the revolution I ought to read a book just published by a young French intellectual, Régis Debray.

The book, it appeared, was dazzling and luminous. It was also naïve and written in a prose style difficult to ingest, full of Marxist jargon—barbarous and pretentious words of the kind thought necessary to esoteric revolutionary doctrines.

It was supposed to be a guerrilla manual and I can just see a guerrilla leader or political commissar trying to explain to *campesinos* and Indians elliptical formulas like, "The guerrilla force is to the jacquerie what Marx is to Sorel," or, "The working class transfer of the model of activist cells and proletarian unions on the peasant reality. . . ."

It was carefully pointed out to me that Régis Debray had only supplied the pen for Fidel's thinking. The book apparently contains some of Che Guevara's ideas as well.

I had also read Che Guevara's *Guerrilla Warfare*. He was mistaken on a number of points: He believed that the fate of world revolution was dependent on what happened in the Sierra Maestra, but at least he was both comprehensible and unpretentious, and gave combatants some practical advice.

I set out in search of Régis Debray. At the French Embassy, nobody had seen him for three months; he had not come to pick up his salary. A philosophy professor assigned to the University of Havana, Debray was doing his tour of military service under a cooperative agreement and was often seen with Castro. Debray had just left on his Bolivian adventure. If he was a soldier like the others, before transforming himself into a journalist to go off and investigate the guerrillas in Bolivia, he should have sought permission from his hierarchical superior, in this case the military attaché. This was pointed out to me by other *coopérants*. But I suppose that he was not subjected to the laws of the common herd. He had his family on the right, his opinions on the left, and he was a friend of Fidel. One night, however, I was told he was in my hotel, the Habana Libre, but it could not have been he.

Our paths were to cross again in Bolivia. We were both looking for the same man, Che Guevara, but not with the same purpose and not for the same reasons. I thought that I could be a spectator of this revolution without participating in it. Every nation has to settle its own problems. But I nevertheless hoped that all Spanish-speaking America would one day form a single nation, a fact that would have permitted the Argentine Guevara to participate in it and even lead it. I wanted to question Che about his adventures, his dreams, to find out what he wanted to do with his revolution.

One morning, knowing that I would not see Fidel Castro, understanding that my direct questions about Che, the guerrilla schools, and the army had made me unwelcome, I went back to Mexico City in a plane crammed full of *gusanos* (on the flight in, the plane had been empty). These people were fleeing their country with nothing more than forty-four pounds of luggage. Even their watches and wedding rings had been taken away from them. But at least they were allowed to leave. It was still better than China, Russia, or East Germany. When the plane was in the air, the women took out their rosaries. Beside me a man still in his youth let out a long sigh of relief.

Four months later, the OLAS, that famous congress of revolutionary movements, opened in Havana. Things didn't go too well in this "seminar" on guerrilla activity, for the star performers were missing. It was supposed to have consisted of guerrilla leaders who had accepted the Castroite theses. Only one came; the others had been detained in their fronts, arrested by the police, killed by the army, or more often yet had merely ceased to be in agreement with the theses of Fidel Castro. These theses are relatively simple. They can be found in Régis Debray's *Revolution in the Revolution?* The revolution can only be brought about by violence—which is probably true. The men and regimes who will govern Latin America will be born from the guerrilla movements. This is somewhat more difficult to believe.

The Venezuelan Communist party had been excluded "for not having followed the principles that must guide the revolutionary movement"; Yugoslavia had been excluded "for having refused unconditional support for the Vietnamese stance in the face of American aggression." The Communist parties of Argentina and Brazil were not participating either. The Colombians had come only after having expressed all sorts of reservations and manifested their solidarity with the Venezuelans. (Since the congress they have broken with Castro.) The leader of the Chilean Communist party, Luis Corvalan, used *Pravda* as a platform and attacked every aspect of the Castroite guerrilla theses. In other words, their Russian silent partners also took a dim view of the matter.

Castroism was trying to spread to Latin America as an original revolutionary movement, refusing all allegiance to either Russian or Chinese theses. It wanted to draw its inspiration from a single experience realized under exceptional conditions—the experience of Fidel Castro. However, what had followed—for example, the intrusion of the *barbudos* into economics and agriculture—had brought about some strange results. In addition, all the more reasonable revolutionists knew that the U.S.S.R. could not afford the luxury of maintaining another such spendthrift revolution on the South American continent. Entrammeled by his desires, his ambitions, his contradictions, and his needs, Fidel Castro saw his popularity losing ground. Even in the universities on the continent, as I myself saw, though the students continued to look on him as a kind of historical figure, they refused to submit to his orders and they questioned the validity of his theses. He was neither a prophet nor a pope, though he did excommunicate people left and right.

Imprisoned by his island and more so by his legend—a picturesque character, muddleheaded, talkative, romantic, and impulsive—Fidel, in spite of his talent, his shrewdness, his generosity, his grip on the crowds, in spite of his successes and because of defeats most often ascribable to his character and personality, sensed that his great dream was more and more escaping him. He would not be able to be Bolívar. To console himself, he should have remembered that Bolívar too had failed —not because of his faults but because of the special character of the Spanish-Americans—and that before he died he said some bitter things.

Today, for the South American continent Castro is merely a Cuban revolutionary who pulled off his own revolution. Che surpasses him in influence as soon as one leaves Cuba, where the Argentine, since his disappearance, has been forgotten, subjected to more than a little criticism, and even detested.

It was this ghost of Che that the Russians feared the most— the ghost of this mysterious and intransigent revolutionary who refused to come to terms with reality, this Spaniard, this son of Iberian anarchist federations who claimed that everything great comes about through disorder. The Russians have means of calming Castro—for example, by refusing him fuel oil. Cuba has no available source of power and would not be able to survive three days without oil. No more oil, then no more electricity, and everything grinds to a halt. But the Russians could do nothing against Che. A myth has no need of diesel oil, nor does a guerrilla. A machine pistol is enough. It was therefore no longer Castro but Che Guevara who was in accord with the basic temperament of the Latin peoples, with the type of revolt they wanted. Che's tormented and ironic personality was closer to that of Bolívar.

Fidel Castro himself, after a period of apparent tranquillity and revolutionary conformism, suddenly dusted off the theses dear to the Argentine doctor, even though they were difficult to apply. He decided to abolish money, to return to barter, to do away with taxes. "What do the notions of cost or price mean in an economy such as ours? The law of value has sense in a capitalist society where the economy is founded on profit. It has no sense in a socialist society. . . . We are already about to do away with financial bookkeeping in exchanges between socialist enterprises. . . ."

It might have been Che speaking: "We must do away with notions of income return, of individual profit, if we are to achieve a socialist conscience. . . ."

But Fidel Castro's great tragedy is to have been born a Cuban. (Actually, in his origins, his character, and his bearing, he is essentially Galician.) He does not really belong to the Latin-American continent. Cuba has been terribly marked for the better, but also for the worse, by the proximity of the United States.

Castro freed himself from the American grip, but in order to maintain this liberty he had to a large extent to transfer title to it by placing himself under the protection of the Soviet Union. He is dependent on the Russians, dependent on their good will and their assistance just as formerly Batista was dependent on the United States. The Latin-American continent cannot accept as leader, as someone who will help it conquer its liberty, a man who is not only bound to another country but who is also a foreigner to the continent.

Che was an Argentine; he was free of all ties. Long before Castro did, he kept his distance from the Soviet Union. He did not want power. One day he said in French—for like all Argentines of good family he spoke French—"Les honneurs, ça m'emmerde." The only thing that interested him was the revolution.

Ernesto Guevara de la Serna (Serna was his mother's maiden

name) was born in 1928 in the city of Rosario in Argentina. However, he was merely born there. His mother, Celia, was one of the richest and most beautiful heiresses of Buenos Aires. She owned not only some of those immense *estancias* that spread for thousands of acres but also thousands of cattle. Argentina was then rich from all the frozen or canned meat that she was exporting to a famished Europe, and money was being thrown out of windows.

Celia de la Serna belonged neither to the world of money nor to the world of grasping emigrants, but to the only real aristocracy in the country, the aristocracy that came from Spain with the first conquerors. One of her ancestors had been the last Spanish viceroy of Peru.

She could therefore flout all the conventions to which "petty people and parvenus" are so strongly attached. It is Celia de la Serna, nicknamed La Rebelde (the rebel), who launched the fashion of boyish bobs, who was the first to have a bank account; her parents were both dead and she refused to have chaperones or guardians. She herself chose as her *novio* the man who pleased her, a certain Ernesto Guevara Lynch who dropped his studies in architecture because they no longer amused him and because, he felt, they would be of no earthly use. He too belonged to this insouciant aristocracy of the "wild" 1920s, an aristocracy that unknowingly ruined itself. His mother was Irish and his grandparents took part in the California gold rush. But they evidently never brought much of the gold back to Argentina. Guevara Lynch was a handsome young man, nonchalant, with just the right touch of insolence and bohemianism necessary to win La Rebelde.

At first their life together was a never-ending festival. They spent without counting, selling farmlands, *estancias*, and herds whenever the end of the month found them short of money. A brilliant court, nonconformist but penniless, followed in their train. They amused themselves by scandalizing Buenos Aires with their pranks. One day they noticed that they had little money left, and Ernesto Guevara Lynch decided to tempt fortune, just as his ancestors had once done in California. However, he went off not to conquer gold, but maté, the national drink of the Argentines. It grows on bushes ten to twenty feet high in the distant province of Misiones, a stretch of land between Paraguay and Brazil. Its shiny leaves are gathered like tea leaves and set to dry. Of course Ernesto and Celia took their friends along with them, and the joyous group started off on this adventure as though to a new kind of party. Ernesto wanted to go on living like a great gentleman in that jungle where huntsmen, down-and-outers, and smugglers of arms, alcohol, and drugs were busy slaughtering one another. He created a village, Puerto Guevara, for himself and his friends. But he never shipped off the piles of *yerba maté* and they rotted on the ground. Having gone to make a fortune, he ended by ruining both himself and his wife.

Celia was expecting a child. She gave birth at Rosario, the city closest to the Guevara concession. Even at that it was more than six hundred miles away, as the crow flies.

The baby was named Ernesto after his father; they nicknamed him Ernestito, or "Teté." Soon after his birth he became subject to serious respiratory ailments, to attacks of asthma which were so intense that his life was constantly in danger. In addition, he was sickly, frail, and very nervous. The Guevaras decided to leave Puerto Guevara, the maté, and the province of Misiones. There were no doctors, the climate was particularly unhealthy, and they had also had enough of playing at being pioneers. They went to live in Buenos Aires in the De las Flores section, but Teté could not stand the climate there either. Finally they settled in the very aristocratic resort of Alta Gracia at the foot of the sierras. Other children were born: Celia and Ana María, who in contrast to their father finished their architectural studies; Roberto, who was to be a lawyer; and finally Juan Martín, who after having tried various careers is now a wine salesman.

Ernesto Guevara Lynch, financially ruined or close to it, could not settle down and go to work. He managed some properties; he let it be bruited about that he was an architect, and he even opened an office. But what took most of his time was politics. He was one of the sixty signers of the Declaration of Alta Gracia, which was thought revolutionary at the time because it was a kind of manifesto supporting the underdeveloped nations. Of his wife, Celia, it was whispered darkly that she might very well be a "socialist."

When the Spanish Civil War broke out, the Guevaras, as non-conformist as ever and still rebels against their milieu, declared themselves for the Republicans, whereas in their immediate society prayers were offered and collections taken up for Franco's armies.

Since Teté was enjoying better health, the Guevaras once more returned to Buenos Aires. The only property they had left was a building in the northern section of the city, away from the best neighborhoods.

The couple no longer got along. It had been money that had permitted them, amid the parties and the hordes of friends, to overlook their mutually difficult, provocative, and proud personalities. They decided to separate without getting a divorce. To save appearances they officially lived under the same roof, but Ernesto Guevara Lynch spent most of his time in a bachelor apartment where he moved for good after his wife's death in 1965. Celia decided to look after the children, and she went at it with passion and enthusiasm, as well as with remarkable incompetence. She was always on the lookout for new educational ideas or methods, and she applied them successively and incorrectly. The house was so badly run that at times the family ate off newspapers doing duty as tablecloths. The pantry was often empty.

Ernestito was always dressed in sweaters and pullovers, his neck swathed in a scarf. He was a silent, reserved child, but he did not lack a sense of humor, and he adjusted quite well to the bohemian life of his parents—to their scenes, their outbursts, their fits of laughter, and their arguments. But when things got too bad, he would seek refuge with his Aunt Beatriz, a woman he venerated. It was to her that he most often wrote.

From his parents, who had spent so much of it, he learned a contempt for money. After they lost their money, they were dropped by most of their friends of their own class; the house, however—a large ramshackle affair, but warm and welcoming— was always filled with people of all sorts, especially young people.

Colonel Perón was in power, and though his government finally paid attention to the *descamisados*, though it instituted social reforms, it did so at the expense of freedom. The army was everywhere. Soldiers replaced professors in the schools, freedom of the press was suppressed, and just as in Germany and Italy, both men and women under the age of fifty were subject to military service. Processions and parades followed one on the heels of the other, and at all of them a strange woman presided alongside Perón: Evita Duarte, a former radio announcer who had more personality than Perón did, and who knew how to speak to the masses of the poor. The oligarchy jeered at her, but once she was Perón's wife she braved all the taboos of good society. She was rather like Celia de la Serna, but she came from the people—some even said from the gutter.

Perón hardly hid his sympathy for the Italian fascists or the German Nazis. He even managed to slip some anti-Semitic measures in among two or three social laws. In some Buenos Aires families it was considered good form for relatives to greet one another with a Hitler-like raised-arm salute.

This was hardly the case in the Guevara home. Here, all this perpetual pomp was definitely frowned on. Ernestito was never to become a Peronist.

In 1947, at the age of nineteen, he began his medical studies, having decided that the best way to overcome his illness was to learn to know it well. He became an allergist, because it seemed to him that more than anything else asthma was an allergy, a psychological malady of the anxious and the anguished. His negligence of dress was such that his friends nicknamed him Chancho, the pig. He never cared about dress, not even when he became a minister. It was in other areas that this mocking, insolent son of aristocrats strove for elegance.

That same year he decided to break the cocoon in which his mother—for reasons of health—forced him to live. He took a bicycle trip around Argentina. He had only a few pesos, but under the guise of offering free publicity, he was able to borrow an auxiliary motor. He set off and lived from day to day, working in hospitals where he was given shelter, but sometimes sleeping in barns or out in the open. Once he teamed up with a tramp who had a fine gift of gab (Che had none), and the latter passed the hat "for this valorous recordholder of the Argentine cycling tour." Ernesto watched him with a mixture of embarrassment and amusement. Later the tramp pocketed half the receipts, gave Che the other half, and the two separated. In the course of Che's trip his motor gave out, and he pedaled his way to the end of his several-thousand-kilometer periplus.

Teté Guevara proved that he could lead a normal life despite his asthma. But he was a bit too quick in believing that he had overcome his malady; even more violent attacks followed. He had to interrupt his studies and return to Alta Gracia, where the climate was so good for him.

In Alta Gracia and in the neighboring sierras of Córdoba, he ran into some former friends of his family. The vagabond was tempted. He fell in love with a young girl of his class, Chichina Ferreyra. Well, not quite of his class; *she* was still rich. Nor was she a rebel like Celia de la Serna. Ernestito was reminded of his pennilessness sharply enough for him to remember it all his life and hate money. He was made to understand just how dirty and shabby he was. Getting the message, he broke with the girl and returned to Buenos Aires. He felt that a woman's love was not worth the sacrifice of his liberty, and his heart speedily mended.

Teté's thoughts were now concentrated on traveling still farther away to see what was going on elsewhere. He went on a motorcycle trip with one of his friends, a medical student like himself. Their goal was to travel overland to the United States. When they ran into motor trouble in the Andes, they tried to continue their trip as stowaways on a ship bound for Panama. They were discovered and tossed overboard while the ship was still in port. And so there they were in Ecuador, treating lepers. They continued their journey by raft and finally reached Venezuela, where Colonal Delgado Chalbaud and Colonel Pérez Jiménez had just seized power in a putsch.

The two students had introductions to other students and professors, all of whom belonged to Rómulo Betancourt's Acción Democrática party, which had just been outlawed. To justify this measure in the usual way, it was said that Betancourt was "lousy," in other words, that he was a communist. Che and his friend wandered around the streets looking for these other friends, but the latter were in hiding. Eventually, the police spotted these ragamuffins, followed them, and realized that they were trying to get in touch with "communists." As a result, they too were baptised "communists," arrested, and expelled.

Ernestito never threw off this label. He had not claimed it, but he didn't reject it. The curious thing about Che was the way he never backtracked. Beginning with his first voyage, he became a voyager forever more. In the same way, he became a communist in Venezuela. The further he went in life, the more he detached himself from his past. He was thrust forward by a heady indifference to self, which may be the mark of fated destinies.*

To his comrades in the school of medicine, Che seemed above all a "vagabond anarchist" bereft of precise political ideas— a beatnik, before it became fashionable. He had their detachment,

---

* "Mon Ami Che Guevara," an account gathered by Georges Dupoy, *Le Figaro*, October 13, 1967.

their anticonformism, and their taste for provocation. But he was also a remarkable student in all areas—even in medicine.

Ernestito left for the United States, accompanying some horses being shipped by plane. And so there he was in Florida. He put his hand to everything—washed dishes, sold newspapers, worked in bars—but above all he watched and listened. He forgot to renew his permit and the immigration police arrested him.

The United States is unlike the rest of the American Hemisphere, where vagabonds always have some chance of darting between visas and frontiers. It's a serious, efficient world in which fantasy, contempt for laws and conventions, everything that Che loved, is not tolerated. Che was never to like the United States, or Switzerland. These countries were much too orderly for him, and order and organization frightened him. He felt that they destroyed man and lulled his sense of rebellion.

For the first time Ernestito, his heart in a rage, had to call on his family for help; they sent the money necessary to repatriate him.

A doctor of medicine, he then did his tour of military service and completed it as a medical lieutenant. He might have gotten discharged because of his asthma, but he did not want to. It was as though this refusal to be considered as an invalid could exorcise his illness. Next he became a wandering doctor and devoted himself to the lepers, because they were even more handicapped than he was and had been completely rejected by society. From the medical point of view, weren't the lepers the symbol of the disinherited of the Third World? In 1953 he was a doctor in a leper hospital in Venezuela, in 1954 in Guatemala. But at the same time he was busy with politics of the only kind that interested him, the kind that fed not on theories but on action. He traveled up and down Latin America, looking everywhere and in every country for that last form of modern, romantic adventure: revolution. His ideas about the world were already a mixture of cynicism and idealism. He believed that in the name of an ideal one could demand everything of people—for example, the renunciation of profit, money, and comfort. He believed that it was possible to create the ideal world dreamed of by Plato and the French Encyclopedists. But he also believed that to obtain it one must never hesitate to use a machine pistol and to make blood flow. At the same time, this idealist, who must have been boring and pontificating, retained a sense of humor. He mocked others as well as himself, and his repartee was often cruel. He went to Peru, where he took part in the rebellion of the naval base at Callao, and to Honduras, where nobody knows just what he did.

One of his friends, the Argentine lawyer Ricardo Rojo, fetched him from a leper colony (leper colonies have always been excellent refuges for professional revolutionaries) and took him to meet Colonel Arbenz, to whom Che became an adviser. Che suggested that he align himself with the peasants and create popular militias, but Arbenz refused. He tried to organize a political police, but it was too late.

Arbenz collapsed under the onslaughts of Castillo Armas, but also because of his own fault; he showed a total lack of character. Che swore to himself that he would henceforth be more careful about choosing the men he served, for—alas!—in Latin countries men are always more important than causes. Che is still remembered in Guatemala. Yon Sosa's Trotskyite-Chinese group was to accuse Castro of having liquidated Che to please the Russians.

After Arbenz' collapse Ernesto Guevara took refuge in the Argentine embassy, which saw to it that they were taken to the Mexican frontier. In the warm and humid climate of Yucatán, Che was suddenly once more laid low by his illness. Hilda Gadea, a Peruvian nurse, tended him with such devotion that she saved his life even though his case had been given up as hopeless. He married her out of gratitude, despite the fact that she was ten years older than he. Later he was to divorce her to marry his second wife, Aleida March, whom he met in the guerrilla forces and who bore him three children. Hilda Gadea was the sister of another revolutionary, Comandante Ricardo Gadea Acosta, a Peruvian guerrilla leader who was to be arrested in April, 1966.

Che went off in search of another revolution. It was then that he met Raúl Castro, who introduced him to his brother Fidel. Che Guevara wrote:

I met him [Fidel Castro] on one of those cold nights in Mexico, and I remember that our first discussion was on international politics. A few hours later that same night—at dawn—I was one of the future expeditionaries.*

Guevara still had no official papers. He was born for the clandestine life and was comfortable in it, but Mexico is a country in which foreigners are checked up on. He was imprisoned, and Fidel Castro had to spend time and money getting him out. The Cuban lawyer was hypnotized by the Argentine doctor, who brought him what many men of action lack—political ideas, clear reasoning powers, and a wider knowledge of the world. Later it would be said in the sierra: "What Che says today, Castro will say tomorrow."

After his defeat at Moncada and his subsequent liberation from prison, Fidel Castro had gone to Mexico to organize a small army with which to disembark in Cuba and overthrow the dictator Batista. Batista was hated by everyone, with the exception of the few thousand men who served him and the American gangsters in Las Vegas who worked hand in glove with him. As a result, after the first difficult days following the *Granma* disembarkment, Fidel was everywhere aided and supported by the population.

It was a Spanish Republican, Colonel Alberto Bayo, who

* Ernesto Che Guevara, *Reminiscences of the Cuban Revolutionary War* (New York: Monthly Review Press, Inc., 1968), p. 37.

trained his small group (eighty-two men). Bayo immediately found Guevara to be his most talented pupil. He was the one who had the sharpest sense of combat and of guerrilla warfare. Unfortunately, Che was asthmatic, and in difficult moments his breath was often so choked off that he could not go forward. But this difficulty strengthened his character and developed his self-discipline.

Che, who had very few illusions about the chances for success of the adventure proposed by Castro, wrote:

My almost immediate impression . . . was of the possibility for victory, which I had seen as very doubtful when I joined the rebel commander. I had been linked to him, from the outset, by a tie of romantic adventurous sympathy, and by the conviction that it would be worth dying on a foreign beach for such a pure ideal.*

The story of the guerrillas and the Sierra Maestra is one of the most beautiful and astonishing adventures of our time. Twelve men, the *Granma* survivors, along with the volunteers that joined them, routed a modern army of several thousand men. Che Guevara commanded one of the columns that took Santa Clara and brought on the collapse of the Batista regime.

At the beginning of the Sierra Maestra adventure, Che had to make an irrevocable choice. He was no longer to be a doctor; he would be a revolutionary. He wrote:

As the troop's doctor, it was my job to treat the men's blisters. I think I remember my last patient on that day. He was Humberto Lamotte, and as it turned out, it was his last day on earth. I can still see his tired and anxious face as he moved from our primitive clinic toward his post, carrying the shoes he could not wear.

Comrade Montané and I were leaning against a tree, talking about our respective children; we were eating our meager rations—

---

* *Ibid.*, p. 38.

half a sausage and two crackers—when we heard a shot. In a matter of seconds a hurricane of bullets—or at least this is what it seemed to my anxious mind during that trial by fire—rained on the troop of eighty-two men. My rifle was not of the best—I had deliberately asked for it because a long asthma attack during the crossing had left me in a deplorable state and I did not want to waste a good weapon. I do not know exactly when or how things happened; the memories are already hazy. I do remember that during the cross fire, Almeida—Captain in those days—came to ask for orders, but there was no longer anyone there to give them. As I found out later, Fidel tried in vain to regroup his men in the nearby cane field, which could be reached simply by crossing a small clearing. The surprise attack had been too massive, the bullets too abundant. Almeida went back to take charge of his group. At that moment a comrade dropped a cartridge box at my feet. I pointed questioningly to it and the man answered me with a face I remember perfectly, for the anguish it reflected seemed to say, "It's too late for bullets," and he immediately left along the path through the cane field (he was later murdered by Batista's thugs). This was perhaps the first time I was faced with the dilemma of choosing between my dedication to medicine and my duty as a revolutionary soldier. At my feet were a pack full of medicines and a cartridge box; together, they were too heavy to carry. I chose the cartridge box, leaving behind the medicine pack, and crossed the clearing which separated me from the cane field.*

During all that period, Che was courageous but in no way boastful. He was often afraid, and he admitted it. He mocked at his own weaknesses and awkwardnesses. His rifle jammed when he wanted to fire. An attack of asthma obliged him to fall behind his comrades and he got lost. But he was forceful when it was a question of eliminating those who were lukewarm or soft.

When the Castro government was established in Havana Che was given high responsibilities for which he was unprepared.

---

* *Ibid.*, pp. 43–44.

There is a story they tell about how he became president of the National Bank, a position that was to make him master over the Cuban economy.

Fidel had reassembled his entire team of original *barbudos* and was trying to see how he could make use of their talents. When he asked, "Which of you is an economist?" Che, who was exhausted and half asleep, thought Fidel had said, "Which of you is a communist?" He raised a finger . . . and was made the financial boss of Cuba. He was the man who most hated money and whose anarchist leanings convinced him that it should be eliminated. The story is probably a joke, but it is characteristic of the way in which Cubans imagined the Oriente rebels handing out offices and functions.

At that time Che Guevara wore the black beret and the little silver star of the *comandante*, the highest rank among the guerrillas. It was to remain the highest rank in the Cuban army because Fidel too is a *comandante* and of course nobody can be higher than he is. Che wore a not very full beard, a long moustache, and extremely long hair. His face in repose was handsome: the features were firm and well fashioned. But when he smiled, his face was transformed into the face of a child who would always be the willing tool of Satan. Then too his eyes were always half-closed. They were mocking, ironic, sparkling with intelligence. Unfortunately, Che, the frenzied idealist, applied his mordant irony only to men and not to ideas, although they too can do with a bit of mockery.

Once in power, Che was caught up in a continuous series of errors. Brilliant as a theoretician, remarkable as a guerrilla leader, he nevertheless had neither the qualities of an administrator nor the skill and sense of compromise of a real politician. However, he maintained his influence over Fidel Castro, and it was he who persuaded him that a humanistic revolution is impossible in the twentieth century. "In order to succeed and to last," he told him, "a revolution must put every aspect of the structure into question and create the irrevocable. It can therefore only be brutal, irreversible, and Marxist."

In *Man and Socialism in Cuba*, Che wrote: "There can be no question of profitability nor of individual material profit. . . ." Like all communist idealists, it is man himself that he wanted to change. He wanted to make him altruistic, and disinterested, without applying any means of pressure other than persuasion.

He eliminated from the Cuban economy all those officials who were not Marxists, and in this way he cut himself off from the best economists remaining in Cuba. He signed the Cuban banknotes with a simple "Che." Like a good anarchist, he refused to file his legal signature with the International Monetary Fund.

After extensive trips abroad, Che became Minister of Industry. An exponent of rapid and brutal solutions, he socialized Cuba in one stroke. He established control over foreign exchange and a monopoly over imports and exports; he did away with private enterprise, nationalizing and regrouping all businesses. He wanted to industrialize the island even though it lacked both power sources and raw materials and was essentially most fit for sugar production and agriculture. It was a catastrophe from which Cuba has not yet recovered. Castro was begged to get rid of Che as quickly as possible; but Fidel could not, or dared not. He still believed in him. Eventually, the overwhelming facts had to be faced and Che was eased out.

To take away some of his prerogatives, another ministry was set up alongside the Ministry of Industry, a ministry over the sugar industry. Instead of the unrewarded Stakhanovism that Che advocated, they began to offer prizes to the workers and to the sugarcane cutters: not quite money, but free vacations, motorcycles, refrigerators, houses. The Argentine doctor's plans for integral communism were shelved, his functions reduced to a minimum, which Che found hard to bear. His irony and his blunt way of putting things quickly made life intolerable for the other *compañeros*, who were urging Fidel Castro to more reasonable solutions. Fidel himself was irritated.

In matters of foreign policy, Che inclined toward the Chinese line since it was the hardest. To ensure the survival of his revolution, Castro went over to the Soviet camp. After his break with the United States, the U.S.S.R. was the only country able to come to Cuba's aid.

René Dumont in *Cuba, Socialism and Development* offers a fine analysis of Che and his problem: Che developed a sort of ideal vision of Socialist Man who had become a stranger to the mercantile side of things and no longer worked for gain but for society. He was very severe on the success of Soviet industry, in which, he said, people work, struggle, and try to surpass their norms in the hope of making more money. He found that Soviet Man did not represent a truly new humanity, because he was not basically different from the Yankee. Che refused to participate knowingly in the creation in Cuba "of a second North American society, even if everything belongs to the State."

It would seem that today, after having somewhat fallen out with the Russians, Castro in his turn is inclined toward the Utopias dear to Che.

On December 9, 1964, Che was sent abroad as an itinerant ambassador of the Cuban revolution. He gave a speech at the United Nations, he went to Africa, he went to Asia—and his pronouncements became more and more sensational. In Algiers he took Russia to task for having, as he saw it, become a selfish bourgeois nation, and he called on her to offer free and unconditional help to the poorer socialist countries. He proclaimed, "We are dependent on the force and unity of the socialist camp, and for this reason the Sino-Russian dispute is truly very serious for us." He asked that the U.S.S.R. reestablish its relations with China.

People began to find that he was involving himself too much

in matters that did not concern him. He was given the responsibility of helping Ben Bella and establishing for him the type of popular militia he had tried to set up in Guatemala, a militia that would enable him to fight against Boumédienne and his threatening army. Che failed. It is hard to see how he could have succeeded. He was under careful surveillance during this whole trip. In Geneva, for example, the Cuban ambassador, an "old communist," did not leave his side for a moment and even managed to see to it that invitations from his family never got to him.

On March 5, 1965, Che returned to Havana. The mystery began shortly after this date.

Learning of his arrival, his Argentine friends came to the plane to meet him. Among them was Yves Daude, the correspondent for Agence France-Presse, who had also been born in Argentina, in Misiones, where Ernesto Guevara had spent his childhood. Che had often been helpful when Daude had run into the kind of difficulties inherent in the exercise of a journalistic profession in a totalitarian country. But neither Daude nor the other Argentines were able to see him.

Fidel Castro, Raúl Castro, and Dorticós, who had replaced Che in all his posts, were waiting for him at the plane and immediately took him off to a small glassed-in room used for the reception of guests of honor. It was obvious that they were determined not to let him talk to anyone or to make any statement—which it seemed he was preparing to do.

Suddenly a violent argument broke out between Che on the one hand and Raúl and Dorticós on the other. Fidel remained the impassive arbiter. Egged on by his entourage, admonished by the Russians, he seemed to have chosen that moment to abandon his old comrade and intellectual mentor. But when Dorticós, furious at Che's stinging replies, supposedly took out his pistol, Fidel intervened and made him reholster it. Che returned under escort to his residence near Havana. From then on he was politically inactive. He disappeared. But he was known to be in Cuba.

On March 22, he was to deliver a lecture on his trip. At the last moment he was replaced by Dorticós, who spoke of commerce with the Third World. Che did not appear. He was seen one last time in the offices of *Revolución*, where he had come to correct the proofs of his book *Man and Socialism in Cuba*. It would appear that during the night he had met Castro and his old comrades and that another altercation had broken out between him and both Raúl Castro and Dorticós, and even Fidel himself. Some people claim to have seen Che around until July. The engineer Alberto Nieto saw him go into the Ministry of the Interior on the night of August 4. On July 26, Aleida, his second wife, was asked by reporters where her husband was and replied, "Everything's fine. We are near Havana."

On October 3, 1965, the day of the creation of the Cuban Communist party, Fidel Castro read from the platform the letter of *despedida*—Che's letter of farewell:

Fidel,

At this moment I remember many things—when I met you in María Antonia's house. . . . I feel that I have fulfilled the part of my duty that tied me to the Cuban revolution in its territory, and I say good-bye to you, the comrades, your people, who are already mine.

I formally renounce my positions in the national leadership of the party, my post as minister, my rank of major, and my Cuban citizenship. . . .

My only serious failing was not having trusted more in you from the first moment in the Sierra Maestra, and not having understood quickly enough your qualities as a leader and a revolutionary. . . .

Rarely has a statesman been more brilliant than you in those days. I am also proud of having followed you without hesitation, identified with your way of thinking and of seeing. . . .

Other nations of the world call for my modest efforts. I can do that which is denied you because of your responsibility as the head of Cuba and the time has come for us to part. . . . I carry to new battlefronts the faith that you taught me. . . .

Che*

During the reading of this letter, Aleida March, who was on the platform alongside Fidel Castro, made no attempt to hide her tears.

However, Che's Argentine friends said immediately that he could not have been the author of certain passages of the letter (those given here in italics). Others went even further and claimed that not a word of it was his. One of them was to tell me, "He humbled himself too much before Fidel—and that's neither his character nor his style. He wouldn't have written it even if a pistol had been pointed at his head."

Important Cuban leaders, one of whom was a minister, declared, "Che is dead, his farewell letter is a historical document." A high official of the Ministry of Foreign Affairs said, "In this way we'll have a nice memory of Che. It's better like that. With his foul personality, sooner or later everything would have gone wrong." Nobody was ever able to see the original of the letter. Typewritten copies were distributed.

When *Granma* officially announced the death of Comandante Ernesto Guevara, to prove the authenticity of the diary found near his body it was not of this letter of *despedida* that a photocopy was published, or of the one that had recently been sent to the Tricontinental Congress; it was of another, very old one, dating from the Sierra Maestra period.

As the mystery thickened, it became obvious that the disappearance of Che was one of the best-kept secrets in Latin America—possibly because only five men were in on it.

They were: Fidel Castro; his brother, Raúl; Ramiro Valdés, the Minister of the Interior; José Abrantes, the nation's security

---

* *Ibid.*, pp. 284–85.

chief; and Comandante Piñeiro Losado, chief of Cuba's special services and known as Red Beard.

In Buenos Aires, Che's parents received a letter from their son.

It must have been sent from Cuba at about the time that his disappearance was noticed. Here are excerpts from the text:

Dear Folks—

Once again I feel between my heels the ribs of Rosinante; once more I hit the road with my shield upon my arm. . . .

Nothing has changed in essence, except that I am much more aware, my Marxism has taken root and become purified. I believe in the armed struggle as the only solution for those peoples who fight to free themselves, and I am consistent with my beliefs. . . .

It is possible that this may be the finish. I don't seek it, but it's within the logical realm of probabilities. If it should be so, I send you a last embrace. . . .

An *abrazo* for you from your obstinate and prodigal son.

Ernesto*

They were never to receive any others. What was happening to Che?

Did he remain in Cuba after July and did he then make a trip to the socialist countries—to Vietnam, it was said—before going to the Latin-American continent? Did he get to the Amazon *selva* by way of Argentina? It seems probable.

It is now reasonable to think (but nothing was ever reasonable or rational in this entire mysterious affair) that Che obtained Fidel Castro's authorization to leave Cuba, since there was nothing more for him to do there, and to once more, as he put it, bestride Rosinante.

Did he agree to remain Fidel's faithful lieutenant, to become the coordinator of the Castro revolution on the continent, in

---

* *Ibid.,* pp. 286–87.

spite of all that separated them? It was not so much their ideas—that would not have been serious—but personal resentments, bitterness, and Che's feeling of having been abandoned along with the revolution as he conceived it.

If it was really Che who was killed at Vallegrande along with the few Cubans who made up his personal guard, it is possible that he and Fidel had reached an agreement, but an agreement concluded on equal terms. There was to be no more *líder máximo*. The revolution was simply to have two faces.

If we go beyond the ideas, the rivalries, the bitterness, we may be able to understand what from their very origins contrasted the personalities of Fidel Castro and Ernesto Guevara.

The one, Fidel, is the son of rich Galician farmers attached to the earth and greedy for profit. His sister Juana is an example. She understood nothing about Castro's revolution and wanted to use her brother to make more money.

Fidel is a realist and has all the qualities and faults of one. He has a taste for action rather than for ideas. He is an empiricist who improvises as he goes along. He is a natural force—people call him "The Horse." His temperament often pushes him further than he really wants to go, but his talents as an orator permit him to outface the ridicule. He is possessive and takes great sensual pleasure in owning the island of Cuba and all those who inhabit it. But he has no interest in the possession of women or money.

He springs from the hard soil of Galicia. His family comes from a village neighboring the one in which was born another man as realistic, as possessive, as himself—General Franco. This may account for the "gentleness" with which the Franco authorities have behaved toward Castro, that "gentleness" which so irritates Washington. Hadn't Fidel Castro avenged Spain by beating the North American *gringos* and chasing them in their turn from Cuba, this island that was Spain's first possession in the New World? This revenge, so sweet to Hispanic pride and bitterness, is well worth a few concessions. Except for some ephemeral ideological notion, isn't Fidel behaving in Cuba like both a madman and a sage, being both crafty and naïve, realist and idealist—in other words like a true son of Sancho Panza, a man who follows Don Quixote but is leery of him?

Ernesto Guevara is the final product not of a long line of rapacious oligarchs but of disillusioned aristocrats. He was known as "The Cat" and he himself used the nickname. Like a cat he claimed to have seven lives. Feline in aspect and just as independent and solitary as a cat, he was contemptuous of the crowd's applause. A great lord, he was cynical and had no illusions about the people, which can be had with a few tricks, a few shouts, and a few clarion calls. But at the same time the idealist in him believed that it was possible to elevate this people—a disincarnate people, reduced to an abstraction—to his own level, where disinterestedness reigned. But this people is not only hungry for bread, rice, and dignity, but also has other desires to satisfy, and the strongest of these is to possess land, money, automobiles—everything they envy in the rich. Che refused them these aspirations. He had been taught to despise money by all his ancestors—those who bought a golden Perichole carriage and those who threw their *estancias* out of windows to amuse their friends.

The one, Fidel, conceived of the revolution as would the son of a farmer. First he wanted to assure his power in Cuba, to manage the island and organize it like a domain. The other, Ernesto, had no more country and wanted no domains. He was Don Quixote, his head was stuffed with dreams and clouds and his revolution began like a fight against the windmills. Fidel is Sancho Panza. Sancho Panza often follows Don Quixote because the latter fascinates him and because at times he himself is a little like Don Quixote. But Don Quixote can never be Sancho Panza. Don Quixote has no common sense. Like Che, he is led only by his holy madness, his taste for the absolute. In truth, like Don Quixote, Che did not even know just what to call his great crusade against injustice.

Was this crusade to be Christian? He dreamed for a moment at Punta del Esta and then at Geneva of the revolution the church had just launched, and at times he felt very close to her. Was it to be Marxist? But his Marxism became so idealistic, so stripped of tricks and the phraseology of the doctors of law and the merchants of the temple, that it had few points in common with that practiced in Russia and the bloc nations.

The two men—Fidel-Sancho Panza and Che-Don Quixote—could understand each other but could not agree for very long.

And so Don Quixote went off all alone, leaving Sancho Panza to the joys of possession, to the applause of the crowds, and to the snobs from the West who came to flatter and cajole him—and occasionally to make fun of him. Yes, make fun of him, because though Sancho Panza is suspicious-minded, he is not always aware of when he becomes ridiculous.

Taking a few friends with him, Don Quixote went to make his revolution, to tackle the power and the organization of North America. But he had no great illusions, for though he might have been mad in the noble sense of the term, as Unamuno pointed out, he was not an imbecile.

This modern-day Don Quixote, astride his Rosinante, an old mule that carried him, sick, into the humid jungle, died a pointless death in a narrow, fusty valley in Bolivia.

But what did Sancho, king of his island, think of it all then? No doubt he regretted not having followed Don Quixote, regretted not having followed the part of himself that was Don Quixote. At first he remained quiet, something not natural to him; then, in a long discourse he confirmed that it really was Che Guevara who died in Bolivia.

He did so with a great many details, a great many analyses, with the pedantry habitual to him. That demonstration is too long to reproduce here. We can only cite a few excerpts:

If we had the least doubt [about the death of Che] it would be our duty to express this doubt; if we felt that the news was false, it would be our duty to state that it was false; if we felt that the news was true, we would then have to consider other questions.

One can imagine that at first it was a painful duty to make a statement confirming news emanating from an oligarchical, reactionary, despotic government, oppressor of its people, ally of imperialism, enemy of the revolution—to see ourselves in the position of having to authenticate and confirm the truth of this news. I believe that this is always painful for any revolutionary. . . .

In our opinion, the diary [found on Che] is absolutely genuine, the photos are absolutely authentic.

It seems to us in every way impossible, it seems to us technically impossible, it seems to us practically impossible, to organize all this on the basis of falsehood. Many imitations can be made, but it is impossible to imitate what constitutes the most subtle traits of personality, the gestures, everything constituting the physiognomy of a person. We feel that by analyzing all these indications, all these details, all these aspects—the diary, the photographs, the releases, the manner in which the news came about, an entire sequence of facts—one can affirm that it was completely impossible to fabricate these proofs. . . .

Neither the most imbecilic nor the most idiotic of all governments—and it is obvious that the government of Bolivia is characterized by its idiocy and by its imbecility—but not even the most superimbecilic would have hit upon anything so stripped of sense, so stupid, so impossible, as to invent and try to prove a similar piece of news, because it would be completely lacking in sense. . . .

We, those who know Ernesto Guevara best, must say—and we say "who know" because it will never be possible to speak of Ernesto Guevara in the past—that we had more than ample knowledge of his character, of his personality. And as difficult as it may be to imagine that such a man, with such prestige, that such a personality, could have died in a fight between a guerrilla patrol and soldiers of the army, even if it seems scarcely logical, we who know him well, know there is nothing extraordinary about it. Because during all the time we have known him he has given evidence of the extraordinary boldness and absolute contempt for danger necessary to accomplish the most difficult and the most dangerous things at the most difficult and dangerous moments. He has behaved this way on numerous occasions during our struggle— in the Sierra Maestra, at Las Villas.

We have often had to take measures, in one manner or another, to protect him. More than once we have had to oppose the realization of certain actions that he wanted to bring off. And given our appreciation of these magnificent qualities as a combatant and the possibility for him to serve the revolution in tasks or missions of the greatest strategic importance, we especially tried to protect him against the risks of falling in a combat of minor importance.

Nobody could ever be sure that he would take the most minimal protective measures. He often went in advance of a reconnaissance patrol. It is possible that, fully aware of the importance of his mission, he thought more of the irrefutable value of the example than of the very relative value of men. . . .

I was saying that absolutely nobody should be amazed that he could have been the first to fall during a guerrilla skirmish, because actually the contrary would have been a miracle.

He has confronted danger on many occasions, and in this domain, a sort of mathematical law is always operative. . . .

Who can deny the significance of the blow that Che's death is to the revolutionary movement, the fact that we now can no longer count on his experience, on his inspiration, on the force of his prestige, which made the reactionaries tremble? It is a severe blow, very hard. But nevertheless we are certain that he was more convinced than anyone that the physical life of men is not the most important thing, but that it is their conduct that is uppermost. And this is the only way in which to explain, this is the only way in which his personality and behavior can be reconciled with, this absolute contempt for danger.

The Council of Ministers met today and adopted the following agreement:

"Given that the heroic Comandante Ernesto Guevara was killed in fighting for the liberation of the peoples of America at the head of the Bolivian Liberation Army,

"Given that the people of Cuba will always remember the extraordinary services rendered by Comandante Ernesto Guevara in both our war of liberation and in the consolidation and development of our revolution,

"Given that his conduct incarnates the internationalist sentiments that inspire the united fight of the peoples,

"Given that his indefatigable revolutionary activity, which knew no frontiers, his communist thought and his unshakable determination to fight until victory or death for the national and social liberation of the continental peoples and against imperialism, constitute an example of conviction and revolutionary heroism that must live forever,

"The Council of Ministers declares:

"First: that for thirty days from this declaration the national flag shall be flown at half mast and that for three days from midnight tonight all public entertainment will be suspended.

"Second: that the day on which he heroically fell in combat shall be declared a day of national homage and that to this effect October 8 will be called 'The Day of the Heroic Guerrilla.'

"Third: that activities designed to perpetuate his life and example in the memory of future generations are to be organized."

Che was buried; they were finished with this myth, which was becoming somewhat embarrassing. Fidel Castro was certainly grieved, and maybe even remorseful.

But the life of his *finca*, his multiple occupations, the applause of the crowd and the flattery of his courtiers, would soon make him forget Don Quixote.

Shortly before this, whenever an American official or a CIA agent was asked what had become of Che and if he was "underground," he would answer, "Yes, he's 'underground' all right, about six feet under."

The first to have announced that he had seen Che alive, that he had spoken to him, and that he had almost interviewed him was Régis Debray. We will return at greater length to this strange and painful affair which may have cost Che his life and which in any case tolled the bell for the Castroite revolution as an export article.

General Ovando, commander in chief of the Bolivian army, confirmed Debray's news and immediately swelled the number of guerrillas involved. There were 110, suddenly there were 400. Then he affirmed that their leader, "Comandante Ramón," was none other than Che Guevara. At a meeting of the Organization of American States held in Washington, the Bolivian minister of foreign affairs, also called Guevara, produced a pile of photographs found in the guerrilla hideouts; these showed that Che was at their head.

With touching unanimity, all the CIA specialists, who only the day before were still denying the existence of Che, admitted that the Argentine doctor was very much alive and that it was undoubtedly he who was in Bolivia. Their haste can easily be understood. The sudden reapparition of Che brought a new argument to the support of their policies. By making a bugbear of him, by proving to all the governments under their control that Che was organizing a revolution that no longer respected frontiers, they were once again able to launch the idea of an inter-American force that would permit them to intervene directly and legally at any menaced point on their continent. Several times during various meetings of the OAS the right to create this force had been refused them by a large majority of the Latin-American nations, in spite of the support of Brazil, Argentina, and Paraguay, three countries in which the army holds power.

The CIA stole Che from the Cubans to use him against them, to force all those countries reluctant to do so to agree to the wishes of the Pentagon. Only a few months earlier, an absolutely amazing story had been going the rounds: Che Guevara had become a CIA agent. The origin of the story was stranger still: Perón's office in Madrid. Of course, it had only been meant as a *chiste*, a joke, but during its transmission to the newspapers it had been deformed into an affirmation. But now one wondered if it was really a joke and not a paradox. Ghosts belong to everyone and to no one in particular; it's what happens to men who play at being ghosts. Che was suddenly helping advance Yankee policy? That accounts for Fidel Castro's haste to bury him so deep that he can never rise again.

Che had in less than two years become the symbol of the revolution aimed at the whole Latin-American continent. He served Fidel Castro, who was chained to the Russians on his island and wanted to free himself at any cost—if only to find new allies on the continent, allies who by making him stronger would make him more independent. He also served the Russians, the Vietnamese, the entire communist camp that was worried by American superpower, and all those who wanted to flank the United States with other conflicts that would oblige it to disperse its forces.

Now the Americans were turning this weapon against their adversaries and resuscitating Che for their own personal use: an avatar he had certainly not foreseen.

Today the opposing forces in Latin America find themselves face to face with an inescapable reality.

The revolutionaries: since the Santo Domingo affair they know that the United States can intervene with impunity at any point in Latin America without anybody's being able to stop them— neither the Chinese, the Russians, nor their Cuban satellite.

They also know that other Latin-American governments, even democratic governments like Costa Rica or Chile, are so economically tied to the United States that they must hold their tongues.

At present, the national armies of all these countries live only for and by the United States, so that a Castroite revolution in any country in Central or South America would not only bring in its wake the intervention of the United States—its navy, its marines, its Green Berets—but also the armies of the neighboring countries.

There is therefore only one way in which the revolutionaries can hope to succeed: to simultaneously unleash revolutions in different countries.

For this to happen, all these countries need a common goal. More than an idea, more than a doctrine, more than a flag, they need a man who symbolizes this goal. On this continent, though they may play with doctrines, or burn flags, in the final analysis they only believe in the man, the leader, the *caudillo*, the *libertador*. For the revolutionaries, despite several timid Cuban attempts at resurrection, this man is no longer Bolívar, he is not Castro, but he might have been Che Guevara.

The United States: thanks to this ghost it suddenly becomes possible to impose its strategic conception. To maintain liberty, national independence, and free enterprise in each country, to lead each of these countries to the very gates of paradise, which is none other than "the American way of life," it must no longer disperse its forces but unite them so that they can fight not on a national level but on a continental one. Of course, for this inter-American force to be efficacious it must have a single command, which can only be conferred on a general of the United States Army. As a matter of fact, there is a General Porter in Panama who would do just fine.

Rarely in history has a man like Che, a man who was not known to be either living or dead, had such influence on the destiny of a continent. But this influence is by no means over. The myth survives the man and already has no need of him.

The course of our civilization has often been determined by the search for empty sepulchers, the search by Don Quixote and many others. Is the quest for another empty sepulcher to decide the fate of a revolution and the future of a continent?

Bolívar
or the Flag **2**

In Latin America, Marxists are currently divided into orthodox communists of Soviet allegiance, Castroites of Cuban allegiance, Maoists of Chinese allegiance, and Trotskyites who follow orders from Mexican headquarters but more often the dictates of their fancy. Trotskyism would seem to have been made for Latin America.

The lines are never rigorously clear cut. For example, one can find Sino-Trotskyites such as Yon Sosa, one of the guerrilla leaders in Guatemala; Castroite-Sino-Trotskyites such as Che Guevara seems to have been for at least some time; Castroite-communists like César Montes in Guatemala.

Among the revolutionists belonging to one of the four categories listed above, one occasionally finds Christian-Socialists who become Christian-Democrats once they are organized into parties, as in Chile or Venezuela. The Christian-Socialists range from the right to the extreme left, but they prefer a position in the center. They are preparing their own revolution and are already in power in Chile with Eduardo Frei. They may well be in power tomorrow in Venezuela with Rafael Caldera.

Reformists such as José Figueres in Costa Rica, Rómulo Betancourt in Venezuela, Julio César Méndez Montenegro in Guatemala, or Fernando Belaunde Terry in Peru are to the communists the allies of reaction and to the reactionaries the allies of the communists. They are no longer considered revolutionaries by those officially concerned with the business of revolution. The position is an uncomfortable one, for though the U.S. State Department has a certain affection for them and makes them all kinds of promises, it nevertheless generally permits them to be deposed by colonels in the service of the Pentagon.

"Oligarquía" is a word constantly used in Latin America. Everybody either wants to get into it, comes from it, or has just left it. The real oligarchs are the large landowners, the *terratenientes*, who in a time when their *peones* can tune in on Radio Habana on their transistors, still want to go on living as though in the Middle Ages. To this group also belong the politicians, the businessmen, the allies of American big business, and the generals and colonels who in return for serving them are permitted to sweep up the crumbs from their tables.

Their disgusted sons often find their way to the university, where they join movements of the extreme left, then sometimes pass over to the guerrillas and become their leaders. These sons occasionally benefit from strange concessions.

No matter what the orthodox communists say, Fidel Castro still enjoys great prestige among the students. None of the communist leaders slowly climbing the rungs of the hierarchy from plenum to central committee, with intervals of autocriticism, has had the good fortune of the Cuban leader who seized his island with a dozen men. Nor has any of them managed to bring off a revolution in his country by following only his own fancy, as Castro did, and by relying almost exclusively on young people to whom he often gave heavy responsibilities.

In any case, as concerns the revolution, heroic and romantic sentiment, as well as temperament, will always win out over dialectical considerations and tactics. The revolution in Latin America is more a matter of sentiment than of political calculations.

Generally, calculation comes with age, and when the young cease to be so, they also cease to be revolutionaries—unless they find death in some adventure or in its other form: the exercise of power. Those in the guerrilla forces generally die very young: A guerrilla rarely survives more than two or three years. The average age of the guerrillas in Guatemala is twenty-two; the oldest of them, nicknamed Viejo, recently turned forty.

In August the meeting of the OLAS (Organization of Latin-American Solidarity) was held in Havana. It was designed to be a kind of vast congress of subversion. It was no more than a guerrilla "seminar," from which were missing the majority of the real guerrilla leaders. Fidel Castro was unable to bring about the creation of a central committee that would have taken over the Latin-American revolution and directed it from Cuba, in other words, under his control. Nationalism is as lively among the revolutionaries as among the oligarchs—maybe even more so. The oligarchs know that their time is past and, already somewhat detached from their countries, feel the stirrings of internationalism within them. By contrast, the revolutionaries hope to accede to power and are adopting as their own the subtle frontier quarrels born at the time of the liberation from the Spaniards, the same quarrels that divided Bolívar's lieutenants and drove them to mutual slaughter.

Many of these revolutionaries, especially the orthodox communists urged on by the Soviets, break their wings against the ambitious unity project of the Caribbean *libertador*. But to the Cubans these communists are no longer revolutionaries. Occasionally one wonders: who is a revolutionary? Fidel Castro's reply is: he who makes revolution. But everybody claims to be doing that.

Sly, crafty, intuitive, Fidel really has no particular political ideology, but he has a fine sense of where the wind is blowing from. Currently it's blowing from the side of unity, but only among his clientele, those well-born young guerrillas who, like himself, come from Jesuit colleges and the universities. Is that why he replaced the traditional portraits of Marx, Lenin, and Engels—those three bearded fellows of another age, totally foreign to the Latin-American continent and the Hispanic spirit— with the long, pale, and romantic face of Simón Bolívar?

No one was fooled. Fidel Castro wanted "his" revolution to free itself of all foreign influences, whether they were Soviet or Chinese, and by reaching across a century of disorders and nationalistic splintering he wanted to tie in with Bolívar's great dream: the United States of Latin America. To do so, his revolution would have had to free itself of economic ties to the Soviet Union, but that was impossible.

In terms of revolutionary propaganda the Yankees had replaced the Spaniards—the *gachupinos* of the Mexicans. Their oppression appeared in the new guise of economic colonialism, and it was against this that Castro launched his crusade. However, many of the revolutionaries were leery of his blundering ambition and refused to consider him as a real Latin "American." He came from the Caribbean, where the blood of the Spaniards had mixed with that of their black slaves. The Indian had contributed neither his violence nor his sadness. Nonchalance, the sweetness of living, and sensuality were stronger there than elsewhere because of the gentleness and the humidity of the climate in those fortunate islands. The problems that Fidel Castro had to solve in Cuba, the very conditions of his resistance against Batista's troops, had nothing to do, they said, with their own problems and their own revolution. They all asked that he limit himself to his role of exemplary revolutionist and that he tend to his own island, where things were not going all that well.

The orthodox communists had small enthusiasm for Bolívar as their new flag. To them the great *libertador* of the nineteenth century had remained a man who had never ceased to serve his own class, that of the rich creoles.

When Bolívar, Sucre, San Martín, and O'Higgins had freed Latin America from the Spaniards, the long and sad history of the continent began.

This Latin America that has painfully conquered its independence, that has witnessed the sudden rise of intrepid, tenacious leaders, some of whom showed the qualities of statesmen, was incapable of organizing itself the way North America had. Not only were the states unable to conclude a mutual and durable alliance, but rivalries grew between them over contested frontiers, and within each of them implacably opposed forces sprang up. The new countries had scarcely been constituted before they broke up. The strong personalities born of the Independence were rapidly consumed in this cruel game. Surprised by events, foreigners spoke of anarchy and chaos. However, they did so too quickly. . . .

The successive revolutions, the contradictory or repetitive constitutions, betrayed this profound indecision of the national societies. The economy itself was too little developed, too exclusively tied to the agriculture of large holdings or to the commercial activity of some large ports, to be able at this stage to create general interests that impose a line of conduct on men in spite of their ideological preferences.

From that time on the individual is to be the determining factor: it is he who will make a constitutional formula efficacious or who will maintain the life of a given government beyond the rules of a constitution. It is he who will spring up in troubled times and lead the always numerous mass of malcontents. As a result, the *caudillos*, political and military bosses, *caciques*, and local clan leaders succeeded one another at a dizzying cadence. . . .*

Bolívar tried to maintain the unity he had dreamed of, but he was unable to, no matter what he did. In 1826 he wrote:

I am not Napoleon and I do not wish to be him. Neither do I want to imitate Caesar, and still less Iturbide.† Such examples seem to me unworthy of my glory. The title of Liberator is superior to any that can glorify men. Because of this I cannot defame it. . . . The nations surrounding Colombia are republics and Colombia itself has never been a kingdom. A throne would cause as much fear by its elevation as by its dazzle. Equality would be destroyed and people of color would see all their rights vanish as a result of a new aristocracy.

Bolívar's best and most faithful friend, General Sucre, was assassinated. He himself was consumed by tuberculosis and even more so by despair. On September 9, 1830, in a letter dated from Baranquilla, he wrote:

You know that I have already been in power for twenty years and I have drawn from it only a few sure conclusions: first, America is ungovernable by us; second, he who serves the revolution plows the sea; third, the only thing one can do in America is to emigrate; fourth, this country will inescapably fall into the hands of a mob of petty tyrants almost too small to be noticed, men of all colors, of all races; fifth, devoured by every kind of crime and beaten down by savagery, we will be disdained by the Europeans,

---

* Victor L. Tapié, *Histoire de l'Amérique latine au XIXᵉ siècle*, Aubier ed.
† A Mexican general who after having helped drive the Spanish from his country had himself crowned emperor and as a result was tried and shot two years later.

who will, however, not disdain to conquer us; sixth, if it were possible for a part of the world to return to primitive chaos, America would do it.

When he arrived, all but dead, at Santa Marta, he stated:

If my death contributes to the elimination of all the factions and to the consolidation of the union, I will go down to my grave in peace—yes, into my grave. It is there that my compatriots are sending me. But I forgive them.

On December 17, 1830, at one o'clock in the morning, he died pronouncing these strange words:

Come, come, this people no longer wants us in this country. . . . Come, my children, my bags. Take my bags and carry them aboard the frigate.

When Fidel Castro placed his revolution under the sign of Bolívar, did he remember the despairing end of the *libertador*?

These days everybody wants to make revolution, but nobody can agree on how to go about it, just as in the time of Bolívar.

In the revolutionary camp, the Castroites and communists attack each other, and not always only with words. The Castroites advocate the revolution first: let's set up guerrilla bands everywhere—two, three, several Vietnams. From these guerrilla forces armies will be born, and from these armies authentically revolutionary governments such as that of Mao Tse-tung in China. "Adventurist" reasoning, reply the orthodox communists. Revolution is a serious affair and must be carefully prepared; the guerrillas can have real importance only if they are supported by an ideology, the apparatus of the party, the unions, the trained and organized masses. In certain cases they are only to be used as an extreme form of revolutionary action. Medicine is always preferable to surgery. A petty bourgeois notion, reply the Castroites. We have to cut into the living flesh, set fire to the four corners of the continent. And citing José Martí, Che Guevara declared, "Once the fires are lit, only the light should be seen."

But what do those who see their farms burn think—all those reeling under the blows of the soldiers, forced to flee, bundles on back, dragging their haggard families behind them?

There are other revolutionaries who hesitate between revolution, with all its subsequent risks, and reformism, a prudent method for changing the social structures. These are the Christian-Socialists. They have the support of a force unavailable to either the Marxists or the Castroites: the grip that the Church, in spite of its errors and compromises, has over the mass of the population and over what is the stake in this revolution—the Indians.

In Guatemala, in Bolivia, and in Peru these Indians are in the majority. They occupy the mountains, they form the most poverty-stricken proletariat of the cities; the failure or success of a guerrilla force depends on them.

What T'Serstevens wrote about the Mexican Indians is equally true of all the Latin-American Indians:

The Indian, the proletarian of all epochs, subjugated in pre-Cortez days by the emperor and his *caciques*, his life compromised, a slave of the Spanish conquerors in spite of the protection of the Fathers, who were not above exploiting his devotion, peon or day laborer on the hacienda and in the mines, pushed by the beneficiaries of Independence into battles about which he understood little, gave his life unstintingly. The agrarian revolution bestowed upon these eternal pariahs a patch of land that was to permit them to survive, but their servitude has made most of them unfit for free labor, and the land they own scarcely gives them more than their dish of tortillas. Others work for a meager salary, a good part of which goes to the churches because their Catholicism has every aspect of idolatry. Often housed in straw huts or in burrows in the earth, dreaming of not so much as a bicycle, they look out on an entire world that lives off their labor, is sheltered in buildings, and rides around in Cadillacs. Is it because of this or for hereditary reasons that they are sad, even when they are amusing themselves, so docile, even when they kill, so pious, because at least the sky belongs to everybody, so prolific in their poverty, because at least that pleasure is available to them, so sober, except in drunkenness, which is no doubt their escape?*

And Alexis de Tocqueville wrote: "The Indians will die in isolation, just as they have lived in it."†

This is no longer certain. The two camps at each other's

---

* Albert T'Serstevens, *Mexique, pays à trois étages* (Grenoble: Arthaud, 1955).

† Commenting on the behavior of the North Americans and the Spaniards toward the Indians, Alexis de Tocqueville wrote: "The Spaniards pursued the Indians with blood-hounds, like wild beasts; they sacked the New World with no more temper or compassion than a city taken by storm: but destruction must cease, and frenzy be stayed; the remnant of the Indian population, which had escaped the massacre, mixed with its conquerors, and adopted in the end their religion and their manners. The conduct of the Americans of the United States towards the aborigines is characterized, on the other hand, by a singular attachment to the formalities of law. Provided that the Indians retain their barbarous condition, the Americans take no part in their affairs; they treat them as independent nations, and do not possess themselves of their hunting-grounds without a treaty of purchase: and if an Indian nation happens to be so encroached upon as to be unable to subsist upon its territory, they afford it brotherly assistance in transporting it to a grave sufficiently remote from the land of its fathers.

"The Spaniards were unable to exterminate the Indian race by those unparalleled atrocities which brand them with indelible shame, nor did they even succeed in wholly depriving it of its rights; but the Americans of the United States have accomplished this twofold purpose with singular felicity; tranquilly, legally, philanthropically, without shedding blood, and without violating a single great principle of morality in the eyes of the world. It is impossible to destroy men with more respect for the laws of humanity." [*Democracy in America* (New York: Schocken Books, 1961), pp. 422–23.]

throats need the Indians, and they are finally going to get some attention.

For their part, the liberals or reformists try to believe in the efficacy of reforms which, as they understand them, can be carried out only with the aid of the United States. But the United States must understand that it cannot intervene in the internal affairs of a country as brutally as it did in Santo Domingo and that it cannot take away with one hand what it gives with the other.

In 1966, the United States made two billion dollars, in the form of loans, help, and assistance, available to the Latin-American continent. It withdrew six billion dollars from it. Under Kennedy the liberals were hopeful; under Johnson they felt hopeless.

The oligarchy exports its capital abroad and invests scarcely anything in its own country. Greedier than ever, in a hurry to grow rich, it no longer hesitates to bleed the peoples over which it rules. Its last hopes are in the national armies, which are more and more under the control of the United States. But the armies' officers, who often come from the lower ranks of the petty bourgeoisie, present a problem. The armies are nests of reactionaries and they have become aware of their importance and of their responsibilities. In most of these countries where the institutions are unstable and the political parties divided, the army represents the only stable, organized, and efficient force.

In Brazil or in Argentina these armies think of themselves as the nation's conscience; in Colombia, as its arbiter. Elsewhere, as in Peru, for example, they assume the social tasks that the administration shows itself incapable of undertaking. Acción Cívica is involved in everything from the construction of roads to the fight against illiteracy, from sanitary aid to the exploitation of unused lands.

The comic-opera armies that were one of the elements of Hispanic American folklore are only a memory now. Since the last war they have little by little transformed themselves into efficient forces of intervention—armed, thanks to American aid, with modern weapons. They are often led by officers trained at Fort Benning, Georgia, or in Panama's La Escuela de las Américas.

During a briefing at Fort Gulick, Panama, the spokesman for the Green Berets told me, "We have engineering courses in heavy materials and construction, courses whose aim is to set up projects designed for civilian use, projects to be undertaken by the Latin-American armies in order to eliminate the causes of subversion. In other words, everything that would improve the standard of living of the various populations and give them hope for the future. As can be seen, it's an enormous program. . . ."

A young Colombian, a member of his country's Communist party and a spokesman for the *guerrillero* movement FARC (Colombian Armed Revolutionary Forces), told me, "In Colombia, the army has changed completely. It no longer wants to frighten, it wants to reassure. In addition, it's a very good army, largely converted to the fight against subversion. Some of its units are capable of living for weeks or even months under the same conditions as the guerrillas. The soldier no longer rapes girls or steals chickens. He comes to the aid of the peasant. He helps him with his work in the fields, he brings him seeds, he builds roads, he clears land. He is accompanied by doctors, veterinarians, dentists, and engineers. Instead of living off the region, these men spend their money there. It's stupid to tell the peasants before the army arrives that it's made up of bands of cruel and greedy looters, instead of describing what it really is: an efficient organization of aid for the population. It only makes us revolutionaries look like liars afterward.

"On the contrary, what we have to make the *campesinos* understand, and this will be a long and hard job, is what's hidden behind that beautiful mask—a more advanced form of reaction, a more subtle form of intelligence activities.

"The Castroites of the ELN (Ejército de Liberación Nacional, the rival guerrilla movement of the FARC) go no further than this old-hat propaganda, and they are wrong.

"In this new army we sometimes find allies and occasionally even efficient leaders for our guerrillas. By fighting against the people and by trying to understand them, these officers and soldiers, who spring from the people or from the petty bourgeoisie, sometimes end by turning their guns against those who employ them—the Yankee imperialists and their straw men."

For his part, Salvador de Madariaga wrote:

There is too often a tendency to believe that the armed forces are probably the only really serious obstacle to the development of democracy in Latin America. . . . Every army has a tradition of liberty that comes from the wars of Independence. Was it not from this struggle for independence, tinged by tricolor ideologies and animated by the echoes of *The Marseillaise*, that the armies of Latin America were born? . . . It is obviously no less true that in numerous cases the army has been an antidemocratic element, especially in those countries where it was less an institution and more like a glorified police force.*

In Guatemala, for example, where the army is really "a glorified police force," most of the cadres of the guerrilla forces operating there come from lower ranks of army officers. The leader of MR 13 (Movimiento Revolucionario del 13 de Noviembre), Lieutenant Marco Antonio Yon Sosa, is a former student of La Escuela de las Américas who obviously learned his lessons well, because he went underground in 1960 and the army has never managed to neutralize the handful of men that he still commands. One of his comrades from the very first days, 2nd Lieutenant Turcios Lima was also a student—and one of the most brilliant—of the training center at Fort Benning.

---

* *L'Amerique Latine entre l'Ours et l'Aigle.*

In addition, these rebel soldiers have numerous friends within the army. For this reason they are somewhat less than aggressive in confronting the detachments sent in pursuit of them, detachments often commanded by classmates. In exchange, these same detachments do not trail them too far. Before his death, Turcios Lima said, "The intelligence services that we have in the very heart of the army are the basis of our survival."

It is no accident that the military has been called upon to play a determining role in the development of subversion in Guatemala. For more than a century the army was the country's only organized political force. Since independence, during more than seventy-five years, Guatemala has been governed by four military dictators: General Rafael Carrera from 1840 to 1865, Justo Rufino Barrios from 1873 to 1885, Manuel Estrada Cabrera from 1898 to 1920, and General Jorge Ubico from 1931 to 1944. The little group of big landowners who owned the country, the *oligarquía*, appreciated a regime that defended their interests. The almost nonexistent and politically divided middle class contented itself with furnishing the cadres for the lower ranks of the army and the administration. As for the Indians, nobody asked their opinion, and they probably did not have one.

The development of the middle class, following World War I, put this form of organization into question. As in France in 1789, these newly enriched members of the middle classes wanted to have their say in the political and economic organization of the country. This self-awareness was shared by the young officers who came from this milieu. These aspirations, mixed with a kind of vague idealism that sharpened during the 1930s, and especially during World War II, brought about the successive upheavals that were to terminate in the present situation.

The history of Guatemala during the course of the last twenty-five years is one of a struggle between conservative tendencies and the reformist élan. The struggle took extreme forms which here more than anywhere else permit us to spot the origins of subversion and the guerrilla bands. We will see that the latter are neither the result of communist propaganda nor the product of Castroite intervention, but a solution born of despair.

Guatemalan subversion illustrates the way in which a handful of guerrillas supported by a solidly organized urban resistance movement is enough to upset the entire economic and social life of a country.

The most important of the guerrilla movements, the Rebel Armed Forces (FAR) commanded in the beginning by Lieutenant Turcios Lima and then after his death by the law student César Montes, is closely allied with the Guatemalan Communist party. The party, unlike that in other Latin-American countries, was forced underground and outlawed, and therefore had no chance to renounce the armed struggle in exchange for legal activity. As a result, the Guatemalan guerrilla forces are constantly cited by Havana as an example to be followed. That does not prevent them from keeping Fidel Castro at a distance, for they find him much too inclined to encroachment.

The official point of view of César Montes and his comrades is that "Fidel Castro is not the *líder máximo*. We understand of course that our fight is for the entire South American continent, and that when the time comes we will need a leader on the continental level. However, when we need him, we will choose him ourselves. To us, Fidel is merely an obvious proof that our struggle can succeed. We admire him, but we absolutely refuse to take orders from him."

In Venezuela and in Colombia, where the Communist party has an official existence, things are different. The communists there have abandoned the armed struggle in favor of legal activity, through which they feel they can more easily bring about the revolution. But in Guatemala the Communist party has no chance of becoming legal; the liberal governments would wish it legal in order to put an end to the guerrillas, but it is too late.

In the past, a particularly active group made up of *terratenientes* and colonels has always managed to torpedo this project, sometimes with the aid of the United States, sometimes in spite of the United States.

Situated to the south of Mexico, Guatemala is one of the most beautiful countries in the world, with ruins like Tikal, Copán, and Piedras Negras. These are all that remain to us of the mysterious and shadowy civilization of the Mayas, who worshiped the stars, the rain, and corn. Because a majority of its inhabitants are Indians, Guatemala is also one of the saddest countries in the world. Officially these small, brown, peaceful, resigned, and often drunk men make up 53 percent of the population. But they make up more than 70 percent if we take into account all those who, on leaving their mountains, call themselves *ladinos*, mestizos, and live in the cities. Despite their name not a single drop of Spanish blood runs in their veins and they have lost their tribal structures and their community-owned land.

Out of Guatemala's total population of 4.2 million these *indios* account for three million; 83 percent of them are illiterate (100 percent of the women) and scarcely speak Spanish. Their language is Quiche. Their per-capita annual income is $10.80, one of the lowest in the world. And nevertheless they hate change, for it can only come from their enemies, the whites and the mestizos. Guatemalan history goes on without them: the liberations, the constitutions no sooner proclaimed than violated, the coups d'etat, the *pronunciamientos*, the political assassinations, the foreign interventions, and now the guerrillas. They have only one doctor per 120,000 inhabitants; in the city there is a doctor for every thousand inhabitants. But the immense weight of their inertia weighs down on the life of the country.

Though badly cared for and badly nourished, though infant mortality and tuberculosis wreak havoc among them, they nevertheless have access to all the alcohol they want.

I remember a village near Lake Atitlán. All the men were drunk and tottering. In front of a small white church they were playing some discordant music on an Indian flute, a marimba, and an improvised xylophone at which a laughing, toothless Indian battered away. Occasionally one could hear behind this cacophony the beginnings of a melody or an extremely pure rhythm coming from the distant past. The women took no part in this drinking bout. They moved in the background, a jug of water on their heads, looking hieratic and very beautiful in their embroidered clothes. These *indios* do not even have Guatemalan priests. Only priests from far-off Galicia have been willing to take care of them. In Chichicastenango, for example, they allow them to worship, in the church of Christ, a jumble of the Blessed Virgin, saints imported from Spain, and their old gods born in the Mayan forest.

The floor of the Chichicastenango church is covered with thousands of small candles that form a carpet of light which dies down and springs up with the wind. On the steps before the entrance, Indians wave incense burners made of punctured old tin cans. A thick blue smoke rises from them; it reminds you of the smoke once offered up by the astrologer-priests to their plumed gods.

But the present-day illiterate Indians know nothing of the secrets of the course of the stars—secrets their ancestors had been the first to discover. They no longer even know the names of their gods. From the fifteenth century on, instead of progressing they have sunk lower and lower.

I asked a priest, "But what could possibly make these Indian masses move?"

"Nothing," he told me. "Neither the army, nor the communists, nor the guerrillas. Maybe one thing . . . maybe we can."

However, the inhabitants of the mountain communities above Chichicastenango recently slit the throats of two priests imported from Spain. Others were driven away because they were impatient to bring the Indians back to more orthodox notions of dogma.

It was the last dictator of the traditional type, Jorge Ubico, who took the first step toward making the Indians aware of their status as second-class citizens. By decree he freed them of all their debts of hereditary bond-service. Because of this, in Huehue-tenango as well as in Antigua, he was affectionately known as "Don Jorge."

Don Jorge liked to visit them in their miserable shanties and share their meals of corn cakes and black beans. Since they liked alcohol and since they now had all the rights of other citizens, in every village he set up gin mills that made them docile by debasing them further. At the same time this very low-grade alcohol also provided tax money to swell the coffers of the state and the pockets of Don Jorge.

Since there was no work for the Indians, he had them construct a network of paved roads in the very heart of the mountains, from which tourists now can contemplate some of the most beautiful landscapes in the world. Twenty thousand *indios* lost their lives there. The government forgot to pay and feed them, but did it really make any difference if they died there or else-where?

Elected for the first time with the support of the United States, Don Jorge refused to leave office when his term was over, and drowned the uprisings of the opposition in blood. To calm Ameri-can anxieties, he made a present to the then very influential United Fruit Company of some of the most fertile land in the country. During the war he confiscated, for his personal benefit or for that of his friends, the well-maintained estates of the German colonials. Today, they all lie fallow.

He was overthrown in June, 1944, by a military junta, but according to custom he was given time to pack his bags and catch a plane. On leaving this country, which as a typical *caudillo* he had thought he held title to until his death, his last words were: "Now beware of the communists and the priests." The triumvirate that succeeded him lasted only a few months. Some young army officers, moved by various motives—ambition, patriotism, a sense of political responsibility—joined with representatives of the liberal professions, trade unions, and students to overthrow this triumvirate and impose democratic elections for the first time in Guatemalan history. Among these young officers was a Captain Jacobo Arbenz Guzmán, the son of a Swiss pharmacist in Quezaltenango.

Juan José Arévalo, a professor in exile in Argentina, was elected. He was an honest man, which was something new. In 1951, when his term was over, he left office without being driven out, which was something newer still. During his term of office he had to put down twenty-eight attempts at putsches and coups d'etat. Arbenz himself, now become a colonel and the Minister of War, was contacted by United Fruit to see if he would not overthrow his president. Hadn't Arévalo been heard to talk in private of agrarian reform. When Arbenz refused the offer to take power, attention was turned to him.

Arbenz succeeded Arévalo as president of the republic in an equally democratic election. At the time, Jacobo Arbenz, thirty-seven, was one of the youngest heads of state in the world. He had a beautiful wife who belonged to the San Salvador oligarchy, the "club of fourteen families," but who had read Marx. He also had friends who had made the pilgrimage to Moscow. He decided to bring about the agrarian reform the country so urgently needed. Twenty-two families and United Fruit had the greater part of arable land, and 300,000 peasants whatever was left over.

The unfarmed lands of the big American trust were distributed, private property limited to what a *hacendado*, a landowner, and his people could farm. The lands were repurchased by the state— and here is where it really hurts—at a price tied to their tax evaluation. Now taxes in this banana republic have a tendency to be figured in inverse proportion to revenue. The enormous profits of United Fruit—sixty-six million dollars in 1950—derived in part from this factor. The tropical fruit trust distributed bribes, but it paid very little in the way of taxes.

Arbenz was immediately accused of being a communist. He wasn't, but the more he was told so the more he tended to be so, as with Fidel Castro in Cuba. He had dared lay a finger on the sacrosanct notion of private property. It was more than a crime, it was a sacrilege—even if that property, as was the case with United Fruit, had been acquired through theft, extortion, lies, and assassination. His reforms were very cautious ones. However, he was surrounded by trade unionists like Pellecer and Gutiérrez, who were communists or communist sympathizers. The Labor Party communists who supported him were hardly numerous. They had only three deputies in the house and they had only won fourteen thousand votes in the elections. But as the only disciplined group, they quickly set the tone. On May 1 they organized parades to protest against the war in Korea and the war in Indochina, and they loudly proclaimed their solidarity with the oppressed peoples of the world. The Arbenz regime was to die as a result of the verbal daring of this small, noisy, excited group that would furnish pretexts for American intervention.

A special American ambassador, John D. Peurifoy, the CIA, which was directed at the time by Allen Dulles, the brother of Secretary of State John Foster Dulles, and the money of United Fruit combined efforts to make an army spring from nowhere, an army commanded by a very sad colonel—Castillo Armas, who had been fetched from the little Mexico City apartment where he had been saying his beads.

Castillo Armas had been imprisoned following an attempted coup d'etat—was it the seventeenth or the twenty-sixth against Arévalo's legislature?—that had gotten nowhere. He had escaped by digging a tunnel (alone?) that led out under Ninth Avenue. From there, a taxi took him to the Colombian embassy, where he demanded asylum. The Colombian ambassador eventually saw to it that he got to Mexico.

Castillo Armas had pursued his military studies in the United States and had maintained solid friendships at the Pentagon.

The Castillo Armas plot was an open secret. Everybody knew about it, including Arbenz, who tried everywhere to procure arms. He wanted to buy some in western Europe but was refused. He found some in the East. When these arms arrived, the signal for the kill was given. The representatives of neighboring banana republics such as Honduras and Nicaragua were recalled. One wonders now if the Arbenz regime would have veered toward communism. It seems probable when we consider what happened afterward in Cuba. The machinations of United Fruit and the American secret services could only have forced Arbenz into the arms of the communists—if indeed he was inclined to resist.

At this time the U.S.S.R. did not have the means of aiding a revolution carried on so far from Russia and so close to the United States. Abandoned by his comrades on the general staff, Arbenz was to defend himself badly. Against the advice of Che Guevara, who was not yet taken very seriously, he refused to create popular militias and to distribute arms to the crowd. Despite his wife and his new friends, he remained a military man who did not care to see weapons floating around the streets. Arbenz capitulated well before Castillo Armas reached the capital. Colonel Armas, with a scapular around his neck, took power, returned the lands to United Fruit, abolished the agrarian reforms, and outlawed the Communist party.

In July, 1957, while the little colonel was on his way to the dining room of the Palace with a group of businessmen, a presidential guard fired on him point blank and then wounded both an aide and a servant before killing himself. Was this guard a madman, an agent of the Communist party, or an agent of the association of discontented colonels? Nobody will ever know.

An engineer corps general who prided himself on being an archaeologist, Miguel Ydígoras Fuentes, took power after holding and reholding elections several times under the pretext that they had been fraudulent. During his term of office, Guatemala was to go through a particularly agitated period. It is true, however, that his election shortly preceded Fidel Castro's victory in Cuba. Ydígoras began by expelling several leaders of the extreme left, having his planes bomb Mexican fishing boats over a question of shrimps, asking that UN observers be sent to the frontier, and accusing Great Britain of having permitted Cuban ships in Belize to load on arms bound for the Guatemalan coast. The Guatemalan government intercepted messages from Castro to Arbenz which indicated the former leader was aiding insurgents in the country in preparation for an attempt at a coup d'etat. Communists were planning phony assassination attempts, which they would blame on the regime, against local extremist leaders.

Finally, in October, a new communiqué announced that the air force had strafed the one-thousand-ton *La Cubana* as it was attempting to land troops on the Atlantic coast. This ship was said to be part of Colonel Arbenz's invasion fleet. The Cubans, it is true, were quite active during this period. They had tried to land in Nicaragua to overthrow the Somoza dynasty, in Santo Domingo to overthrow Trujillo, in Venezuela to seize petroleum sources. The heroes of the Sierra Maestra thought at times that anything was possible, not only in Cuba but elsewhere in South America.

The other side was by no means inactive. On the Helvetia plantation, where an airplane landing field had been constructed during the Castillo Armas operation, anti-Castro Cubans were training under American instructors. They were equipped with Polish and Czech arms bought by Arbenz and captured after his defeat.

These are the troops which after having been discreetly transported to Nicaragua were to embark on the disastrous Bay of Pigs expedition. Ydígoras formally denied the participation of Guatemala in any project to invade Cuba.

On November 13, 1960, came the real outbreak of guerrilla

warfare in Guatemala. In the middle of the night, two officers—
Captain Chur del Cid and Colonel Pereira—imprisoned in the
Matamoros barracks for acts of rebellion managed to escape
from their cells, shot down two other colonels who were about
to give the alarm, and with the help of some members of the
Guatemalan Labor party (communist) and the Revolutionary
party (reformist) set out for the Atlantic. They had several jeeps,
an armored car, and some automatic weapons.

On arriving at the Zacapa base they pretended to be reinforcements and captured the garrison without firing a shot. Some of
the soldiers joined them, others fled. Colonel Ramón Gonzales,
commander of the base, managed to reach the capital and give
the alarm. Nobody had suspected a thing.

Meanwhile the rebel convoy set out for the coast again. They
camped outside Puerto Barrios, posing as rice dealers. The next
morning the base and the port were taken and occupied, the
colonel who commanded them was shot, and mimeographed tracts
were distributed to the population.

It was the first attempt at a military coup d'etat that staunchly
affirmed its communist and Castroite sentiments and tried to set
up a political platform. When the city was taken, the Guatemalan
fleet of three ships—two of them really personal yachts of the
president—got away from shore in time and established radio
contact with the capital.

Ydígoras was banqueting in the country with a few colonel
friends. As soon as he was alerted, he gave orders for his air
force to intervene. Puerto Barrios is a small agglomeration of low
wooden and cement houses scattered between wastelands and
swamps; it has a red-light district for sailors and a Negro quarter
that looks like a primitive tropical village.

The planes skimmed over the ground, bombing the fuel tanks
and the aircraft runway to prevent any eventual landing of Cuban
planes. The local radio station, which had been launching appeals
to rebel, was destroyed. But on Radio Habana, Arbenz announced his return.

The entire Guatemalan army remained faithful and, once mobilized, some thirteen thousand men set out by plane and overland with modern American armament that had just been delivered. Elements of the advance guard entered into contact with the rebels. Ydígoras flew over the combat zone and made helicopter landings to encourage unit commanders; his followers begged him not to risk a life so precious to the country. It was a great moment of lyrical delirium in the Hispanic-American manner.

But the boldness of the chief of state was measured. He allowed himself to be restrained. The six hundred colonels whom he had created, some of whom were merely bookkeepers or even orderlies in the Ministry of War, and some of whom were illiterate, clung to their new advantages. Ydígoras himself was not eager to lose his $150,000 salary, plus the million-dollar personal retirement fund he had set up for himself.

During this time, between bombardments, the rebel leaders in Puerto Barrios held a public meeting that discouragingly drew only two hundred people.

Two days after the launching of the rebellion, after a twenty-five-minute pretense at resistance, the Zacapa base surrendered. The next day, government officials aboard a light aircraft landed at Puerto Barrios waving the white handkerchief of truce. They discussed the matter heatedly while the pilot and his plane prudently took off, abandoning the passengers.

The following day, Ydígoras made a triumphal entry into Zacapa, the capture of which had not cost a single victim, but merely led to the taking of eight prisoners and some uniforms. During this time the rebels also abandoned Puerto Barrios and fled to the mountains. Ydígoras and his liberating troops made a new triumphal entry, this time into the port. Total government losses are estimated at four colonels.

It was only then that the students tried to demonstrate, both in the capital and in Antigua, the old Spanish colonial city. Some were killed and others imprisoned. They were too late; the game had already been played and lost without them. Colonel Pereira and a small group of the faithful managed to reach the Izabal mountains. Their encampment was surrounded and the rebels lost eighteen men. Eventually Colonel Pereira was able to reach Mexico. Soon no more than a handful of soldiers and a few students under the command of Lieutenant Yon Sosa and 2nd Lieutenant Turcios were left. The small group sought refuge in the Sierra de las Minas, a deserted region of about one inhabitant per square mile, a region pocked with caves. The road below facilitated contacts with the capital and the arrival of supplies.

The Guatemalan reporters who had sent out dispatches did not even know the names of the real leaders of the rebellion. It was only afterward that Yon Sosa, Trejo Esquivel, Lt. Colonel Argüeta, Captains de León and Chacón, and 2nd Lieutenants Turcios Lima and Eva Zaldivar were to enter into the news bulletins. Argüeta, de León, and Chacón were later killed in the course of skirmishes with the army.

Replying in writing to a questionnaire I had sent, the political committee of the MR 13* maintained that "apart from all political influence, the uprising of November 13 was provoked by the corrupt rule of the Ydígoras Fuentes government and by the existence at Helvetia of a training camp controlled by the Americans. Initially, this uprising was aimed merely at replacing one military government by another military government, one that would be further to the left and free of North American influences.

"But in the Izabal mountain hideouts, the best of us," explained

---

* The MR 13, founded after the failure of Colonel Pereira's putsch, initially included all the "rebels." It was directed by Lieutenant Yon Sosa, whose second in command was 2nd Lieutenant Turcios. As the result of political and personal rivalries between the two leaders, the movement split into two groups: Yon Sosa retained the leadership of the MR 13, which adopted a Trotskyite stance, and Turcios Lima created the Rebel Armed Forces, the FAR, which passed over into the communist camp.

the leaders of the movement, "will find ties with the peasants, become aware of the conditions of exploitation under which they live, and thus be won over by the idea of fighting for their liberation. The very evolution of our struggle led us to understand that bourgeois politics will never permit us to rally around us the masses of the country. . . ."

It is likely that this attitude was created, maintained, and oriented by the more politically minded students who had joined them and by the cadres of the Communist party, which had been underground for six years.

In its beginnings, the movement was formed of different elements with different political pasts but urged on by a common goal—the overthrow of a regime based on corruption, prevarication, and submission to the big American interests. This time the military rebels did not want to limit themselves to a putsch, but to replace the government by another type—one that would be socialist and Castroite, for Cuba had already imposed itself on them as an example. By refusing to change his methods, by continuing further along the road of corruption and militarism, Ydígoras was to give the nascent movement reason to survive and grow until the internal ideological quarrels caused enormous splits.

At the request of the Guatemalan and Nicaraguan governments, for a month after November 13 the American fleet cruised along the Atlantic coast to prevent a possible Castroite landing, something that, of course, never happened. Arbenz simply launched a radio appeal inviting the Guatemalan people to destroy the Helvetia base, whose existence had finally been revealed in the United States press. Helvetia was primarily a direct threat to Castro.

For about a year, the rebels—they were not yet known as guerrillas—did little to cause talk. The two young officers and their men were hardly uneasy. Their classmates and some of the leaders of the latter continued to protect them.

Operations against them did not really begin until 1962. At the beginning of February, a garrison on the Atlantic coast in the Izabal province was attacked by fifty guerrillas who had regrouped in Honduras. The 2nd lieutenant on duty was killed, and three men were wounded. The leader of this commando force was Yon Sosa; it was the first time he was to cause a stir. Without attempting to exploit his victory, he regained the Sierra de las Minas.

At almost the same time, the chief of police of Guatemala City was assassinated, and bombs began exploding everywhere. Toward the end of the month two radio stations were occupied by armed commandos. For a few minutes they broadcast ideological professions of faith and invited the population to rebel. One of these radio stations was about three hundred yards from the Presidential Palace.

These events were followed in March by strikes in which students stretched across the roadways and blocked traffic, and by tussles between the police and several thousands of demonstrators. Cars were overturned, windows broken, and demonstrators killed and wounded.

This time the army seriously entered into the struggle. There were several skirmishes in the mountains. Spokesmen for the general staff announced dozens of deaths, but—Turcios Lima claimed afterward—they were for the most part peasants who had been shot down because of their sympathies for the guerrillas.

The most serious encounter took place in the region of Granados in March, 1962. A group of guerrillas had been betrayed to the army. Their encampment was surrounded during the night, and in the early hours of dawn an attack was launched. Eight guerrillas were killed. Among the prisoners was Rodrigo Asturias, son of the writer Miguel Ángel Asturias, who is now Guatemala's ambassador in Paris and who recently received the Nobel Prize. Ydígoras, a friend of his family, came to see him. He lectured Rodrigo as though he had been a schoolboy on a spree, but agreed to intervene with the military in his favor. A short time later, Rodrigo was released and went to Mexico. The striking students decided to organize a big funeral parade through the streets of the city: the Burial of Democracy. The police intervened: three deaths. Requests for Ydígoras' resignation came from both the right and the left; the former thought he was too soft, the latter saw in him a fearsome *caudillo*.

During this time, profiting from the disorder, Turcios' commandos swept through the capital, attacking military patrols and police stations, taking prisoners for ransom. But what most worried the conservative right, as well as the army, was the possible candidacy and probable election of Juan José Arévalo, the former liberal president who had been cleared in Washington of charges of Castroism and communism brought against him and who now benefited from the official support of the Kennedy government.

In November, 1962, the officers of the Aurora military base rebelled and their planes machine-gunned the barracks in the capital. One even strafed the Presidential Palace. Several bullets dug into the walls and furnishings of Ydígoras' office and bedroom. The government responded by bombing the general headquarters of the rebels. At the end of three hours the aviators surrendered by stretching their white parachutes around the runway. This time the putsch came from the extreme right and was financed by the big landowners: Ydígoras had decided to divide about five million acres of unfarmed land among a hundred thousand Indian families.

It was into this atmosphere of disorder, corruption, widespread strikes, summary executions, attacks, and attempts at government overthrow that on March 31, 1963, came former President Arévalo's announcement of his return. Ydígoras had authorized it. Why? Pressure from the United States? A new about-face? Weariness with his overbearing colonels?

That same day, Sherman tanks surrounded the Presidential

Palace. A delegation of colonels led by the Minister of War, Colonel Peralta Azurdia, demanded entrance. The president refused. A tank climbed the marble steps of the palace, battered down the monumental door, and installed itself in the patio. Ydígoras Fuentes was forced on board a military plane that landed him in Managua, Nicaragua. On his arrival he declared, "The same thing that happened to Napoleon happened to me. But he had to go to Sainte-Hélène, whereas I at least find myself among friends."

The rightist group formed by the colonels and the big land-owners could scarcely have done otherwise to salvage their privileges. All the liberals and the entire left were in agreement on the candidacy of Arévalo, and for once Washington had given its benediction. Arévalo could not have failed to be elected. Nobody really knows what he would have done once he was in power, but it was possible to hope that he would declare a general amnesty which would have put an end to guerrilla operations. The Kennedy government saw in its support of Arévalo a means of increasing its prestige in Latin America. The bell was once again tolling for the colonels and the *caudillos*, just as it had in Roosevelt's day. The Alliance for Progress had just been launched. Maybe everything was going to change. A handful of colonels decided otherwise.

The most important consequence of the Peralta coup d'etat, in spite of the attempts at democratization made by the regime that followed, was to have made the guerrilla bands an irreversible phenomenon. After March 31, 1963, there were only two possible solutions: the crushing of the rebellion or the installation of an extreme-left revolutionary regime.

For ten years the political and social life of the country had been marking time. Whether or not he had been a communist, Arbenz had aroused many hopes by taking measures to improve the deplorable condition of the urban and rural proletariat. The most privileged members of this proletariat were those who worked for United Fruit. But after having lobbied in Washington and bribed officials and colonels to conserve its privileges, the big American company, struck by the antitrust law and by an epidemic that ravaged its banana plantations, had to liquidate its holdings one after another. Its discharged employees swelled the ranks of the discontented.

Power continued to be held by the army of six hundred colonels and an oligarchy that was again breathing easily after having feared briefly that it would fall once more into the hands of Arévalo. The oligarchy followed a simple principle: "If the Indians learn how to read, they will become vulnerable to Castroite propaganda, hence it is an error to build schools." All the social legislation that had been set up was abandoned. Social security was no more than a memory, agrarian reform no more than a conversational gambit.

In the beginning, the armed struggle was not an end in itself but merely a means to reestablish these advantages and to put into action those reforms written into the constitution. Shortly before the coup d'etat, the central committee of the underground Communist party affirmed, "Revolution is not a synonym for armed struggle. Its essential feature is the passage of the power of property and the principal means of essential production from one class to another."

Since the army was once more in power and all their hopes were now frustrated, the communists participated in the struggle with a new vigor, placing at the disposition of the guerrillas their underground organization and their urban infrastructure. In the country, it was the well-organized former United Fruit workers who were able to offer the most efficient help.

For the combatants themselves it was no longer a question of pressuring the political system for popular reforms, but of obtaining a victory over the colonels. They wanted to overthrow the regime.

A resolution of the Communist party reaffirmed:

The reactionary classes having resorted to extreme means and placed the army in power, the revolutionary forces have also decided on extreme means. . . . It is the stubborn resistance of the forces of reaction to democratic changes that has forced the people of Guatemala to adopt the path of armed struggle.

The guerrilla bands reorganized. New fronts were established in the provinces of Izabal and Zacapa, and units scattered in other regions were regrouped under the command of Yon Sosa and Turcios Lima. The Sierra de las Minas, with its inaccessible mountains, its few and easily watched-over roads, its scant population, became the ideal zone for the establishment of an itinerant general headquarters.

Itinerant because mobility was the essential element of this new tactic: marches, countermarches, lightning raids, improvised meetings in the villages—meetings designed to accelerate the political education of the *campesinos*. To avoid army reprisals against the latter, they pretended a certain brutality toward them. However, this in no way prevented alerted military detachments from murdering peasants sympathetic to the guerrilla cause.

Occasionally after army raids the survivors would tie their belongings into bundles and abandon their village. Some joined the guerrillas; others, accompanied by their wives and children, scattered and went off to live in other Indian communities in other provinces. As a result, several small villages in the Zacapa area slowly fell into ruins as the tropical vegetation reclaimed what had once been farmed land.

The army intelligence service was primarily dependent on *comisionados militares*, retired soldiers or noncoms who benefited from certain advantages. The guerrillas decided to make an example of them and executed several in the village square late at night, with their neighbors invited to attend. The guerrillas would disappear into the night while the Indians stood motionless around the corpse, thinking of the calamities in store for them.

Some of the plantation overseers met the same fate for having taken the interests of their bosses too much to heart.

The army had not been inactive either. Operations increased in the entire zone held, but not controlled, by the guerrilla bands. The list of those killed in various engagements grew daily.

But a new factor intervened—the presence of Green Berets alongside the army detachments. These detachments received modern arms, the same given American soldiers fighting in Vietnam. The arms excited the envy of some guerrillas, who managed to "salvage" a few.

The arrival of the new reinforcements, often camouflaged as surveyors assigned to make a map of the country or as topographic engineers laying out new roads, was to modify the nature of the struggle. It was already a bloody one, but it had a certain tropical insouciance about it; sentimental considerations sometimes overrode strategic ones. It was to become pitiless. The Green Berets did not act directly. They were aware of the unpopularity attached to them, their country, and their mission. They skillfully took the army in hand by means of their former students in Panama and La Escuela de las Américas. The "weekends" in the guerrilla forces came to a brutal halt. Several arrested members of the revolutionary organization were "worked over" and agreed to betray their comrades.

Small army detachments accompanied by these men, whose faces were hidden by hoods, stopped cars and taxis on the Puerto Barrios road. The hooded man would point out those whom he recognized as liaison agents or sympathizers of the guerrillas. Those so identified were shot against a hillside.

The bitterness of the struggle brought two guerrilla personalities to the fore. One of them was Yon Sosa, nicknamed "El Chino" because of his physical appearance. He was the son of a Chinese and a native woman. A remarkable military leader who had benefited from the training provided in American instruction centers, he now tried also to become a political leader.

"Yon Sosa," his comrade Turcios Lima was to say later, "claimed to be the only one to represent the revolution. For him the guerrilla forces are a stimulant designed to modify the political context. . . . El Chino talks of the 'socialist revolution,' whereas from all indications there is not a bit of socialist awareness in the entire country. He talks of 'soviets,' of the Union of Socialist Republics of the Caribbean. . . . He's dreaming."

What was held against him was something more serious. He was becoming a Trotskyite, unwise in a subversive movement that took its watchwords from Cuba and its example from Fidel Castro.

Denouncing this tendency at the end of Havana's Tricontinental Congress, Castro was to say, "If at one time Trotskyism represented an erroneous position, but one within the framework of our ideas, it has subsequently become a common instrument of imperialism and reaction."

Régis Debray, who in *Revolution in the Revolution?* made himself the critical interpreter of Fidel Castro and his ideas, wrote:

Trotskyism attributes great importance to the socialist character of the revolution, to its future program, and would like it to be judged by this purely phraseological question, as if declaring a thousand times that the revolution should be socialist would help call it into existence. But the nub of the question is not theoretical, it lies in the forms of organization through which the "Socialist Revolution" will be realized. It is here that we discover not only that the revolution which they speak of is utopian, but that the means employed lead not to the revolution but to the scarcely utopian liquidation of existing popular movements. . . .*

---

* Régis Debray, *Revolution in the Revolution?* (New York: Grove Press, Inc., 1967), p. 37.

Trotskyism comes especially from Mexico, where the old revolutionary leader was assassinated, but where he left many disciples. Members of the opposition constantly cross the border in both directions. They are in frequent contact not only with opponents of the Mexican government who have remained attached to the memory of Emiliano Zapata and who are disappointed by the Mexican revolution's conversion to middle-class values, but also with Spanish refugees of the POUM, survivors of the civil war.

The other figure who came to the fore in Guatemala was Yon Sosa's former subordinate, Turcios Lima. As the uncontested military leader of the Armed Rebel Forces (FAR), Turcios, with his boyish laugh and his spoiled child's notions, was the image of a kind of Robin Hood who punished the colonels and helped the poor *campesinos* by stealing money from the pockets of the rich. He gave press conferences in the city. He let himself be seen in cafés. He appeared in places where people least expected to see him, and though tracked by the entire police force, he disappeared with no trouble at all. He was accompanied by at most one or two bodyguards. The day his class graduated, he even dared take part in the great ball given in the rooms of the officers' club. He came in uniform and, after having checked his pistol at the door, mixed with the guests. Nobody arrested him or even tried to, although there was a $25,000 price on his head. Turcios had retained a great many friends in the army, especially among the young officers, and he did nothing to lose these friendships. He never attacked the lower ranks.

Turcios condemned a colonel to death and had four of his men follow him continuously. The colonel tried to escape by reaching the airport, but the plane had already taken off and he had to return to the city, where he was shot down. It was not the right colonel but his brother-in-law, who was also an air force colonel. Afterward it was claimed that he had bombed villages held by the rebels—which proved that they had been right, after all, to kill him. Still another colonel, the commander of the military police, was shot down in Puerto Barrios.

Seduced by the $25,000 reward, a former U.S. Marine back from Vietnam tried to assassinate Turcios by passing himself off as a reporter. His brother worked for *Life* and he took advantage of the fact that their names could be confused. He knew that Turcios was fond of the company of reporters. But the American incautiously talked too much in front of some military men whom he naïvely believed hostile to Turcios. They may have been enemies of the communist Turcios, but they were still friends of the 2nd lieutenant. The American's body was found with a bullet through the head.

In an attempt to capitalize on the dissensions among the guerrillas, the government of Colonel Peralta Azurdia tried new liberal measures. But the possibilities for action were extremely limited. In spite of himself, Peralta was the man of the right, which owed its salvation to him. He managed to restrain their demands, but he could take no step that would engage the more dynamic elements of the middle class. There could be no question of income taxes, even though they were called for by law, nor could there be any question of agrarian reform. All he could do was improve the functioning of the administration, fight corruption as well as he could, avoid a crisis, and fight communism.

In order to be recognized by the American government, Peralta had made vague promises of elections in 1965. To begin with, he proposed to elect a constituent assembly in 1964. In addition to Peralta's own group, two others—the National Liberation Movement, composed of partisans of Colonel Castillo Armas, a pro-American and extreme right party; and the Revolutionary party, a leftist reform party—accepted the gambit after deliberation. As for the others, after ten years of executions, imprisonments, and exile, it was difficult for them to express themselves. They could only do so by means of another party tolerated by those in power. So thought the *licenciado* Mario Méndez Montenegro, who had been mayor of Guatemala City under President Arévalo. He felt that it was better to join in a pseudo-democratic congress than to refuse and "legalize the guerrilla forces" by forcing the communists, their real support, to remain underground. Needless to say, all these events and bargainings took place in an atmosphere of kidnappings, assassinations, and communiqués regularly announcing the death of dozens of guerrillas. Bombs exploded in the city, grenades went off in movie houses on the outskirts, and many were wounded. The Minister of Defense, Colonel Molina Arreaga, was shot down in the street.

The leftist and the extreme leftist opposition had asked the voters to protest by leaving their ballots blank, but though the majority of the ballots were blank, the assembly was nevertheless elected. Supporters of Peralta had forty seats, those of Colonel Castillo Armas had ten seats, and those of Méndez Montenegro had ten seats. One of the first decisions of the new constituent assembly was to outlaw communism. As for the presidential election that was to be held the following year, Mario Méndez Montenegro appeared the most likely candidate to succeed. However, Peralta felt, probably incorrectly, that the *licenciado*'s compromise with the military government would cost him the support of the left and that his own candidate would be a shoo-in.

An unforeseen event upset everything. Early in November, 1965, Mario Méndez Montenegro was shot down in front of his door. The police immediately claimed it was a suicide. Then, going back on its previous declarations, it said that he had been assassinated by the communists, who could not forgive him his betrayal. A more likely rumor had it that he was eliminated by the oligarchy, who preferred to eliminate the reformist candidate rather than take the least chance of his being elected.

From being a traitor, Méndez Montenegro became a martyr. The left, which had decided to abstain from the election, was ready now to support the candidacy of his brother, Julio César Méndez Montenegro, a centrist liberal and professor at the university. After having taken part in the 1944 revolution, Julio César Méndez Montenegro had been made Arévalo's secretary, then had quit the political scene. More reassuring than his brother, he was also adopted by the right, which counted on him to end guerrilla activities. The left and the right having agreed on him, his election was assured. Only the extreme left opposed him, claiming that no matter what the result of the elections, the future president would be a prisoner of the army.

It was during this period of search for an impossible political solution that the underground, despite its ideological division, organized and carried out a scheme for financing its activities. Big landowners, industrialists, and rich businessmen were kidnapped and held for ransom. The sums demanded ranged from $50,000 to $100,000. (The latter sum was what was required for the lawyer Roberto Serrano.) But in March, 1966, a rancher, Manuel Ralda, had to pay $250,000 for his freedom. Thanks to this method, all the financial problems of the revolution were suddenly resolved.

Unfortunately, ideological problems were insurmountable. By the end of 1964, there were pro-Chinese Trotskyites on the one side and Castroite communists on the other. The first of these two groups explained this separation in its Marxist-Leninist jargon.

"In July, 1964, the Movement of November 13, having attained ideological and political maturity and having analyzed the national and international situation, decided to assume the program of the 'Socialist Revolution' and withdrew from the Armed Rebel Forces, inviting the masses to take up arms and put a peasant-worker government in power. . . . History teaches, and national experience confirms, that Imperialism and its allies within the country are opposed to any solution that would go against their interests, and that they are determined to use any means to prevent such a solution."

As for the point of view of the Castroite-communist faction,

it was explained by Turcios Lima, who at the Havana Tricontinental Congress had been promoted to commander in chief of the
FAR. According to him, the split was a consequence of "Trotskyite infiltrations, which provoked division and confusion in the
country's liberation movement."

Turcios Lima also explained some of his personal ideas, which
must have seemed strangely unorthodox, especially at Havana.

"First of all," he declared, "I am not a communist. . . . I am
a revolutionary. I have five years of experience in the guerrilla
forces, and an analysis of all the errors made since the beginning
of the armed insurrection in Guatemala has led me to my present
position."

Two out of the three guerrilla groups active in 1962 had been
completely destroyed because they had not gone sufficiently deep
into the mountains. Turcios cited the example of one guerrilla
force that had set itself up in the Huehuetenango region on November 13, 1962, in commemoration of the November 13, 1960,
uprising.

"It is a very mountainous zone with a high population density.
The men at the head of the guerrilla band had made no provision
for political preparation. They scarcely knew the terrain and
could count on no peasant organization. They wandered around
outdoors, vainly trying to explain the sense of their struggle to
peasants at brief, improvised meetings. The results were disastrous; they were all captured or killed."

During this time, Julio César Méndez Montenegro, accepted
by the right as the lesser evil, supported by the left because he
was the brother of the man assassinated for his liberal ideas, was
elected president. With the center-left faction in power, one
could at last hope for a truce.

Before accepting his election, the right forced the new chief
of state to sign a "secret pact" under the terms of which he was
not authorized to undertake any structural reforms. He had no
authority to intervene in the affairs of the army without the

authorization of the general staff; he could neither appoint nor replace officers, and he had no control over the fight against the guerrillas. In short, he was offered the chance to be, like his predecessors, a simple administrator who had the advantage, so far as foreign countries were concerned, of providing a democratic screen for the regime of the colonels.

Like his brother Mario, Julio César Méndez Montenegro thought he would be able to get out of an inextricable situation by first accepting power under any conditions and then freeing himself from these conditions thanks to external and internal support.

So far as he was concerned, the pact was an expedient from which he could liberate himself whenever he wanted to. However, this pact, which nobody took the trouble to keep secret, quickly became his prison and made any step he took meaningless. Nobody believed in him or in the support of the United States, nor did his trip to Mexico increase his political stature.

Once more the situation was hopeless. Méndez Montenegro offered the guerrilla leaders an amnesty if they would lay down their arms, but he could give them no guarantee. The proposal was rejected.

At the same time the association of students revealed that twenty-eight communist leaders who had disappeared since the presidential election had been assassinated by the army secret services and the police.

The government awkwardly began by denying everything. When requested to produce the prisoners, it could only come up with some vague excuses. The opposition specified that the men had been shot at the Retalhuleu military base and that their bodies had been dumped into the sea by military planes.

Thus this election, which was to have deprived the guerrillas of popular support, actually reinforced the tendency to armed insurrection, which now seemed the only possible solution. Assassination attempts began again, bombs exploded, and kidnappings increased. The election of Méndez Montenegro had done nothing except destroy the last flickering hopes for a peaceful solution.

It was in this atmosphere that in October, 1966, the death of Turcios Lima occurred. The hero who had carried out so many wild schemes and made a legend of his invulnerability stole a sports car parked in front of a restaurant and drove it into a wall at 125 miles an hour. His funeral cortege in Guatemala City was followed by an immense crowd. At his grave, one of his comrades gave the funeral elegy of the *comandante*.

"Friends, Guatemalans, *compañeros* . . . like all real revolutionaries, Turcios knew that life was to be lived at its fullest in the service of a high and noble ideal. . . . Comandante Turcios loved life, for it gave him the opportunity to use revolutionary means to bring about the future victory of all Guatemalans. . . . In him the Guatemalan revolution loses one of its youngest and most seasoned leaders. . . ."

There was a great deal of weeping, especially among the women and the common people, but also among several of his classmates who had secretly dreamed of doing as he had. One of his lieutenants, César Montes, succeeded him.

Perhaps this change of leadership facilitated a certain rapprochement between the two rival movements. According to MR 13 leaders, "Relations between FAR and us are now fraternal, though limited. They include the exchange of information and the mutual protection of the members of the two groups. We are currently discussing the possibilities for joint action. . . ."

To political kidnapping was soon added gangsterism and pranks. Phony guerrillas set up on their own. Some youngsters from good families kidnapped themselves and pocketed the ransoms they had cronies collect from their parents. The leaders and most of the members of the guerrilla forces, of course, all belong to the country's best families, those who have both power and money. Everything took place between people of the same social world, and whether they wanted to or not, the parents had to come to the aid of their sons. Slowly but surely, everybody was involved.

To save their sons from the guerrilla contagion, some wealthy Guatemalan families sent them abroad to complete never-ending studies. Most often a student's chance of a scholarship is in direct proportion to his opposition to the government. But it often happens that returning students go off to fight and die in the guerrilla forces.

One young guerrilla was to tell us,

"What do you want me to do, go on with my studies? What for? To accomplish what? Every path is blocked and barricaded. Joining the guerrillas is the only way out."

This young guerrilla and his girl friend were shot down a few weeks later. I read about it in the newspapers on my return to France.

However, when you arrive in Guatemala, you are unaware that this is a country in a state of latent civil war. At first glance, Guatemala looks like a peaceful little tropical republic drowsing in the sun—happy and welcoming with its Mayan ruins, its colorfully dressed Indians, and its troublesome drunks.

During the day one sometimes hears distant rifle shots, machine-gun bursts, and sirens, but the Guatemalans go about their business. The next day one hears that there was a skirmish and that several people died. Summary executions are carried out even more discreetly.

The Guatemalans' only luxury is the transistor radio. The Japanese have shipped over boatfuls in exchange for farm products, and there are enough of them in the country to satisfy demand for the next twenty years. They are inexpensive, and in most stores stockpiles reach the ceiling. There are a few fancy dress shops in the center of the city, and that's about it. The only other things are the leprous facades of the small shops set up by Lebanese or Spanish emigrants. They had been attracted by the stability of the currency, the quetzal, and though driven to despair by the absence of clients, they don't dare return home. However, they have no illusions.

Nobody undertakes anything, nobody invests a cent. Economic life has come to a standstill. There is no visible danger, but a vague menace discouragingly floats everywhere in the air. In the evening the streets are empty, and there are scarcely more than a handful of spectators in the movie houses. The bored police spend their nights chasing after prostitutes, who are probably among the fastest runners in Latin America. If they are caught, they have to pay a bribe known here as in Mexico by the flavorsome name of *mordida*. If they escape, they have won. This little game takes up a good part of their night.

Restaurants are rare and even the most luxurious of them look like suburban snack bars. Though the food may be served under gleaming neon lights, it is not very good. In the few bars open at night, drunks linger because they haven't the strength to go another step. The police sit around with the prostitutes they have managed to nab while the latter negotiate for their liberty over a bottle of cane alcohol.

Away from the center of town, in zone seven or ten, the evening drags on until midnight. This area is an annex of Los Angeles, with its luxurious pavilions, its shiny supermarkets, its daily round of parties, its new bowling alley, and its sports cars.

There are few young people at parties here. The children are in New York, or in Europe, or even closer, in another zone, where they are busily blowing up an electric power station or executing a spy.

It used to be good form for young Guatemala City students to go off for a weekend in the guerrilla bands. The "weekend" was actually a training period of several days of military instruction. They were in no particular danger, and they had the excitement of participating in the guerrilla adventure. In private cars or in taxis they drove off toward Puerto Barrios. Halfway there, in the

Zacapa region, they got out and climbed up the sierra. After hiking a few hours, they were there. As for the guerrillas, it was said that those who had large financial resources would hire mercenaries to take their places for five dollars a day while they went into town.

However, the situation deteriorated when Colonel Peralta, represented everywhere as one of the mainstays of fascism and reaction, left for exile, and the democratic Professor Julio César Méndez Montenegro came to power. Peralta had distrusted the Americans and tried to limit their military aid, but Dr. Méndez Montenegro, struggling with both the opposition of the right and the left, was obliged to call on them to maintain himself in power. And that is how the Green Berets arrived on the scene.

One has only to live a few weeks in Guatemala to see that the social life of the country is in a state of upheaval. Scenes of violence and disorder are everywhere; entire communities are decimated, particularly in the northwest of the country; every day the number of widows and orphans increases, victims of mysterious struggles and vengeances. Many men are torn from their homes by unknown bands and either kept prisoner in secret places or summarily executed. Afterward their mutilated corpses are found somewhere far from the spot in which they were kidnapped.

We are very disturbed about our peaceful population, which has for too long now been subjected to brutality, terror, and anguish. . . . The ruling climate of insecurity merely aggravates our country's moral, social, and economic problems, holding down all efforts at development and causing an increase in the cost of living, unemployment, and famine. The new generations are unable to find work, while the older ones are often forced to abandon it.

These "pastoral exhortations" from the Guatemalan episcopacy give some idea of the situation in the country during 1967.

Three thousand Guatemalan men and women of all ages, social conditions, and political allegiances were victims of the policy of

repression practiced by both the government and the army. Nobody knows how many were victims of the guerrillas. It became
difficult to know to whom the corpses belonged. Of 256 corpses
whose discovery was recently announced in the newspapers, only
140 could be identified. Their terrorized families had not dared
to enter a complaint, and the police had not cared to press their
inquiries. The faces of the corpses had been smashed, their papers
stolen, and their clothing torn off to make identification impossible.

Peasants were killed in the course of military operations
launched against the guerrillas. Forty-three people, twenty-eight
of whom could not be identified, were shot down in the streets of
the capital in the course of skirmishes between the urban guerrilla forces on one side and the army and police on the other.

After being arrested, eighteen people died of "natural causes."

One hundred and two people were kidnapped by secret anticommunist organizations: the NOA (Nueva Organización Anticomunista); MANO, also called Mano Blanca (Movimiento
Anticomunista Nacionalista Organizado); and CADEG (Consejo
Anticomunista de Guatemala). All were tortured before being
killed; sixty-nine could not be identified.

The same organizations also claimed seventy-one summary
executions. To complete these figures we must include the legal
arrest of ninety-eight people, nine of whom were tortured. Thirty
people disappeared without leaving so much as a trace.

During this same period there were thirty-five dynamitings,
eighteen against private homes and three against pharmacies that
were probably suspected of furnishing medicaments to the guerrillas. Nor was the university, an active center of opposition,
spared. There were four explosions in university buildings or in
the homes of university administrators.

During my April, 1967, stay in Guatemala, one morning I
discovered all the walls of the capital covered with posters pasted
up during the night by the Mano Blanca. They included the

photos, descriptions, and university titles of all the political and military leaders of the guerrillas, as well as of their sympathizers. A threatening text below affirmed their responsibility for the current misfortunes of the country.

This sort of operation could hardly have been undertaken without the complicity of the police, which constantly patrolled the streets. And yet the Méndez Montenegro government has categorically condemned the subversive antiguerrilla movements. It has even arrested one or two colonels—colonels without a command, that is, colonels of no importance—who had been officially compromised by the movements.

The following month, on May 9, 1967, the NOA pronounced twenty-two death sentences: two journalists, seven union leaders, eight members of the Communist party, and five members of the university. It was no bluff; these condemnations were to be carried out.

It was necessary only to look over the local press—*El Imparcial, El Gráfico, La Hora, La Prensa Libre.* Horrible bits of news could be garnered—for example, the discovery of the ossuary in Los Amates in the Izabal province: three young women and a man. In Gualán, another corpse was found, the body of a twenty-four-year-old woman with ten bullets in her— executed "for reasons unknown" said the communiqué from the Minister of Justice. A little farther off, the body of a young man with a bullet in his head was dug up. On the old El Salvador road four other bodies were found: two had been decapitated, two had been shot.

It was soon discovered that most of the victims belonged to the guerrilla forces or had been in liaison with them. The guerrillas were losing their most active sympathizers, if not their cadres. Leaders of student or union associations were disappearing or being arrested. Eleven were kidnapped the same day. The Mano Blanca applied the law of retaliation. It declared that for every anticommunist shot down, five communists or so-called communists would be killed.

The police were helpless and incapable of maintaining order. How could they arrest even an assassin caught in the act without running the risk of reprisals from guerrilla or antiguerrilla forces? It was more prudent to close one's eyes.

Thefts, kidnappings, and holdups were organized on private initiative. Gangsterism developed and phony guerrillas amassed fortunes.

As a result, after each assassination or kidnapping announced by the press, the political leaders of the FAR or of the MR 13 had to send the newspapers communiqués claiming or denying responsibility for the crime. At least that way one knew whom to hate, who had to be paid off, on whom vengeance had to be taken. But the government, nervous at this tacit legalization of the guerrillas, forbade the newspapers to publish any communiqué that did not come from an official source. From then on, nobody knew anything, nobody knew whom he was dealing with, and uncertainty was added to despair.

Intellectuals, professors, engineers, and technicians who were not interested in the political struggle preferred to work in other less disturbed Latin-American countries—in Mexico, or in the United States if their diplomas were good enough.

And so the country began to disintegrate. Only a few hundred men deep in the mountains with a mixed assortment of weapons were needed to bring matters to a head. Both the guerrillas and those who fight against them are the result of a political and social evolution that has now entered a new stage, that of the "dynamics of violence."

On the side of repression, the instrument of these "dynamics" is now the Minister of Defense, Colonel Rafael Arreaga Bosque, who "with the collaboration and aid of U.S. Army military technicians and special agents of the American Intelligence Services—especially the CIA—has built up a gigantic and onerous repressive apparatus in which participate not only members of the regular army and the various police groups—which have currently mobilized thirty thousand men—but also about one thousand

Green Berets who form the cadre of the antiguerrilla units under the control of the North American strategists. To these must be added parallel anticommunist organizations such as NOA, MANO, and CADEG, formed of delinquents and criminals recruited from the lowest strata of society either by the *terratenientes* or by other privileged groups of the oligarchy and elements of the national army's extreme right wing."

In the above communiqué from the extreme-left opposition, certain figures were clearly exaggerated, especially those concerning the number of Green Berets. There were probably only about two hundred of these Green Berets at most.

On the side of the rebellion, we have two groups of guerrillas: that of Yon Sosa, between forty and seventy men, and that of César Montes, a guerrilla force of about two hundred. To these should be added the "urban groups," about whose number very little is known.

As can be seen, the two groups, that of repression and that of subversion, are unequally matched. About one hundred soldiers are required for every guerrilla, to say nothing of enormous sums of money. True enough, it is the Pentagon that pays, and where the antiguerrilla struggle is concerned the Pentagon spares no expense.

In the middle stands the great majority of the population, including the Indians (70 percent), which tries to keep out of the way. Its only desire is to avoid being hurt.

However, the government, the army, and the very administrators of the country, those who officially fight for the defense of liberty and for democratic free enterprise, are more deeply infected by violence than the core of revolutionaries. The latter at least give the impression of fighting for some sort of ideal.

The Church itself is being forced to take part, if not at first directly, then at least through the political organizations that appeal to its authority.

I met René de León Schlotter, head of the Christian-Democrat

party, in the grayish back room in which he had set up his headquarters. His mother is an Alsatian and he himself studied at the
University of Strasbourg. It was therefore rather strange to hear
him say in a broad Rhineland accent, "The guerrilla forces in
Guatemala are marked by original sin. In the beginning they were
only another military insurrection. Overnight this insurrection was
transformed into a Marxist movement. It all happened very
quickly. Who are these Marxists? City people scattered throughout the countryside and distrusted by the peasants, although they
do not mistreat them. They pay for what they buy, they have
propaganda meetings. But their arrival immediately brings the
army into the area, and it beats and arrests peasants without
much discrimination. The guerrillas are in a sorry plight everywhere. But if the government continues to call everybody who
wants reforms a communist; if the army, which is detested, continues to control this government; if the Pentagon continues to
use national armies as a means of directing the politics of the
countries of Central and Latin America—then guerrilla bands
will only spring up more and more powerfully everywhere. Even
for us Christians the guerrilla bands are the only way out. American intervention—disguised as it was here in the days of Arbenz,
or brutal, as it was in Santo Domingo—will force the whole
population to join the guerrillas. Including us. We know that if
there were to be the least hint of a coup d'etat from the right or
the left in Guatemala, the U.S. Marines would intervene—either
because a rightist coup d'etat could unleash a communist or
Castroite counter-coup d'etat, or because once the communists
and Castroites were masters of Guatemala they would set the rest
of Central America on fire and the Panama Canal would be
threatened.

"Christians in the guerrilla forces would be a much more
serious business than the communists. At least we would have
the support of the population, and thanks to the Church, which
finds the old society harder and harder to put up with, we could

count on at least the neutrality of the Indians, if not on their help."

René de León smiled peculiarly.

"Imagine the Green Berets firing on Christians who carried crosses alongside their flags and had priests with them. It would be enough to drive a President of the United States out of office."

The Guatemalan episcopacy has again broken its silence and in its "Pastoral Exhortation to Find a Peaceful Solution" does not hesitate to assign blame.

Nobody can deny that our current social and economic situation is profoundly unjust and unbalanced and that a change in our vitiated structures is necessary. It is especially necessary to change the mentality of many of our fellow countrymen. The necessity for a change, for a radical change, can be felt in places far removed from our country. . . .

Against the bishops, against the revolutionaries or reformists, against the twenty-year-old guerrillas and rebellious students, stand all those who, to defend their privileges and to prevent any social transformation, advocate the peace of the cemetery.

"They are afraid of change, they have no confidence in social evolution and want the present situation to be maintained by force. They call anyone who argues in favor of justice and a better distribution of wealth a communist. The imbeciles are only forcing them toward communism."

Let us hear what the Guatemalan bishops have to say:

Such an attitude is both absurd and suicidal. They may be able to hold things back for a little while and sometimes even cause an aggravation of the most unjust living conditions, but their policy is a hopeless one and sooner or later, by voluntary revolution or a violent cataclysm, the present situation will have to end.

But nobody listens to them.

The Guatemalan army was regaining its assurance. It no longer tried to avoid encounters with the guerrillas but increased its operations. The Sierra de las Minas ceased to be a safe refuge. The guerrillas might have been willing to negotiate, but the amnesty proposed by Méndez Montenegro was defined by the military men who would theoretically have applied it: the rebels were to surrender with their arms—with no guarantees for what might happen afterward.

The army owed a great part of its success to American aid and advice, but it alone got the glory, and it immediately profited from the situation to once more tread on the civil authorities. Nevertheless, the guerrillas managed to pull off a fine operation by rescuing a former president of the students right off the city streets as he was being taken to trial.

However, Turcios' sister and three friends, who had been arrested by the police and freed by the court, refused to leave prison. They were afraid of being shot down. Eventually they found refuge in the Uruguayan embassy and from there they were gotten out of the country.

A former army sergeant, a specialist in antiguerrilla combat who had joined the guerrillas after having committed murder, surrendered to the army. He was known as "El Gallo Giro." On being presented to the press, he provided the following figures and information:

"In January, there were four hundred guerrillas in the entire country—one hundred *campesinos* and three hundred students. Some of them did not stay with the guerrilla bands but only came for periods of training and military instruction. There have never been any Cuban instructors in the Guatemalan guerrilla forces. Che Guevara was never seen or heard from. On the other hand, twenty-five Guatemalans were recently sent to complete their military instruction in Cuba. The guerrillas receive no pay."

El Gallo claimed not to know where the money and arms came from.

It was evident, when the army struck with unerring certainty at a number of guerrilla hideouts, finding stores of arms that only

El Gallo could have uncovered for them in the zone he had come from, that the guerrilla was a traitor. Apparently, César Montes had suspected that El Gallo might already be in league with army security and was getting ready to pass sentence on him when he fled. Turcios would not have hesitated. He would have killed him first.

The guerrilla forces then entered a dormant period. One of the leaders of the FAR told us, "We have to think of our fight in terms of a long, hard struggle that will continue for ten years, maybe twenty. Our first objective is to last, and for that we have to survive."

The United States became more and more involved in the antiguerrilla struggle, all the while closely controlling the political life of the country. It merely wanted to help Méndez Montenegro's regime, which was not as democratic as it seemed. The number of imported U.S. military advisers and technicians kept growing. It was they who organized a new mounted police corps. Large sums were allocated to the reorganization of the security forces. Even though the government denied it, it was Americans who piloted the jet planes that bombed guerrilla bases.

Ydígoras had once said, "Just because my aviators are blond and blue-eyed doesn't mean they're not Guatemalans." Julio César Méndez Montenegro could have paraphrased him, "Just because my aviators have a Virginia or Texas accent and come from West Point or Annapolis and are either lieutenants, captains, or majors in the U.S. Air Force doesn't mean they're not Guatemalans."

Reporter Ann Geyer of the Chicago *Daily News* cabled her paper that in the Zacapa region, where five hundred men of the Guatemalan army were carrying out operations, there were also one hundred Green Berets, Vietnam veterans.

Antiterrorist organizations sprang up like mushrooms, and one of the recent ones claimed to draw inspiration from methods used by the Special Forces in Vietnam; it said that its ranks included parachutists and specialists in antisubversive warfare.

The NOA, the Nueva Organización Anticomunista, reinforced its troop disposition. It maintained armed bands that spread terror in the Teculután, Gualán, and Río Hondo regions. These bands kidnapped or executed all guerrilla sympathizers and all those who formed the infrastructure of the guerrilla forces. The other antiterrorist movements, not wanting to be left out of things, participated alongside the army in antiguerrilla operations. Everything conspired to aid the forces of repression: the presence of the Green Berets, who not only inspired the army officers with confidence but also forced them to make war seriously by refusing all pacts with the enemy; the help of the "white underground," whose members never hesitated to use torture to make their prisoners talk; the indifference or mistrust of the Indians; and finally, the weariness of the population.

Yon Sosa, whose army friends were no longer able to protect him, was wounded in the leg and his base destroyed. In September alone, forty guerrillas belonging to the two movements were killed in the course of six skirmishes with the army.

The army men made no attempt to hide their relations with the rightist underground. Members of these organizations, which had officially been condemned by the government, did not spend much time in prison when they were arrested. A colonel declared, "The guerrillas claim they are enemies of neither the president nor the government, but only of the army. The army therefore has the right to defend itself by whatever means available to it, and to give arms to those who support it, especially to all sincere anticommunists."

As a result, army supplies in the Zacapa region were tapped to arm antirevolutionary groups. The Guatemalan ambassador to Honduras, Urrutia de León, a partisan and friend of Colonel Peralta, arranged agreements with the Somoza brothers, the Nicaraguan *caudillos*, by which the latter supplied him with everything necessary to equip other extreme-right underground movements.

Hirelings and mercenaries were recruited from the former

volunteers whom Castillo Armas had collected to fight against Arbenz with United Fruit money, from survivors of the disastrous Bay of Pigs expedition, from all those illiterate, landless peasants who were ready to serve anyone who paid them cash. Nor did their training present any problems. Cadres were recruited from the national police, among G-2 agents and the secret services of the army, and also among the *comisionados*, soldiers who had survived the guerrilla purge.

The PUR, Unitary Revolutionary Party, an organization which had undertaken to unite the guerrillas and centralize the actions of the two groups, stated in one of its clandestine bulletins:

The oligarchy, especially as represented by the upper bourgeoisie and the *terratenientes*, has chosen armed confrontation. . . . The clique in power doesn't even understand that in the interior of the country the civil war taking place is being fought by the people against the army and its civilian allies, the anticommunist movements. In the city, the situation is even more confused: Here it is the left against the forces of repression, the right against the government, the right against the left. Everything merges into the general illegality, and this unstable climate permits all kinds of individuals to commit acts that have nothing to do with the social struggle. . . . Once the right has been armed, without government objection and with the support of the army and its protégés, all under the friendly eye of the American Military Mission, Méndez Montenegro will have lost all popular support for his policy. This situation is aggravated by the positions taken by a part of the clergy, which deliberately ignores the evolution of the Church undertaken by Pope John XXIII, and the Guatemalan clergy's change of direction, at least so far as their words are concerned.

Plots proliferated. The extreme right decided to get rid of Méndez Montenegro, though he hardly got in their way. All colonels with commands of any importance took part in the plot, as did also, according to reports, the Minister of Defense, Arreaga

Bosque. The U.S. secret services warned Méndez Montenegro and somewhat shook his imperturbable optimism. The president took action, and since he had no right to arrest officers (because of the secret pact), he called in the Minister of Defense. Under the threat of pistols held by members of the presidential security services, the minister signed a warrant for the arrest of the plotting colonels.

One of the leaders of the conspiracy was to say later, "Another five hours and we would have won."

He was wrong. Times had changed since Jorge Ubico, Ydígoras, and Peralta. Americans held all the positions of command and more and more closely controlled the real army—the one capable of fighting—as well as the secret police and the army's G-2.

It has taken Guatemala only six years of struggle between the subversives and the anticommunist forces—a struggle which took place more on the political than the military plane and which involved a ridiculously small proportion of the immense population—to arrive at its present situation.

On one side there are the guerrillas, on the other side the army and the various paramilitary services it has established. In support of the two confronting forces there is on the one hand the oligarchy plus the civilian and military "technicians" in its employ; and on the other hand the Communist party, the students, the intellectuals, and the more dynamic elements of the urban petty bourgeoisie which stands to benefit from the economic development—should it ever come about.

That leaves two unknowns: first, the United States, whose policy is completely conditioned by the Vietnam war. For the moment, one can say that in a way the State Department has lost interest in Latin America, that it has no time to spare for it and that it has given the Pentagon only one order: "Don't make waves!"

Second, there is the Guatemalan people, whose capacity for

revolt equals its capacity for submission. Therefore, anything is still possible in Guatemala today, despite the semiannihilation of the guerrilla forces. Let us imagine, for example, that the lower-ranking officers once more arrest their colonels, proclaim the advent of socialism, and take the lead together with the survivors of the guerrilla bands of a popular army.

The U.S. Marines would land immediately, and the country would be occupied. Since its experience in Santo Domingo a few years ago, the United States knows that it can intervene with impunity at any point in the hemisphere and that no country will raise a hand to prevent it from doing so. Its enemies know it too.

The occupation of Guatemala would unleash a popular revolt. A war of liberation would probably shake off the time-honored inertia of the Guatemalan people. In addition, one would have to take into account the backlash that shockwaves would cause in neighboring countries. However, the American services are on the alert, disarming all explosive situations on both the left and the right, all putsches and plots in preparation.

If the various subversion movements in the different Latin-American countries want to pull off their revolutions, they now have only one way of doing it: simultaneous action over the entire continent so that the American intervention forces are scattered and swallowed up in the immensity of the forests, the mountains, and the deserts.

That is exactly what Castro hopes for, and it is what Che Guevara dreamed of doing.

Then why do the two guerrilla groups in Guatemala continue to fight even though they have no chance of success? They still want to survive, to affirm their existence, and to continue to bring pressure to bear on the political and economic life of the country. The reprisals and executions that follow each of their operations help maintain an atmosphere of civil war in which everything is possible, in which yesterday's vanquished may be tomorrow's vanquishers.

Initially the current situation was foreseen by neither side. It just came about empirically, as the sequence of events has shown. It was only afterward that ideology contributed justifying arguments and a more general sense of political direction.

The subversive movements have undertaken a heavy task. Since they call themselves socialist, this uncertain political climate requires them not only to make war but also to become involved in the education of the masses in order to prepare them for the advent of socialism. Insofar as the Indians are concerned, it is a hopeless task unless years and years could be devoted to it. On the other hand, if this political education is not undertaken, there is no possibility of carrying with them the Indian masses, those indifferent arbiters of the entire conflict.

There is only one possible solution: the union of the Christian Socialists, whose priests give them influence among the Indians, and the "Marxists," who in Latin America often remain very Christian. But the new Church is getting its own revolution underway and so far, unlike the Marxists, it has not wasted its energies in exhausting struggles and internecine quarrels. It has conserved its hierarchy. First it must obtain command over the universities, those citadels of the revolution. It almost succeeded in Guatemala during the 1967 election, when out of eight thousand students, only 50 percent of whom voted, the Christian Socialists got 25 percent of the ballots and the Marxists got 25 percent.

The secretary of the Guatemalan Communist party, which controls the FAR, summed up the situation as follows: "Time is on our side. All we have to do is last it out. We are in the mainstream of history. The oligarchy, the army, and the United States are fighting a rear-guard action, and they know it. They do not believe in the ultimate victory and it is their greatest weakness."

But they still have to last it out!

True enough, the guerrilla bands do not cost much. Their coffers are filled by the ransoms paid for kidnapped members of the oligarchy. Some guerrillas may be mown down, but replacements will always be found among the ranks of the despairing young who see no other way out for themselves.

As long as social, political, and economic conditions remain unchanged, the guerrilla bands will always be reborn from their ashes. Even if they change labels, it will still be the same revolt against injustice.

But what sort of life do these guerrillas lead?

Let us take as an example the Edgar Ibarra Front, a Castroite-communist group first commanded by Turcios and then by César Montes. It operates in the Zacapa region and still rather tightly controls the Sierra de las Minas, a mountain chain that follows the road to the Atlantic. Along this wide, modern road—studded with recent works of art and paralleled by a railroad line—race the trucks that supply the capital or bring plantation products to Puerto Barrios.

Along the way there are half a dozen military posts, most often occupied by seven or eight soldiers sprawled over crates or straw chairs, dreaming, drinking, but keeping their weapons close at hand. Children in tattered clothing surround them and are always ready to do the daily tasks that these soldiers consider beneath their dignity.

Depending on how they feel, they will either lazily wave their hands in authorization for cars to proceed along the road, or with machine pistol ready, make the passengers get out with their hands in the air. After scattering baggage and merchandise about, they saunter back to their shacks, leaving the children to earn a few centavos by helping the drivers get their things together. No doubt the tips made in this way are afterward shared more or less equally between the soldiers and the *niños*.

About fifty or sixty miles outside of Guatemala City, you enter the mountain by turning to the left and following a path, now sown with sharp rocks, now buried in sand, now lost in the bed of a tiny stream. The slope is a sharp one, and it is impossible to drive more than about ten miles an hour. For hours you go up, you go down, you plunge into valleys smothered by vegetation hiding miserable shacks. Occasionally you cross an Indian in embroidered pants, then you climb almost bare slopes only to plunge again into a landscape of amazing grandeur. On the horizon, black peaks are silhouetted against a dark-blue sky.

It is on these seemingly inaccessible slopes that the guerrillas live—seventy-five miles of mountains that lead to the immense Lake Izabal. It was on the shores of this lake that on October 29, 1963, Turcios Lima created the embryo of what was to become the Edgar Ibarra Front with a group of students, professors, peasants, some workers, and some former soldiers.

Today the front represents the largest guerrilla group in Guatemala—about 350 men. (Estimates vary to double that figure, depending on whether they come from the headquarters of the army or of the insurgents. Leaders of the guerrilla forces said 350.)

As it grew, the front divided into zones and the guerrillas split into three groups, each with a chief in liaison with headquarters.

In addition to its "liberated" zone, each group "covers" a part of the neighboring departments: Chiquimula, Jalapa, and El Progreso. These groups of a hundred or so men are further divided into smaller units whose number varies with the importance and nature of the missions given them. Except for its liaison with the commander in chief—only yesterday it was César Montes, now nobody is really sure who it is—each of these groups is perfectly autonomous and takes responsibility for the operations and maneuvers it carries out.

There is a fourth group that has no fixed encampment, but remains in an area near Lake Izabal. This is the training group responsible for the political and military formation of new recruits and for completing the education of semiexperienced guerrillas. This group is involved in neither propagandistic activity nor military action. The courses taught include the tactics of the people's war, the elementary principles of organization, security methods, and the objectives of the revolution.

The other groups are always on the move, not only out of fear of betrayal, but also to maintain morale by a constant climate of activity. And it's an old trick to impress an enemy by constantly parading the same troops past him. The bases that the army claims to have destroyed are most often caches of supplies and medicines left under the guard of a handful of men ready to scatter upon the appearance of a military patrol. This mobility is also necessary because of the size of the zones and the number of missions to be carried out.

These missions aim to unite the *campesinos* and to explain the aims of the revolution, to choose local cadres to continue the work of the guerrillas and the search for information about troop movements or antiguerrilla groups—information that is transmitted from village to village.

All this information is studied, classified, and collated. If it does not call for immediate action, it is sent to general headquarters, from whence it reaches the political leadership of the underground in the capital. From the other direction come decisions made in Guatemala City and operation orders: a raid on a post or the execution of a local individual who is a member of Mano Blanca or some other "white underground" group.

The severe discipline is intended to increase the value of guerrilla resistance. Every halt on these long marches is used for discussions designed to get to the core of the political doctrine.

"When we make camp," one guerrilla told us, "we get up at five in the morning. After breakfasting, cleaning our weapons, and checking our equipment, we start out. Our pace is about three miles an hour. Sometimes for three hours at a stretch we will go at a 'Vietnamese step'—five miles an hour. At nightfall we stop and have our second and last meal. We listen to the news on the radio and discuss it before going to sleep.

"Sometimes we make night marches from seven in the evening to five in the morning. This generally happens after an armed propaganda session in populated areas, and it is done to avoid possible betrayal.

"Our most pressing problem is medical treatment and medicines. But this life has hardened us and we manage much better now than we did in the beginning. Sometimes when a guerrilla is seriously sick, the urban underground rents a small plane to take him to a hospital or a clinic in the city, or to deliver the necessary medicines."

Food supplies are also a problem. The poverty of the Guatemalan peasant makes it impossible for the guerrillas to live off the inhabitants, except for corn tortillas or an occasional chicken they are able to buy. The rest comes from the city, and the establishment of a supply network is one of the principal problems of the urban underground. These supplies are generally carried by vehicles that speed along the road to the Atlantic, and they are delivered to fixed rendezvous along the way.

Aid from Cuba seems unthinkable to anybody who knows the topography of the region. The coast is narrow and carefully guarded. Unloading in places other than the ports is difficult since the waters are not very deep and the thick forest comes right up to the shore. Transport across the Petén *selva* first and then over the mountains poses practically insoluble problems.

What is true for food supplies, however, is less so for arms. In Guatemala arms from every source are found everywhere: stocks pilfered by rebellious officers, as in Zacapa and Puerto Barrios; weapons distributed by Arbenz to his volunteers against Castillo Armas, or by Ydígoras Fuentes to the peasant militias that he had brought to the city to protect him; and arms captured after a skirmish with the military. The choice is vast.

Naturally, clothing is equally disparate. It ranges from Guatemalan army uniforms to American surplus, from blue jeans to trousers of *campesino* cloth, from a straw hat to a Cuban cap. The same is more or less true of equipment. The important thing is to have warm clothes, for though the sun in the sierra may be hot, the nights are freezing.

All guerrilla activity is based on the life of the peasant. "The revolutionary war," said one of the officers of the front, "began and developed among the peasants because Guatemala is essentially an agricultural country. The working class is much too susceptible to the influence of demagogues. It is a weak and ridiculous force."

In spite of this theoretical stance, the life of the guerrilla band now obviously depends on the help given them by the urban underground. For the last two years the two fronts on the northwest have suffered incessant staggering blows from the army, and their fine organization has often been destroyed or scattered. During the same time the "urban guerrilla forces" have been able to defend themselves better; they still maintain some degree of operative initiative in Guatemala City.

"To provide relief for our comrades who fight in the mountains," one of their leaders told me, "we try to concentrate the greater part of the government's repressive apparatus in the city. It is easier for us to hide and counterattack. In addition, we have massive support from the students, workers, and various levels of the population.

"For example, in the country it is considerably more difficult to execute those condemned by the FAR for murder and torture. With the support of the army, these people terrorize the peasants, who fear that their liquidation will bring army reprisals on its heels. But from time to time they come into the city to relax. They get drunk and make the rounds of the bars and the brothels. That's where we lie in wait for them," concluded my informant with a gentle smile.

In addition to the execution of enemies condemned by the leaders of the movement, the urban guerrilla also takes care of essential propaganda, of sending FAR communiqués to the newspapers, of kidnappings for ransom to feed the funds of the subversive movement, of sabotaging business firms that cooperate with the antiguerrilla struggle, of making and setting off bombs, of organizing strikes, of watching over guerrilla leaders when they come to the city, of attacking police patrols, of taking over radio stations from time to time and making announcements, and of freeing arrested *compañeros.*

The communist leader Gutiérrez, who had been arrested, was freed by the urban guerrillas and then recaptured; he died as a result of "the hood torture" favored by the Guatemalan police. The victim's head is covered by a hood filled with quicklime and insecticides.

In addition to the Unitary Revolutionary party, which controls all subversive activities, the urban underground has two separate organisms.

The first group is made up of the permanent combat brigades that are on the alert twenty-four hours a day, its members living in scattered places, awaiting convocations that can unite them in a matter of minutes at previously fixed points.

The second group is composed of self-defense units whose aim is to organize—within legally recognized professional and social organizations—those elements that can exploit the social agitation and the political propaganda. Like the guerrilla units in the mountains, these groups must maintain absolute secrecy, and the initiative comes from them alone. Obviously, the members of this group are those most threatened. When one of them seems on the point of being "burned," he is immediately assigned to a permanent brigade and ceases all political activities in his social group.

Since the arrival of the Green Berets and the creation of the "white underground," the situation of the guerrillas has become difficult. The umbilical cord that tied them to their matrix, the city and the university in Guatemala City, has often been cut. Bands that had suffered great losses dissolved into the countryside or were forced to change zones, something that is always dangerous. But despite its efforts, the army has not been completely successful. Let me point out again: the guerrilla forces are above all a political, economic, and social problem—a problem the army cannot resolve.

The future of Guatemala is tied to that of the continuation or the end of guerrilla activities. If the guerrilla and counter-guerrilla forces continue to keep the nation, and especially the cities, in this atmosphere of disorder and terror, Guatemala will be further emptied of its substance. Soon it will no longer have any existence as a nation.

The guerrilla bands can only cease activities by integrating themselves into a political party—not a secret one, but an official one—and insofar as the largest group is concerned, this now means the Communist party.

First, however, it will be necessary for the Communist party to be able to cease being a clandestine party and to obtain some guarantees before reentering legally recognized activities. The Guatemalan guerrilla forces now follow Fidel Castro only because the Communist party to which it adheres cannot do otherwise as long as it is hunted down and has to fight for survival.

But like the other Communist parties, this one keeps its eyes fixed more on Moscow than on Havana. The Russians have been quite clear about it. Unlike the Cubans, for the time being they want no more guerrilla activities in Latin America.

If Méndez Montenegro could, he would be ready to give the Communist party the opportunity of what might be called "settling down." But he cannot, because he is a prisoner of the army and the army won't hear of it. The army thinks it can do away with guerrillas—with guerrillas maybe, but not with the guerrilla forces. For the moment, nothing can change the situation, unless, perhaps, the Americans and the Russians—the former having become masters of the Latin-American armies, and the latter having regained control of this Guatemalan Communist party which is torn between the official line and the practical situation imposed on it—come to some agreement over the heads of the peoples, the parties, and the governments involved. Strange things are already happening in all the countries except Guatemala; steps are being taken to eliminate all those nuisances who long for justice rather than discipline, who consider their country before considering the needs of worldwide strategy.

That leaves only the Indians, the *campesinos*, and, above all, the Church. In its old form the Church evangelized the Indians, and, though it maintained traditions and privileges, it became entrenched in both the land and the daily life. In its new form the Church thinks of itself as revolutionary. Its proposed solutions are often as radical as those of the communists or the Castroites. Just as the Castroites were able to find a banner in Che Guevara, the Church in turn has been able to find one in Father Camilo Torres, a priest who went off to fight and die among the guerrillas.

"Saint Camilo Torres" 3

The scene was Havana—not in the modern city of big hotels for American tourists, where since there are no more Americans everything is crumbling, but in the old Spanish quarter where nothing has changed since the days of the viceroys. Carlos Puebla's cabaret fronts on a small, narrow, badly lit street paved was unequal cobblestones. From it comes an odor of rum, fried pork, and cigar smoke. It's the kind of place where you expect to see barefooted sailors with red neckerchiefs tied around their heads, all dead-drunk and being tailed by recruiting sergeants ready to shanghai them onto the king of Spain's heavy galleons.

The dark walls are covered with photographs, some still fresh, others yellowed by time. The fresh ones, the more recent ones, are of Fidel Castro and his brother Raúl; of Che Guevara, with his mocking smile; of Camilo Cienfuegos, with his long beatnik hair; the old photos are of a bushy-bearded Hemingway, of a blonde-haired Ginger Rogers, of a self-consciously smiling Martine Carol, of Margot Fonteyn in her tutu and doing a dance step, and of a grimacing Bob Hope.

In 1958, while the latter group came to amuse itself at Carlos Puebla's place, the former were still in the mountains. The U.S. ambassador kept insisting that nothing would happen, that the regime had never been more solid, and the French ambassador made Batista an officer of the Legion of Honor. These days a violently colored poster with a background of cannons, machine guns, and red flags is pasted on the walls: "1967, Year of Vietnamese Heroism," and Carlos Puebla is an influential member of some sort of union or cultural organization and sings revolutionary songs. At his place you can hear all the Latin-American guerrilla anthems—even if the guerrilla bands themselves have ceased to exist, as has happened in Peru, or have not yet gone into action, as is the case in Bolivia. (A few days later news came of the first skirmishes in the Ñancahuazú region.) In his domain, Carlos Puebla follows the Fidel Castro line. He has set all the guerrillas marching to Cuban rhythms.

To catchy, light, and rhythmic tunes songs are sung about Guantanamo, songs about Comandante Che Guevara and how his love of revolution led him into new ventures, songs about guerrillas in Guatemala, in Colombia, in Venezuela—those, of course, who follow Fidel, not those who are reactionary guerrillas allied to the "orthodox" Communist parties.

Carlos Puebla, massive, round-faced, and rosy-cheeked, struck two or three chords and, then, accompanied by two other guitars and a maraca player, suddenly began the ballad of Camilo Torres. "Oh . . . oh . . . I am going to tell you . . . something really true. . . . In Colombia a wonderful guerrilla died. . . . I am singing about Camilo Torres who went off to find liberty . . . on the spurs of the *cordillera* . . . oh . . . oh. . . ." Near us there was a black girl with a large mouth and dazzling teeth, very shapely, simultaneously ugly and magnificent. She could have been taken for a priestess of the ancient Voodoo cult, which has been lost in Cuba but which is coming back with the encouragement (why?) of the government. She stamped her feet and swayed her shoulders. Suddenly, unable to bear it another minute, she leaped up on a table and began to dance, her heels drumming, her skirts flying around her long legs. Bending back and forth she thrust forward her breasts. She was no longer anything but music, rhythm, movement, and sex. Her swirling long hair almost brushed against our faces. "Oh . . . oh . . . *Camilo Torres en las guerrillas de Colombia* . . . oh . . . oh. . . ."

I had just come back from Colombia. During my stay I had tried—by means of his friends and enemies, those who had understood him and those who had rejected him—to retrace the memory of Camilo Torres. Along with Che Guevara, he had in one year become the other symbol of the Latin-American revolution, the symbol that waved the cross instead of the red flag. Camilo Torres had taken the road to martyrdom and had uselessly fallen in an ambush, betrayed by a peasant who did not even know him, just as Che was in Bolivia. The myth was growing, but one could still distinguish behind it the man—the man who resembled us, who had hesitated, who had fooled himself and who had been fooled. Charming, naïve, idealistic, and above all an authentic Christian, he had hoped to change the world. He had accepted help from wherever it came, made any alliance, never been suspicious of anyone, and one day he had found himself with his back against a wall: either reenter chastened into the bosom of the Church, or follow his course to the end.

Camilo Torres Restrepo was born in Bogotá, on February 3, 1929. His father, Calixto Torres, was the most famous doctor in the city. It was said of his mother, Doña Isabel Restrepo, that she bore herself so proudly that she seemed to be a duchess. She was quick-witted, free-spirited, and strong in character. Like Doña Celia de la Serna, Che Guevara's mother, she was an aristocrat. She had the same contempt for conventions, the same carelessness about money, the same way of doing as she pleased.

Camilo Torres spent his entire childhood in Bogotá society's top level of twenty-four powerful families. These families are all Hispanic, proud of the purity of their blood and convinced that their privileges come to them by divine right. As a group they possess most of the large landholdings on which some of the best coffee in the world is grown. Colombia produces 20 percent of the world's production. Camilo Torres, after brilliantly completing his studies at the Cervantes School, began his law studies in 1948. It was the same year in which the *violencia* and repression by the army and the police broke out in Colombia. Fidel Castro, then also a student, witnessed this tragedy. He did not become involved; he had just come from Cuba and was traveling for pleasure. But he had entree into the liberal milieu of Jorge Gaitán, who had just been assassinated.

Camilo Torres did not become involved either, but like the future Cuban leader he never forgot this bloody outbreak. He felt that all strength resides in the people, and that even when they seem resigned, once they rebel they are capable of overthrowing the most well-established regime.

Camilo Torres was handsome. He had the build of a soccer player and a somewhat heavy face, but the strange, gentle, long-lashed eyes of a woman—eyes that seemed out of place in this athlete. He was softhearted and was always to remain so, even when he spoke of violence.

In the society he grew up in, the young people were not in agreement with their elders. There were frequent references to the Biblical saying, "The fathers have eaten sour grapes, and the children's teeth are set on edge." Among the young people was Alfonso López Michelsen, son of a president of the republic, who hated this oligarchy of which he was one of the richest representatives. But López already preferred cynicism and hardness of heart to the noble indignation of Camilo. While still very young, he joined Carlos Lleras Restrepo, the present president of the republic, and went off to fight, and make his peers fight back. At present he is the leader of the MRL, the Liberal Revolutionary Movement, the extreme-left wing of the Liberal party. It is said of López Michelsen that he will soon be president of the republic and that he will make peace with the communists.

López Michelsen identifies the *violencia* with a sexual repression that exists only on the high plateaus, where Spanish and Indian blood were mixed. The *violencia* does not exist on the coast, where the Negro and the Spaniard mingled their bloods. According to him, the Church is guilty of this orgy of blood and atrocity. It forces the country to live in the times of Isabella the Catholic, and its hold on the people is considerably stronger there than in Spain or in any other Latin-American country. He has no use for anybody connected with the Church, even when, like Camilo, they leave it. He said, "Camilo was marked by his sick relations with his mother. They both incessantly played at the game of stormy relationships. They loved and hated each other.

"As an unfrocked priest, Camilo interested the crowds and became something of a spectacle. We have another unfrocked personality here, General Ruiz Novoa, who commanded the Colombian battalion in Korea, tossed away his military uniform, and then went off to preach his revolution from city to city.

"But the crowds always want a new spectacle. They are easily bored. Ex-general Ruiz Novoa, like ex-father Camilo Torres, has ceased to be box office.

"In the beginning forty thousand copies of Camilo's newspaper were printed, then twenty thousand, then five thousand. Like General Boulanger, Camilo died heroically and pointlessly. Like

Boulanger, he didn't understand politics. His speeches were always childish and always the same. As I see it, Christ committed suicide because he thought his suicide necessary to the victory of his cause. In order to give some value to all the ventures in which he had failed, Camilo wanted to do as Christ had done."

In Camilo Torres' circle, politics is the source of power as well as money. It provides women, land, and a clientele—the courtiers who surround those in power. Every peasant in his far-off *pueblo* is linked to politics for his survival, and his life or death, as well as that of his family, will depend on his choice of party.

Camilo Torres therefore decided to go into politics. At Cervantes, he had already founded a newspaper, *El Puma*, and somewhat later he had unionized the bootblacks. It was at that time that he met and became betrothed to the daughter of Dr. Montalvo, but they did not marry. In Colombia, which, like Mexico, is the land of *machismo*,* it is not the woman who chooses; she can only be chosen, so one might assume that it was Camilo who ended the relationship. In any case, the young girl became a nun. Camilo's mother, "The Duchess," was single-minded and jealous in her love for her son. She may have precipitated the break.

Camilo Torres withdrew to a monastery to make a retreat. Then he left law school and entered the chief seminary, where he took the cassock. His friends already said of him, "Camilo can become anything—a saint, a great mystic, a dangerous anarchist—anything but a mediocrity."

Camilo violently resented the injustice that reigned in his country, and he often spoke of it to his mother, who was his confidante.

---

* *Machismo*: an intolerable cult of virility. It consists of a contempt for women, an exaltation of men, and the use on the slightest provocation of a knife or a pistol to defend an honor—or rather a touchiness—always on the alert for offense.

She encouraged him in his rebellion, and once she proclaimed with her usual pride, "In his day, my ancestor José Félix de Restrepo freed the slaves. My own son, who you say is strange, will one day free the slaves that we have all become."

In 1954, Father Camilo Torres said his first Mass in the Bogotá cathedral. All the best Colombian society was present. Then he left for Europe. For the next six years he studied sociology at the University of Louvain.

Miss Olivieri, who met him during this time and who was afterward to become his secretary and help him when he was with the guerrillas, described him. "He was an amazing man. He had the gift of human contact and exercised a great attraction over all those around him. Everybody felt it—men, women, and children. He was a man of joy. He always had a big smile and he adored life. I remember one night on the Paris Métro. We had just come from a concert and Father Camilo was not wearing a cassock but was dressed as a clergyman. We were speaking Spanish to each other. Suddenly a man of about forty came up and said to Camilo, 'Father, I absolutely must speak to you immediately.' Camilo got off with him at the next station. Because he was used to people coming to confide in him, he was in no way surprised. The next day he told me simply, 'This man and I walked around in the night and talked for three hours. He had need of a priest.' "

Father Camilo Torres led the sons and daughters of wealthy Colombians studying in Paris to Villejuif, a parish of shanties. He wanted them to understand the miseries of poverty, a poverty they would find even worse in their own country. He was already something of a Boy Scout leader, a quality that exasperated some and charmed others.

In Belgium he became friendly with Belgian-Colombians. He told those young people studying there, "You are the privileged ones. You must make your country and its people profit from the education that you were able to acquire thanks to the situation of your families. You are going to return to live in a country where poverty and social injustice reign, a Christian country where what is happening is the absolute negation of all forms of Christianity."

He was referring to the *violencia*, in which hundreds of thousands of people were slaughtered. Camilo Torres returned to Colombia in 1960. He was named chaplain of the University of Bogotá, and at the same time he held the sociology chair. He quickly became the leader of the students, a factor that somewhat worried the Marxist groups which had until then controlled all the organizations. But the charm and name of Camilo Torres worked its spell. He came from good—very good—society, just as did all those studying at the university. There were no *campesinos* there. The students were among themselves, among their own social class. Even among the revolutionaries, family precedence continued to play a role. Oh, those Latin-American "clubs" that reconstitute themselves even among revolutionaries! Though the conflict between generations often enters into the political conflict, everything happens within this closed circle.

Camilo Torres did not preach wisdom and resignation to his students; they would not have listened and he felt no such inclination. He preached what they wanted to hear: the rejection of misery and injustice, and the means of opposing it with violence, if necessary. He was already convinced that charity merely perpetuates misery instead of curing it. It is the medicine given to tuberculosis victims to keep them from coughing. Camilo Torres soon connected the violence and injustice not only with the important families to which he belonged but also with the country that protected them, the United States. He was therefore forced to take a frankly anti-American stance, a fact that could only lead him to fight alongside the communists.

Initially, Father Camilo Torres asked for reforms; seeing that nobody listened, he went further, repeating what so many others before him had said. On December 23, 1965, at the university's student living quarters he declared, "Only armed revolution can bring about the transformation of the political system."

He also said, "The oligarchy knows that it is finished. Either it agrees to turn control over to the people, who are the custodians of all power, or it refuses and we will have to resort to violence to rid ourselves of it."

But he never stopped saying, "I do not want violence." He was even to repeat it a few days before joining the guerrillas.

Miss Olivieri explained the process by which Camilo Torres was forced to join the guerrillas. "Because he was a priest, because of his profession as a sociologist, and also because of his family situation—that counted and it still counts in Colombia—Camilo was in on the beginning of all the more or less honest projects conceived to improve the situation of the Colombian people. Year after year he saw these projects blocked by the very government that had voted them, turned from their original meaning by those who were supposed to carry them out. He saw himself imprisoned in a sort of diabolical circle, in which all those who like himself wanted to do something, and who were well equipped to do so, were annihilated. Seeing the circle tighten around him, he wanted to break it. The only means left to him was to break with his past and with everything his life had consisted of. He therefore asked to be returned to a lay state. That still left politics, but he was not interested in playing a political role. Whenever he was asked if he wanted to be president of the republic he would break into his great hearty laugh. Whatever he did was for the Colombian people alone. Where outside the Church and politics was he to go? With the guerrillas."

The church hierarchy reacted against his "revolutionary tendencies." It removed him first from his post as chaplain and then from his chair in sociology. The students demonstrated in sympathy with him. There were riots and arrests.

It was then that Camilo Torres asked the primate cardinal for permission to revert to a lay state for an indefinite period of time. This in no way meant that he ceased to be a priest, that he could marry, or that he could no longer say Mass. He was not under an interdict. He was on "an unpaid vacation" and could at any time ask to be reintegrated into the Church.

Even after he became a guerrilla, he said, "I am first of all a priest and a Christian. I have merely asked to be relieved of the disciplinary laws of the clergy, but I consider myself bound to behave as a priest."

There can be no doubt that his superiors, when they agreed to his renunciation of the cassock, knew that he would end up with the guerrillas. They did nothing to prevent him. What they feared more than anything else was scandal, and they felt there would be less of it if Camilo quit his cassock.

Camilo Torres established a newspaper, *Frente Unidó*, whose program called for the union of all parties of the left, liberals and communists included. He demanded basic reforms that could lead only to total revolution. He organized propaganda tours to make known what he called his "platform." His violent tone and very *fidelista* style provoked riots along the way. Camilo Torres himself was arrested and detained for several hours at the prison in Medellín. Camilo loved to talk before crowds. His speeches lasted three and four hours. Unfortunately he was also disorganized, and one has to know how to bring these crowds together, how to transport them and put them in a proper frame of mind. His party, the United Front, was nonexistent. He had many friends, but no followers. He knew nothing about political organization, the work of agitation, how to build cells and clandestine networks and prepare for a meeting. The communists took over the organization of his tours and procured a public for him just as the public was beginning to weary of him.

El Colombiano, the most important daily newspaper in the capital, was soon comparing him to Fidel Castro. It wrote, "Like him, Torres is a dangerous adventurer ready to take extreme measures to gain power."

However, at about the same time, Camilo Torres declared, "I am not a communist. I do not believe in historical materialism and even less in dialectical materialism. But I think the simple fact of being against the government and against the United States policy that it defends immediately places you as a communist. As far as the government is concerned, the thirty thousand school teachers who went on strike last year to demand wages that had not been paid for seven months are communists. The twenty-five thousand students who went on strike to protest against the intervention of the Marines in Santo Domingo are communists. The fifty thousand unemployed who demand work, the hundreds of thousands of peasants who die of hunger in a very wealthy country, the parents who demand schools for their children, the nationalists who protest against a foreign policy that makes our country into a United States colony and our army into a sort of foreign legion under the command of the Pentagon—all these are communists. A minority of twenty-four families holds the entire economy of the country in its hands. It is they who make the decisions, and these decisions are always in their own favor, never in favor of the Colombian people. Does refusal to accept this state of things make one a communist? Eighty percent of the Colombian people are dying of hunger. We have no schools and in some provinces illiteracy is as high as 65 percent. The rights of man are not respected and never have been.

"Because people have to eat, thousands of children in Bogotá live in the gutters, prostituting themselves by the time they are twelve, stealing and killing, because it's all they know how to do, it's all they have been taught. And one day Europe will hear that a band of unscrupulous adventurers has revolted, sowing disorder in Colombia. We will be baptized as communists and lined up against a wall. But this time we will not let ourselves be slaughtered like so many sheep. The most legitimate of the rights of man is the right of legitimate self-defense."

When he was asked if the fact that he was a priest did not

hinder his political activity and if he did not run the risk of serious trouble with his superiors, he declared, "Our Colombian Church is the most retrograde in the world, infinitely more so than the Church in Spain. It follows a so-called opportunistic policy and supports whatever government is in power. In Colombia, and I believe this is unique in the world, a priest can become a bishop only with the consent of all the other bishops. To be accepted unanimously by fifty people, a candidate must certainly be mediocre. It is through this system of co-option that mediocrity is perpetuated at the head of our Church.

"Do you know that our bishops here were scandalized by the Council's decisions? They are strongly opposed to the use of the vernacular in the liturgy. They are against even the most superficial reforms. What then can be said of the fundamental reforms asked for by this same Council? In our country, every Christian must wear a scapular. Attendance at processions seems more important than all that makes up Christianity: love, compassion, and justice. This is the road that leads to fetishism."

When mention was made to him of the Alliance for Progress, Kennedy's plan for helping Latin America, he made this violent and unfortunately all too just criticism, "The reforms proposed by this Alliance are careful not to touch on the private interests of the North Americans. As a result, we have to repurchase the oil that comes from our own subsoil, and in dollars, at that. When this Alliance makes a loan, it is never in ready cash. Of course one can read in the newspapers that American aid to underdeveloped countries amounts to so many billions annually. This is not true. In practice we are immediately forced to convert these loans into purchases of American surplus production: outmoded machines that do not correspond to the needs of modern technique. These machines are to be transported by American ships. The necessary technicians and spare parts are to come from the United States, and both will be expensive."

On being asked what motives led him to quit his cassock, he

replied, "I was led to ask my bishop for an unlimited leave of absence. It is true that the objectives of a revolution are not reconcilable with the doctrine of our Colombian Church. What I propose has long since been established in Switzerland, France, Belgium, and all the other countries of western Europe, which so far as I know are not communist: free education for all Colombians, progressive taxes, industrial planning, equal salaries for all Colombian and foreign workers, the right to establish diplomatic contacts with every country in the world, social security, etc.

"I've been told that I was marked for assassination. I do not believe that my adversaries will resort to this means—they are much more likely to put me in prison. Please note that I do not want to be thought a martyr. I do not have the soul of a martyr. I love life too much to sacrifice it stupidly for a word. . . ."

On November 8, 1965, after a disastrous propaganda tour in the province of Santander, Camilo Torres mysteriously disappeared. Three days later, Camilo joined an ALN (National Liberation Army) guerrilla unit operating in the San Vincente de Chucuri region of the same province.

It is difficult to learn just what made Camilo Torres take the final step. According to some of his friends, Camilo suffered a great deal when he realized that people came to see him not because of his ideas but simply as a curiosity, a priest in mufti, preaching revolution in this very Catholic Colombia.

In addition, his communist supporters had withdrawn those crowds which had formerly come to applaud him with remarkable discipline. They wanted him to ally himself more closely with them, to follow their own tactics and discipline.

Father Camilo Torres knew that he could not obtain a single reform, that he had been "burned," that he was thought a communist, that his United Front attempt had failed due to the lack of solid base and cadres. But he had no desire to become an unconditional hostage of the Communist party, which was simultaneously clandestine and official, and whose subtle tactics and compromises sometimes frightened and sometimes disgusted him. It was then that he announced he would join the guerrillas.

The communists—realizing that they had gone too far with him, that they had once too often played cat and mouse, donkey and carrot, with this idealist—tried to recapture him. They felt that Camilo could be an excellent ally, one who would help them attract other parties and other noncommunist forces that could be digested and absorbed.

They in no way wanted Camilo Torres with the guerrillas. It seemed a childish stunt to them. Insofar as they were concerned, you only joined the guerrillas when you had no other choice. They also felt that those who did so should be trained specialists and not amateurs. The formation of the masses was considerably more important. And it was on this point that they were in opposition to Castroite doctrines. In addition, the Colombian Communist party has not only an official existence and organization, but a clandestine organization with its own guerrilla forces, the Colombian Armed Revolutionary Forces—the FARC.

The leader of the Communist party, Gilberto Royos, met with Camilo Torres. He explained to him that in the interests of the revolution he ought to give up his idea of playing at being a guerrilla, that he ought to continue his unity movement. This time they would help him—if, of course, he agreed to follow a certain line of tactics. Royos warned him that in any case, both for his own good and for the good of the cause he defended, he would permit no unit of the revolutionary army to accept him into its ranks.

The FARC is the most important guerrilla movement and is closely controlled by the party. It includes six hundred men "permanently in the field,"* plus all those who belong to the underground movement of the cities—the self-defense zones that

---

* These figures were furnished to me by the communists.

operate in Bogotá itself (as in the Polycarpe section, where ten thousand men and women live under the control and with the aid of the communists).

Royos left, feeling certain that he had won over Camilo Torres. Until that point, Camilo had only been in contact with the communists, and not with the Castroites. The latter had only the two hundred men who made up the ALN, the National Liberation Army. Of these, 80 percent were students.

Initially supported by the communist-controlled oil unions but then abandoned by them, the ALN could now count only on outside aid, either from Cuba by means of the coast or from the university by means of the road. But the communists had seized control of the university and were trying to dry up this source of supply.

The two leaders of this guerrilla force, Comandante Victor Medina and Fabio Vázquez, had only a very local following. The Castroite rebellion needed a big name to relaunch it. It was stagnating because it had not yet found its leader, its *caudillo*. Rejected by his own, cheated by the communists, heartsick, knowing that only death could bring about the triumph of his ideas, Camilo went off. The guerrillas were his last chance, and since the communists did not want him, he would join the others. The Castroites had two representatives at the university. They laid siege to Camilo and never lacked for arguments. They spoke of generosity instead of tactics. Without even informing Monsignor Guzman, his best friend and a man who leaned toward the communist theses, Camilo joined the Santander guerrillas. The communists had had Camilo Torres stolen from them because they had been much too Machiavellian. The Castroites thought they finally had a banner to rally around. They were not to keep it long.

According to the Santander guerrillas who knew him in the sierra, Camilo proved himself to be the nicest and the most agreeable comrade possible. He asked to be considered as a simple private. Of course, he had absolutely no military training and his first attempts to learn how to handle a weapon were hardly encouraging. But nobody was asking him to fight. His role was not to make war but to make contact with the peasants and explain to them what the guerrillas were really after. In point of fact, he was a kind of political commissar. Since he was also a priest, his following became very large. He operated under the sign of both the Church and the revolution.

The army soldiers, knowing there was a priest out there, did everything possible to avoid meeting up with him. To primitive believers, killing a priest is the worst crime in the world. The patrols sent off to make contact with the guerrillas with whom Camilo was thought to be, would trudge a few miles, get their boots dirty, fire a few rounds in the air, and return. And then one day a peasant betrayed the guerrillas. He had been taken in hand by Civic and Military Action, a fighting plan established in Panama.

These methods of psychological warfare had already been used in Algeria, where they were first developed. They were designed to help the army win over civilian populations by supplying them with everything they lacked and should have had: doctors, dentists, teachers, agricultural advisors, roads, substantial housing, and food supplies when famine threatened.

As a result, this peasant felt that the army was worth more than the guerrillas, that it was finally giving instead of taking; he therefore informed a Civic and Military Action team that a small band of the National Liberation Army was making regular forays into a village to resupply itself. An ambush was set up. A patrol of seven men was sent forward as bait. Behind them, sixty more men were hidden along the sides of the path. Camilo Torres was supposed to be with the two guerrilla leaders in some other region, but at the last moment he remained behind. Another mischance made him follow the small group that went down to the village, which until then had been considered safe. The guerrillas swooped down on the patrol, killed or wounded three men, gave chase, and fell into the trap. Camilo was killed just as he was picking up a soldier's rifle.

In great embarrassment, the army published the following communiqué:

On Tuesday, February 15, 1966, in the course of an encounter with the guerrillas, a unit of the Fifth Brigade killed five armed men. One of the bodies has been identified as that of Camilo Torres Restrepo.

In Bogotá, I heard another version of the story. According to this account, Camilo Torres was betrayed to the DAS, the political police, by a student who told them where his guerrilla band was located. This student did it for money. There is another variant of this version. The student was a communist and he betrayed him because the communists preferred Camilo Torres dead rather than with the Castroites. In any case, the incident occurred at a bad time. Elections were in full swing. The body of Camilo Torres was buried secretly, just as Che Guevara's was to be later. That was foolish. To this day there are insistent rumors in the countryside that Camilo is still alive and will come back. Attempts were made to discredit his memory by claiming that he was shot down while trying to kill off a wounded man. That was also foolish. The Bolivian military were to do no better when they burned the body of Che Guevara to keep his grave from becoming the site of pilgrimages.

I questioned Colonel Angarita, who commanded this Civic and Military Action group, about this. He replied curtly, "Camilo Torres was an unfrocked priest and a communist. He was killed while under arms. That's all there is to it."

But it was not quite so simple.

Dead, Camilo became considerably more of an embarrassment than he had been alive. The priest in mufti had become a martyr of both the revolution and the new Church. The myth quickly spread beyond the Colombian borders. In Cuba it became the subject of a musical ballad to which beautiful women danced; for the Church in Peru, Mexico, and Brazil, it became an example set them by Rome.

His death was to mark a profound change not only in the Colombian Church but in all the other churches on the continent. He was the banner this new Church born of the Council needed in South America in order to detach itself from its former clientele—the oligarchs, the military men, and the rich bourgeoisie— and to find new faithful among the disinherited, the poor, all those who were subjected to violence and who occasionally practiced it themselves. It was to them that Christ had addressed himself when he preached.

In contrast to Che Guevara—a revolutionary without a frontier, a man who never claimed to be Argentine and seldom spoke of Argentina, a Christian if Christianity turned revolutionary, a communist only as long as communism remained revolutionary— Camilo Torres was first and foremost a priest and a Colombian. It was his country and the tragedy it had just lived through that obsessed him and determined his actions. Che belonged to no church—unless by church is meant a certain feeling of revolt against injustice and misery, and by dogma, a means for making his revolution.

He said, "If communism were not designed to bring about the birth of a new man, it would make no sense."

Camilo Torres would never have dared proclaim that "if Christianity were not designed to bring about the birth of a new man, it would make no sense." For him, above the Church there was still God.

To understand Che, it is necessary to understand Latin America as a whole. To understand Camilo Torres one need understand only the Colombian revolution and the reformist tendencies stirring in the Church. That in itself is no small task.

The "exemplary" adventure of Camilo Torres, his tragic end—
which the communists (who have perhaps renounced the new
man) wrongly judge to be useless—could only have been possible
given the particular situation of this country.

Colombia had been bathed in violence for too long to allow
mere reforms. You don't give wine that has been sugared and
watered down to a man used to drinking straight rum by the
bottleful. Camilo Torres chose the guerrilla forces as a solution
born of despair; he accepted martyrdom because it was the only
way open to him.

Behind the origin of the *violencia* in Colombia and the tragedy
of Camilo Torres, which was that of an entire people, there is
an idiotic and lamentable tale of cuckoldry and *machismo*.

A certain Roa Sierra, who wanted to be known as a *macho,*
carried on "undetermined professional activities" (according to
the police report) in Bogotá. On April 9, 1948, he quarreled
with his mistress, who was cheating on him with the local postman.
This lady let him get away with nothing; she shouted louder than
he did, and said that he was a man *sin cojones,* in other words,
without balls.

In a mad fury, Roa took his revolver, slipped it into his pocket,
and ran down the steps of her house shouting, "You'll soon see
if I'm a man *sin cojones.*"

At the same time, a lawyer and politician who had risen to
fame in the past few years, Jorge Eliécer Gaitán, was getting
ready to leave his office in the center of town. A member of the
left wing of the Liberal party, generous, demagogic, romantic,
he was gifted with the kind of magnetism that galvanizes crowds.
Like many before him, he demanded the suppression of privileges
and the participation of the masses in political power. In a few
months, his followers had multiplied.

He was the man of the hour, the man most spoken of, the
man whose death would cause the greatest stir. Roa Sierra had

141 / "SAINT CAMILO TORRES"

to show some dazzling proof of his virile qualities. He therefore decided to kill Gaitán.

Some time in the afternoon, as Gaitán was leaving his office building, Roa took his revolver from his pocket and fired. The liberal leader sank to the ground.

This insane gesture by Roa Sierra was to trigger a chain reaction that is still going on today. A few figures will give some idea of its seriousness: five thousand dead in Bogotá in three days, plus three hundred thousand in the entire country during the course of the next seven years. According to a Red Cross report, sixty thousand houses were destroyed. This bloody delirium was called *la violencia*.

There are many other variations of the real reason behind the death of Gaitán. According to some stories, Sierra was a communist agent charged with unleashing a revolt that would permit his party to take power; according to other tales, he was hired by conservatives who wanted to get rid of an annoying adversary. It was true that Gaitán had every chance of being elected president during the next elections. Other people said that Roa Sierra had been used by Liberal party leaders who resented being shoved into the shadows by this tribune of the people.

Whatever his motive, less than a minute after having fired, Roa Sierra was lynched by a maddened mob. Still attached to the rope, his body was dragged through the streets of the city to the Presidential Palace, before which the crowd massed shouting, "Down with Laureano Gómez!"

Laureano Gómez was the leader of the Conservative party, to which belonged the president then in power, Mariano Ospina Pérez.

Within a few minutes the demonstration degenerated into a riot. The palace had to be cleared with bayonets. The city exploded. The capitol was overrun and the guards disappeared; somebody had forgotten to distribute weapons to them. Dossiers were scattered, windows and mirrors broken, and typewriters thrown from windows.

When about a hundred soldiers finally arrived to clear the area, the sky was already heavy with smoke. Nine ministries were burned, as was the Franco-Colombian Lycée. Trucks equipped with loudspeakers rode up and down the streets, calling the people to revolution. Stores were looted and merchandise was scattered over the sidewalks.

The facilities of Radio Bogotá were taken by assault and the Revolutionary Committee of the Liberal party broadcast an announcement proclaiming, "We have taken over the government."

During the chaos the army was mysteriously absent. Later it was said that the unit on duty had been overwhelmed, but actually the government preferred to let the riot develop. The more damage done, the more ferocious the repression that followed could be. Some said the *falangistas* of the Conservative party's extreme right were busy feeding the flames. Equipped with red insignias, they mixed with the crowd, led it, and opened the prisons.

At one in the morning the president of the republic announced that the government had regained control of the situation. A hundred people were dead. "The troubles," he affirmed, "are the result of a communist maneuver." Martial law was proclaimed.

In most of the country's other population centers, the crowd, believing that the Liberal party had carried the day at Bogotá, took over the public buildings and created popular juntas. This ephemeral power, which lasted several days, was in many places accompanied by savage murders as vengeance against some of the members of the Conservative party. These acts were to serve as a further pretext for repression.

"Gaitanism" almost took power, but Gaitán had always refused to make use of his popularity to organize a political party. He used to say, "I am not a man, I am the people."

On April 10, the repression began. In the night an armored

division arrived at Tunja, and by dawn it had penetrated to Bogotá. The machine guns of the tanks strafed the large avenues. *Comisiones* composed of civilians and commanded by noncoms held trials on street corners and carried out executions against the nearest wall. The rioters, refusing defeat, fought on with machetes. After two days, order was finally reestablished. On April 15, the Pan-American Congress, whose meeting in the city had been interrupted six days before by Gaitán's murder, went back to work as though nothing had happened.

The Conservative government set to work to draw all possible benefits from the affair.

Generally speaking, observers have tended to set the beginning of the *violencia* in Colombia at the murder of Jorge Eliécer Gaitán, as though the Colombian people had suddenly liberated itself from its traditional inhibitions in one fell swoop. In point of fact, the *violencia* was deeply anchored in the spirit and mores of Colombia and had shown itself at every stage of its history.

It was already in evidence among the cannibalistic Indians on the coast, a people expert in torture. Then the Spaniards came and contributed their own violence:

"Violence," wrote José María Samper, "was the only means of conquest in Colombia. Violence against the nomad tribes who refused to submit, violence against the simplicity and blind confidence, the love of peace, of the sedentary populations of the high plateaus."

For centuries, everything conspired to maintain this climate: slavery, Indian revolts, upheavals, furious repressions, the suppression of slavery but the use of forced labor to furnish the metropolis with gold and precious stones, the confiscation of lands granted by the crown to Indian communities, the imposition by force of Catholicism with all its sexual constraints on these primitive peoples who had heretofore enjoyed complete freedom in this area.

Independence did not put an end to the *violencia*. Civil war replaced Spanish repression and the anticolonial rebellion. Even before the death of Bolívar, conservatives and liberals were already confronting each other. During the course of the nineteenth century, Colombia was the scene of nine national civil wars, fourteen local civil wars, two international wars, three coups d'etat, and a conspiracy—which failed.

"The political convulsions of the nineteenth century," wrote Diego Montana Guellar, "have turned the life of Colombians into an existence of poverty, privations, and frustrations. . . . Neither large landholdings nor commerce could of themselves have led to the creation of great fortunes. Fortunes above the average were built in the shadow of State deals.

"This necessity revealed itself as a social factor of the greatest importance. The bureaucracy weighs more and more heavily on Colombian public life, and it is of capital importance for the ruling classes to have control of the administrative apparatus of the State."

As a result the struggle between the liberals and the conservatives became inexpiable. It was not a question of groups with profoundly opposed economic interests; beneath the ideological conflicts there was a profound need to limit the number of those who would have the right to some of the spoils. What separated the two parties during the last century may well seem laughable today. The conservatives wanted a strong central government, the liberals were federalists; the conservatives supported the Church, the liberals were anticlerical—which did not keep them from being deeply Catholic. According to a saying much in vogue at the beginning of the century, the conservatives went to Mass at nine o'clock and the liberals at ten o'clock. It was all that distinguished the two groups.

Despite all this political activity, the real power was in the hands of about one hundred families who controlled more than half the country: lands, banks, industries, and commerce. This oligarchy is known in Bogotá as the *sistema*. Its only criterion is wealth, and certification is proven by membership in the Jockey Club or the Gun Club. This is why it is also said that Colombia is governed by the Jockey Club.

As one moves from the very rich to the most rich, one goes from one hundred families to thirty, to twenty-four, or even to five. One of the members of these *richissime* five families has said, "In addition to my own, I know of only two others." His name was Lara and his domains were larger than all of Switzerland.

Unlike the major parties in England or in the United States, which they superficially resemble, the Colombian Liberal and Conservative parties have always rejected change and tried to ignore all social upheavals, both technical and political. Their only concern is wresting from side to side the power which is the key to wealth.

The origin of the *violencia* is in the depths of the Colombian soul, in the melange in Indian and Spanish blood. The most recent resurgence of turbulence can be said to begin with the conservatives' return to power in 1946. They had been kept at a distance since 1930, and once in power they decided never to lose it again.

During those sixteen years numerous events had modified the social physiognomy of the country: the establishment of the Communist party, tolerated by the liberals; the temptation of fascism and nazism, which under the form of *falangismo* was to influence the comportment of the Conservative party; economic expansion and industrial development due to World War II; and the development of unionism. In short, too many changes had come about to allow either the liberals or the conservatives, tied as they were to traditions that went back centuries, time enough to adapt themselves.

In 1946, a conservative, Ospina Pérez, was elected president, but he had to deal with a liberal majority in the House of Representatives. His problem, therefore, was to destroy this opposition permanently, to eliminate its cadres and to disorganize its electorate. A political police was created, and to a large extent its members were recruited from among the underworld—the hired killers, the pimps, the unemployed, all those men like Roa Sierra who had "undetermined professional activities."

In two years, more than fifteen thousand people were killed; lands were confiscated and houses burned down, a factor which was to bring about an exodus of entire regional populations, driving them to the poverty-stricken suburbs or to neighboring countries. A small village in the valley of Cauca, Celian, was destroyed, and all its inhabitants burned alive. In Cali, on October 22, 1947, a public meeting of workers and peasants was broken up by machine-gun-armed bands, and hundreds were killed. The villages from which the demonstrators came were pillaged, their women raped, and all inhabitants executed.

The first bands of *pájaros*, those "birds of passage," appeared; they were organized, trained, and commanded by falangist elements, and they were the precursors of the *bandoleros*, which we will discuss later. As social agitation grew, strikes spread.

The Communist party could do very little. Its leaders admitted that their "compromises with the Liberal governments had destroyed their popular support." A few weeks before his death, Gaitán organized his long, silent march of more than a hundred thousand demonstrators through the streets of Bogotá. No protest signs, no banners, no slogans, no shouting—simply thousands and thousands of hands waving white handkerchiefs.

It took only the action of Roa Sierra to turn this heavy silence into an explosion.

In organizing a violent repression, the Conservative party was avenging itself, as had the Liberal party when it obtained power in 1930.

The oligarchy, out of self-interest, might have consented to reforms and prevented much of the chaos, but it was trapped in a kind of medieval pride, an unhealthy love of the past, in the name of which it thought it could prevent Colombia from entering a new individualistic, materialistic, and capitalistic world which it saw as being without traditions, without a hierarchy, and without honor.

It wanted to keep this world from crossing the Colombian frontiers, but as the years passed, the country's traditional structures were shaken. The two old parties were pulled to the left and the right; other doctrines tried to find a wedge in this political block. Eventually, the two-party system, which was rooted in the rural life of the country, seemed a mere fiction in the capital.

The *violencia* became an epidemic. In one place, all the passengers of a bus were decapitated and their heads carefully placed on their knees. In another place, all the men in a village had their throats cut and their tongues pulled through the opening. This sort of thing was called a "tie cut."

Once, all the musicians of the Bogotá Conservatory traveling in a bus were decapitated by Liberal *bandoleros*. Since they belonged to the conservatory, they were obviously conservatives.

Gutiérrez Anzola's study on the *violencia* speaks of the passionate hate that developed in this ignorant and emotional population without political ideas. From earliest childhood the Colombian child belongs to one of the two parties by birth and ancestral tradition. His hate for the neighboring family or village is an ancient one—the motives long forgotten, but the emotion so ardent that the slightest incident reawakens it.

The *violencia* spread after the death of Jorge Eliécer Gaitán, and it led to the creation here, as in Guatemala and in Venezuela, of a permanent guerrilla force.

The essential goal of the repression following April 9, 1948, was not to punish those who had obeyed the Liberal Revolutionary Committee by driving out the local conservatives and massacring their political enemies, but to destroy systematically all organized opposition and to secure, in the following year, the election of the conservative and falangist leader Laureano Gómez.

The liberals are as responsible as the conservatives. The liberal leaders urged their followers to revolt, then disavowed them publicly and refrained from supplying the military and political support while continuing secretly to encourage them.

The police was given this assignment of extermination, while the army was kept on alert. At Belalcazar, 112 people were shot in one day. At Tolima all those who attended the burial of a member of the Liberal party who had died under torture were cut down by machine-gun bursts.

People were pulled from their homes, beaten, tortured, and executed. Contingents of armed civilians, *comisiones*, were sent from the capital to help the police. Often drunk, these men pillaged and killed for their own pleasure. And everywhere there were rapes of little girls and children, disembowelments of women. Entire regions were victims of this delirium, and their fleeing inhabitants were pursued like so many rats. During this time the conservatives seized control of all the country's land.

Photographs taken during this period show laughing policemen waving freshly cut heads; smiling groups of *comisionados* posed before rows of aligned corpses whose throats have been cut; mutilated children, heads lined up on the edge of a fountain; the bodies of old men swaying from the branches of trees.

There seemed to have been a special penchant for crucifying children against barn doors. The seed must be destroyed so that it cannot grow up to claim the lands stolen from the parents.

It was in this atmosphere that the first guerrilla groups sprang up, shortly before Castro's victory in Cuba. They had as yet no political goal. Their only goal was to save the population from general massacre.

In the El Cucuy region it was the sons of the patrician families, the intellectuals, the lawyers, the doctors, who created an armed group of 250 men. They fought victoriously against the police and its auxiliaries. Initially solidly ensconced in the natural fortress at the foot of the mountain, they eventually ascended into the *llanos*, those endless, semisavage pasturelands in the eastern part of Colombia.

The rebellious groups, initially motivated by instincts of conservation, multiplied and in turn took part in the general genocide. Revolutionary commandos sprang up just about everywhere. Mounted militias sped through the *llanos*. Whether or not they volunteered, peasants who had lost everything were enlisted, most often by force. Groups that ought to have united in the common struggle fought against one another. The revolutionary élan dribbled away into improvised actions and unplanned, uncoordinated operations.

As for the large liberal landholders, they went on living in Bogotá, but they hired mercenaries to protect their herds and their lands. However, the forces they had created soon escaped from their control and took the lion's share of the goods they had been assigned to protect.

A young liberal leader, Franco Isaza, decided to organize this revolt, to unite all the scattered forces, all the liberal bands, and have them converge on Bogotá to overthrow the Conservative government. He went to see the leader of the most important of the guerrilla bands in the *llanos*, a man named Velásquez. But Velásquez, who was now front-page news, refused to share his glory with this *avocaillon*.

The election in 1949 of Laureano Gómez, to be known as "The Tyrant of the Andes," solidified the power of the Conservative party and provided new impetus to the struggle. This time the army took a hand in it. Until then the Liberal-party guerrillas and the military had avoided a confrontation. The first intervention of the army took place at the behest of the big landowners in the Boyacá province who were worried by the independent spirit of the *quadrillas de bandoleros* which they themselves had created. They agreed to pay a contribution to compensate for "the sacrifices of the soldiers in their task of pacification."

Groups of twenty to fifty soldiers were sent to the various ranches. Better armed than the *bandoleros*, they were easily able to fend them off. But they quickly ceased "guarding the cows" and organized themselves into "guerrillas of peace." Led by their officers and noncoms, they took a hand in pacifying the region. They arrested or massacred *campesinos* suspected of complicity with the armed opposition. Rewards were offered to informers. Areas were "cleaned" of their dubious elements.

It was still possible to believe in the pacifying mission of the army. However, the massacre of twenty agricultural workers in a hacienda which a battalion happened to be passing marked the real entry of the soldiers into the *violencia*, which soon spread to the entire country. Once again peasants were burned alive in their houses, prisoners thrown out of planes over zones occupied by guerrilla bands, women raped en masse and then disemboweled with bayonets. In the areas under their control, the regional army commanders started a lucrative traffic in cattle, and the *hacendados* soon began to ask themselves if the military remedy was not worse than the *bandolero* disease.

Operations in the *llanos*, bombings, the destruction of all living things, forced the "guerrillas" or *bandoleros* to take to the mountains. Since they had no food supplies, they were soon obliged to fight. At first they tended to ambush *comisionados*, thus procuring automatic weapons, uniforms, and watches. In order to survive they had to coordinate their efforts. Leaders such as Guadalupe Salcedo sprang up. A good strategist of insane audacity, he did not hesitate to take on the army in open-country battles, and so brought the guerrillas their first victories against the military.

In the course of this struggle, old liberal concepts were slowly dropped and abandoned. Among the guerrillas the men began to call one another comrade and to talk of "revolution." This revolution had no program, no goal, and no political cadres. The intellectuals of the Liberal party who might have been able to organize it preferred to remain in Bogotá, where the risks were still not so great as in the *llanos*.

The Communist party attempted to fill this vacuum. It began initially by organizing a popular front between liberal and communist guerrillas. Then it spread to a class-conscious movement based on the defense of the land. Food supplies for all were assured by the participation of the guerrillas in agricultural labors and the participation of the peasants in the guerrilla struggle. According to the Communist party, "For the first time the rural populations discovered that the guerrillas were their only defense against the abuses of repression."

In 1950, this led to the creation of the first mass self-defense group at Chaparral, in the province of Tolima. The group quickly became important, even though due to some errors it had at times to fight against liberal guerrillas.

This was nothing new in Colombia, since in 1930 the Communist party had already established in Viota a rural zone which it controlled completely and in which it had its own administration. This autonomous "republic" was destroyed not by force but—in the jargon of the autocriticism that followed—"by internal bourgeoisification due to compromises with the Liberal party aimed at creating a popular front."

Once again, this time while the *violencia* was in full swing, the Viota region was taken in hand by the party.

In the course of the Fourteenth Congress, the communists declared:

The persistence of guerrilla bands and the inability of the reactionary dictatorship to liquidate them has stimulated armed resistance to abuses of the regime and spread the guerrilla movement to other areas. The struggle would now be able to enter a new phase, if it could combine with the peasant struggle and if we Communists could become the spokesmen for the claims of the peasants and proletarians against the oligarchy.

At the same time, the party created a coordinating junta that tried to organize, aid, and orient the "combatants of the people's army." In 1952, it organized a "National Guerrilla Conference" in Boyacá, which a number of guerrilla leaders participated in. The order of the day associated the armed struggle with agrarian reform and called for the formation of governing committees in zones controlled by the guerrillas. However, only those sectors that were already politically organized followed these orders.

Buenaventura, a former journalist turned stage director, told me, "At that time the government and the army paid off assassins on presentation of a photo of the victims they had just executed. The result was a brisk business in doctored photographs and duplicate prints. It was therefore decided that payment would be made only upon presentation of the victim's ears. At the Conservative newspaper for which I worked, I myself saw men show up at the pay window with skewers of ears, which were carefully counted before being paid for."

The brotherhood of *pájaros*—like the "white underground" later in Guatemala—terrorized the Cauca Valley. They were motorized and operated in the cities, eliminating well-known people who were either Liberals or guerrilla sympathizers. Then they extended their activities to the coffee plantations so that they could get their hands on the crop. They belonged to groups of the extreme right and enjoyed official support. Finally, they took to the countryside and undertook "work" for local political bosses. According to Monsignor Guzmán, who has written a famous study on the nature, causes, and psychology of the *violencia*, this creole Ku Klux Klan showed "remarkable efficiency in murder."

In all this time the rest of the world heard nothing about it, except for occasional brief paragraphs denouncing some armed band or describing the assassination by persons unknown of some more or less famous people.

By unleashing army intervention, Laureano Gómez had increased by tenfold the ravages caused by the *violencia*. He felt no qualms about the 200,000 dead for whom he was indirectly responsible. But he made the error of announcing his intention of standing for election. On June 13, 1953, Gustavo Rojas Pinilla, a general who seemed to have no political ambitions, took over the operations. He occupied Bogotá with armored cars, pulled the indignant Gómez from his palace, and expelled him. Rojas Pinilla then had to choose between creating a government based on the national union of the two big parties or remaining in power himself. He chose the latter course and surrounded himself with moderate conservatives, seemingly settling down to the essential business of pacification.

By bringing the army into the *violencia*, Laureano Gómez had given it a taste for power. Under General Rojas Pinilla, most officers saw before them honors and wealth instead of merely their meager salaries.

This army takeover of power created an immense hope in a population wearied by several years of cruelty, insecurity, and misery. It welcomed Rojas Pinilla as a savior. By means of promises that he was not to keep, the latter convinced many guerrillas to lay down their arms and turn the sectors under their control over to the army. Exhausted, sick, eager to return home, 3,540 of them in the *llanos* alone surrendered. In Santander, Antioquia, and other regions, guerrilla units were dissolved. Elsewhere, *bandolero* leaders let the army buy them over.

The only ones to continue the struggle were the guerrillas south of Tolima, who were now threatened by both the army and the *bandoleros* who had gone over to the government. These *bandoleros* wore thick beards and had been nicknamed *barbudos*. Then the *pájaros* went back to work.

On June 8, 1954, to protest the death of a member of the University of Bogotá who had been killed during a demonstration, the students and their professors joined in a silent march through the streets of the city. When they reached the center, the Colombia Battalion, which had recently returned from Korea, fired into the marchers, killing three and wounding forty.

Immediately afterward, university people, members of the Communist party, and leaders of the extreme right were thrown pell-mell into prison. The return of the *violencia* was at hand. According to experts, this return was because soldiers participating in operations received double pay, advanced in the ranks more quickly, and accumulated certain material bonuses.

In the regions of Tolima and Sumapaz rich lands had been developed by groups of peasants organized by the popular leader Valencia and were now coveted by several neighboring large landowners and some of their officer friends.

An advance guard of *pájaros* was sent ahead; then on November 12, 1954, eight hundred soldiers invaded the zone, massacred a few *campesinos*, and arrested the leaders of the peasant organizations. Once again the peasants took up arms. Self-defense units were spontaneously organized; in turn the repression bore down more heavily. A concentration camp, or rather an extermination camp, was set up at Cunday, a military operations base. A few liberal leaders such as Herrera and Orjuela died there, and this contributed to detaching their party from the Rojas Pinilla dictatorship.

Almost five thousand soldiers, forty tanks or armored cars, and a few bombing squadrons were put into the field against the peasants to no avail. The army laid siege. Finally the peasants and their families took refuge in the virgin forest. The region had become a desert. The fugitives were bombed with napalm, and most of the survivors of this exodus either died in the forest or were killed by disease and hunger.

But other guerrilla bands formed in the provinces of Tolima,

Huila, Caldas, or Cauca, and one after another they organized into "self-defense groups" that were to be called "independent republics."

General Rojas Pinilla might have triumphed if he had been given the time. But he was beginning to worry those who had put him in power. The people who had backed him because he brought peace were disillusioned: the university by the machine-gunning of the marchers; the conservatives of the extreme right by their removal from power; the liberals because of his sanctioning the execution of some of their best leaders; and the communists because they had been made the scapegoat.

In addition to everything else, this good soldier, initially unambitious, was beginning to take himself for Perón. He tried to attract the good will of the Church. He turned his daughter María Eugenia into an Evita and sent her off amid great fanfare to distribute charity to the poor. He even created his own political party. In 1957, he suddenly decided to prolong by four years a mandate that was to expire the following year. Since in spite of everything he had a certain respect for legality, he convoked a constituent assembly. It was his undoing.

As we have seen, in Colombia, he who holds the government controls all the wealth of the country. For more than a century the liberals and the conservatives had been fighting over the division of a cake which the army, until then, had had no share of. And now this little nothing of a general, who had merely been hired to put an end to the disorders that inhibited the functioning of the dollar-making machine, wanted to make this machine work for him. The situation was inconceivable.

The Constituent Assembly docilely voted as Rojas Pinilla asked it to. He was reelected for the period of 1958–62. Three days later the leaders of the army visited him at the San Carlos Palace and politely but insistently asked him to leave. He no longer had the support of anybody. His officers, also eager to get into the *sistema*, had all been bought off. Just for the form of it, before his departure Rojas Pinilla turned over power to a military junta. The latter very honestly transmitted it into the hands of a coalition of conservatives and liberals. After all, weren't these two groups the actual owners of the country?

The two former enemies, the liberals and the conservatives, weary of killing one another off, of losing instead of making money, of bleeding this country which they considered their private property, suddenly discovered the advantages of fraternity. They were reconciled, but in such a way as to keep political groups other than their own from power. The constitution they worked up specified:

1. A sixteen-year truce—until 1974—with the president alternating every four years, a conservative succeeding a liberal, then a liberal a conservative, etc. The vice president had to be a member of the party opposed to the president's party. At every echelon of the administration, from ministers down to post-office clerks, the same alternation had to be followed. If a departmental manager was a conservative, his chief clerk had to be a liberal. However, the Minister of Foreign Affairs had to be a member of the same party as the president—but the Minister of the Interior had to be a member of the opposition.

2. A law could only be passed by a two-thirds majority, which meant that any move by either party had to be approved by some part of the other party.

Strange as it may seem, the system has been in force to this very day. The first into office was a liberal, Alberto Lleras Camargo. A conservative, Guillermo León Valencia, succeeded him. But the system has its faults. For example, it's difficult to interest the electors in voting when the outcome is known in advance. It creates a state of apathy and dissatisfaction. In addition, the required two-thirds majority prevents the passage of numerous laws at a time when basic structural reforms are necessary.

On the other hand, this suffocating system has allowed new

political groups, which have not participated in the pact—for example López Michelsen's MRL—to establish a following (16 percent of the vote) and conserve a dynamism that the two big traditional parties have lost.

Only one problem remained unresolved: the *violencia*.

The return after the dictatorship to a lame constitutional democracy—that is to say, to the *sistema*—could in no way stop this violence.

Even though there had been neither a formal truce nor an amnesty, the agreement between the conservatives and the liberals was considered a sign that the battles were over. Some liberal guerrillas surrendered. But others had developed a taste for illegality and intended to continue the struggle without troubling themselves about political opinions.

To protect their lands, the big landholders therefore continued to maintain private bands. In some regions, conservative officials, who may have felt that the struggles could end only with the complete elimination of the adversary, had their men hunt down the very liberals whose leaders were in power in Bogotá. The *bandoleros* took to the roads, pillaging and burning farms, arresting and robbing travelers. Former guerrilla leaders who had abandoned the struggle were killed by hired assassins.

Initially the fight was directed against this "bandolerism" which followed the armed revolt. Journalist Santiago Solarte has given this explanation of how the situation deteriorated:

. . . the lack of political formation and social awareness, guerrilla romanticism, the thirst for vengeance or personal ambition, the lack of coordination and even the existence of antagonisms between the various armed groups, and above all, the fact that the armed struggle was isolated from the political and social struggles in the cities. For these reasons, the guerrilla movement was incapable of controlling the political events to which it had given rise.

Though the Communist party had accepted the principle of a tacit truce, it had not surrendered its arms. It was little by little to orient itself toward the systematic organization of self-defense groups by aiding hunted guerrillas, and peasants whose land had been expropriated, to clear new lands in regions difficult to reach. Nearly sixty thousand men participated in this undertaking.

During this time in the city the leaders of the party, which finally had a legal existence, were demanding an agrarian reform that would sanction this situation, and trying to tie their organization to the claims of the working classes.

The Communist party had never done anything but follow the lead of these guerrilla-peasants, who were acting instinctively in trying to create outside the zones of violence new villages and new farmlands that would enable them to feed themselves and their families. In 1954, considerably before the agreement of the parties, while repression was in full swing, a column of guerrillas, chased by the army for more than 250 miles, had managed to disappear into the El Pato forest. The guerrillas had been under the command of a member of the central committee, Comandante Ciro Trujillo Costaño.

These men began to clear the *selva*. In two years the zone was transformed into a network of prosperous farms. The new colonists were soon joined by their families. They set up an agrarian union, a collegial administration, women's organizations, schools, and youth movements; they made the forest into a small Marxist universe.

In 1956, under the same conditions, in Guayabero in the heart of the Cordilleras, another group of farms was established. Just as in El Pato, these "small" communist leaders in Guayabero, left to their own devices, followed the example of Viota, the first "independent republic" created after the 1928 peasant revolts, before the birth of the Colombian Communist party. The government had initially kept its hands off, thinking that inexperience would soon put an end to this collectivist enterprise. But the latter had continued to flourish, furnishing fruits and vegetables to the capital and even entering into agreements with wholesalers and neighboring large landowners.

When the army was sent to destroy this "state within a state," it was fought off. The government contented itself with condemning the Viota peasant leaders in absentia for "criminal association." In 1953, while the *violencia* was at its height, by one of those remarkable contradictions in Colombian justice, these same leaders were acquitted with expressions of praise. The new self-defense groups could find no better justification than this acquittal.

It was a parliamentarian of the extreme right, Alvaro Gómez Hurtado, who invented the term "independent republic," a term which fits the situation perfectly. Actually, the situation was a strange one. In areas where the official authorities did not oppose the collective peasant ventures, the new organizations and the administration coexisted peacefully. In some zones there were small military garrisons. But where officials tried to oppose those who had taken the local interests in hand, only the revolutionary authority counted.

According to an English scholar who went to Colombia to study the situation there, the communist zones were armed, organized, and disciplined; they were identifiable by the fact that even when they were surrounded by territories in which violence reigned they were perfectly peaceful. Their principal strength, the Englishman found, lay in their manifest efficiency and their equitable laws, which attracted neighboring populations.

The leaders made efforts to avoid political sectarianism. They tried to conciliate the more progressive elements of the Catholic Church. Everybody shared in the maintenance of roads and bridges but the right to property was not questioned. Nonetheless, the basic doctrine remained communist. In 1961, in Cunday, communists, parish priests, liberals, and conservatives for the first time confiscated lands that were not being sufficiently exploited and drove off their owners. This first step toward an illegal agrarian reform was to help accelerate the government reaction. "All those fleeing persecution," wrote Monsignor Guzmán, "came to Gaitanan. The revolutionary organization gave them land, medicines, and protection. The only condition placed on new arrivals was to not put others in the wrong because of their political or religious opinions. None of them renounced his former political or religious designation—he merely added a new one: that of communist."

During my stay in Bogotá I met a student who had lived for two years in the "Independent Republic of Marquetalia." He told me, "In 1959 the Republic of Marquetalia was just beginning to get organized. I stayed there two years. Nothing really worked well until we got some Chinese and Cuban instructors. They came in a C-47. The land in the Marquetalia Valley was flat enough to construct aircraft runways 2,500 feet long that look like potato fields from a distance. These instructors separated us into different groups of specialists—the group that wrote tracts included the typographers, the printers, and the Indians who would eventually distribute the tracts throughout the entire region.

"But after these instructors left, we sank back into 'tropicalism,' into the easy life. We had built our own palm-thatched houses. Food was no problem, but we had to raise money in Bogotá from sympathizers. We never kidnapped anybody for ransom. We sold stamps, collected taxes on alcohol or tobacco, and when we were completely broke, we could always launch an attack."

These "independent republics" were simultaneously a challenge to the army, the *sistema*, the government, and U.S. policy in South America. For the last two years Fidel Castro had been in power in Cuba and he hid neither his political sympathies nor his intentions. The expedition sent to overthrow him had been driven into the sea, and he was beginning to loom much too large.

It was the army, intoxicated by its successes against the *bandoleros*, that was the first to break the truce. In the beginning of 1962, the Sixth Brigade launched an attack in the Marquetalia region.

Specialized antiguerrilla units, "pioneers" officered by men trained in Panama or in Texas, participated in this operation involving more than five thousand men. The peasant self-defense groups valiantly absorbed the shock, inflicting heavy losses on the army. They even managed to capture some heavy equipment.

Before ceding office to his successor, a conservative, Lleras Camargo ordered the retreat of his troops. This engagement was to make the leader of the self-defense groups, Manuel Marulandia Velez—better known under his *nom de guerre*, Tiro Fijo (Sure Shot)—famous throughout the country. The army's defeat was followed by a long period of calm that was nevertheless marked by skirmishes between military patrols and elements of the self-defense groups.

The new Minister of War, Ruiz Novoa, with the aid of the Southern Command, its advisers, and its instructors, completely reorganized the Colombian army, which was furnished with excellent equipment. Ruiz Novoa, however, did not receive the reward of his labors. He was superseded at the beginning of the general offensive in 1944 for having become the leader of a "Nasserist" military group that advocated an energetic government and real social reforms.

Ruiz Novoa affirmed, "The war of the future will be guerrilla warfare. . . . Sometimes it will be communism that will attempt to seize power by means of subversion. At other times communism will have to face guerrillas who are trying to recuperate land for the West. At the moment, it is the West that has to recuperate Colombian lands which have fallen into the hands of the communists."

The U.S. government is giving this undertaking its full support; Colombia figures immediately after Vietnam in the preoccupations of the Pentagon. Forty percent of the Colombian budget is devoted to the army. The purchase of arms and military equipment in the United States has absolute priority. The influence of the U.S. Military Mission over the Colombian general staff is complete. I was able to judge this for myself by visiting the large military barracks on the outskirts of the city; they are crammed with American equipment, American advisers in battle dress, and Colombian officers who imitate their style. Everything is American, even the way in which we were received, "briefed," and carted from one office to another like counters being moved over the immense squares of a computer chart on which absolutely nothing is left to chance.

In the meantime, according to the Miami *Herald*, the region controlled by the "Independent Republic of Marquetalia" had doubled its territory and tripled its population.

The strategy carefully worked out by the army and the Southern Command is known as the "Laso Plan." According to a Communist report, the following are its main objectives:

1. Preparation and organization: Once the troops have been trained for action against the guerrillas, spies are to be sent out to gather information in the region. To this end, a "civic military-action program" has been organized to present the army as a benefactor, bringing the peasants gifts (clothes, medicines, and Yankee foodstuff from associations such as Care and Caritas) and providing them with medical and dental services. It is even building them bridges, roads and schools.

2. An expanded program of psychological warfare is then set on foot and use is made of the factor of surprise. Measures are taken to control the civilian population. This is the initial phase of a blockade of the region.

3. Next military operations aimed at isolating and then exterminating armed rebel groups are undertaken.

4. The armed rebel movement is systematically divided by means of psychological propaganda aimed at emphasizing internal divergencies due to political differences, the ambitions of the leaders, base

passions, or errors of the guerrilla command. Attempts are made to win over elements capable of betraying the guerrilla movement.

5. Finally, economic, political, and social "reconstruction" of the operations zone is undertaken with the same North American aid that has previously been used to destroy the zone.

This plan was first successfully put into action against a guerrilla group installed near the Venezuelan border. The time then came to use it against Marquetalia. Journalists from various countries were invited to follow the forces involved: sixteen thousand men—a third of the Colombian army.

Fighting began on May 1, 1964. A month and a half later the peasant stronghold was still resisting and the army had been unable to infiltrate it.

Then, with the aid of U.S. Army helicopters, a vast airborne operation was launched to capture Tiro Fijo. But the latter withdrew into the mountains with his men without sustaining heavy losses. The villages of Marquetalia were occupied, but the economic organization set up by the communists continued in force despite repression.

The army pursued the self-defense groups, but the latter solidly entrenched themselves in the mountains. They once more became guerrillas. The "Laso Plan" had partially failed. The Marquetalia operation alone had cost seventeen million dollars.

Encircled for six months, the self-defense zone of El Pato was attacked on March 22, 1965. The fields were laid waste and domestic animals were confiscated. More than a hundred families pursued by the commandos took refuge in the forest. Ninety-six women, children, and old people died in the course of a seventy-two-hour forced march.

Shortly afterward, in the Santander province, a group of young students set up the ELN (Ejército de Liberación Nacional). The communists held the newborn child over the baptismal font since they brought to it the support of the petroleum unions under their control. But the day was on hand when they would become brotherly enemies because of Fidel Castro, the Russians, and the theft from them of Camilo Torres. Today the two organizations have split, but the Colombian Castroites have obtained some help from the Venezuelan Castroites on the other side of the border. Venezuelan and Colombian guerrillas fight in either or both countries. It is the first practical attempt to apply the "Bolívar Plan," which sets the subversive struggle a continental goal that supersedes national interests.

The communists, those in the official party as well as those in the clandestine party and the Colombian Armed Revolutionary Forces, all know that the Colombian people want peace and an end to guerrilla warfare. For the last few years the communist guerrillas have merely defended themselves; they never attack the government forces.

It is difficult for the Castroites—students who come from the university and are born into good city families—to understand just what these illiterate *campesinos*, half-breeds to whom they will always remain strangers, want or reject.

Perhaps because they have peasants among them, and because even their leaders in the guerrilla bands are men trained by long years of underground struggle, the communists have a better appreciation of the real situation in the country.

Everybody in Colombia agreed on the need to end guerrilla warfare, except of course the two hundred members of the Camilo Torres Front.

They all almost came to an agreement: the communists, President Lleras Restrepo's liberals, López Michelsen's MRL, and the Russians who had come to help. But the "Castroites," who wanted to continue the *violencia* because they had no other solutions to propose other than intensified guerrilla activity, and the Colombian military, whose peacetime powers would have been considerably diminished, caused this attempt to fail—as certain Americans looked on approvingly.

Things continued as before. No, not exactly as before. The communists were now determined to eliminate the Colombian Castroites, and the Russians were determined to put an end to Cuban guerrilla activities on the continent. At the end of this chain, there was the miserable death of Che Guevara.

The situation between the communists and the Castroites continued to deteriorate rapidly. Following a violent indictment published in *Pravda* on October 25, 1967, Fidel Castro refused to attend the celebration in Moscow of the Fiftieth Anniversary of the October Revolution. In early November the Colombian Communist party stated in its publication, *Vox Proletaria*:

No factors justifying a real revolution exist in Colombia. . . . Despite the evident crisis, it is untrue that the revolutionary struggle of the masses is growing—on the contrary. . . . Because of this, Communists must take part in the coming legislative elections—that is where their duty lies. . . .

It was in this atmosphere impregnated with violence that Father Camilo Torres was raised. His social group was the scene of many bloody struggles between conservatives and liberals —sordid struggles aimed solely at seizing power in order to make money. He found these same struggles in the bosom of the Church, a Church made sluggish and sleepy by the weight of its wealth, its gold-threaded copes and its golden vessels. Instead of trying to smother the violence, the Colombian Church was merely concerned with its own safety. It supported all the governments, particularly that of Laureano Gómez, a former student of the Jesuit fathers, a man who revered the memory of Hitler and Mussolini, who had asked Franco to train his police, and whose entourage was made up exclusively of priests. The village clergy were so involved in collaboration with this regime that they gave peasants safe-conducts certifying that they "did not belong to the Liberal party and that in consequence their lives, their families, and their property are to be respected." The Church had always lived in the shadow of the oligarchy. Camilo Torres' sacrifice was to permit it, first in Colombia and then in the rest of Latin America, to keep its distance from this outmoded form of power condemned by all, even the United States.

Then, swept along by its own dynamism, the Church was to go even farther along the path to revolution. But let's not exaggerate—instead of "the Church," let's say its "advance guard."

Some forty miles from Mexico City, about three thousand feet nearer sea level, among flamboyant gardens and their flowery jacarandas, is spread, or rather strewn, Cuernavaca. It is the city of eternal springtime, the home of painters like Siqueiros— who wanted to kill Trotsky—of artists, rich beatniks given over to drugs, poor beatniks chased by the police but nevertheless able to find drugs, and old Americans who come to end their days in the sun. It is also the city in which the buses make more stench and noise than anywhere else in Mexico. Some kind of mad notion of *machismo* makes the bus drivers' union of Cuernavaca want to turn one of the most pleasant cities in the world into an unlivable one.

As for the priests of Cuernavaca, they seem to have agreed to turn this little city into the most fiery center of the revolution in the very heart of the Church.

To begin with there is the Bishop of Cuernavaca, who faithfully protects all those who are for change, whether it be political or religious.

For example, let us take the case of one of "his" revolution-aries, Monsignor Iván Illich, who went beyond the limits allowed a member of the sacerdotal hierarchy by writing:

The Roman Catholic Church is the most important nongovern-mental bureaucracy in the world: it has 1,800,000 fulltime employees, priests, monks, and nuns. . . . But the Colossus is tottering. This system which absorbs so many priests and bishops in more and more complex administrative tasks is no longer a persuasive one. Many Christians, even priests, do not find the Gospel in it. Sacerdotal defections are multiplying. Ten years ago they were the exception. Tomorrow they may be the rule.

The Bishop of Cuernavaca reacted by publishing in the Mexican weekly *Siempre!* an open letter in which he limited himself to condemning this "dangerous caricature based on hasty generalizations." But he continued to back the work of Monsignor Illich with all his support and help.

The Bishop of Cuernavaca feels that the Mexican Revolution and the persecutions that followed it saved the clergy from mediocrity. He therefore continues to render it homage.

In the Cuernavaca Cathedral, the new liturgical reforms are followed and Mass is said in Spanish. This change has been most successful. In a small neighboring church, the Mass is accompanied by the sound of maracas. Yesterday the churches were empty; today they are full.

Another of the religious "curiosities" of Cuernavaca is the Emmaus Center, where Dominicans practice psychoanalysis under the direction of Father Grégoire Lemercier.

The venture has turned out rather badly. Father Lemercier has been returned to a lay state. The Church feels that it has no need of psychoanalysis and that confession offers the faithful sufficient relief. As for the communists, they feel that auto-criticism is sufficient to free their comrades from guilt complexes.

Since I agree with them and find little of interest in intro-spection, persuaded as I am that it is only through others that one finds himself, and since I was making an inquiry into a precise political subject, I left the Dominicans to their troubles. I opted for Monsignor Illich's seminary. I in no way expected to find that here too a kind of political revolution was being prepared.

In principle, the priests who live in this seminary belong to clerical groups from all over the world—Europe, Canada, the United States—and come there to learn Spanish. But this excellent and modern school of living languages is also a "documentation center," and its students are taught many other things.

One day in Mexico City I was told, "It's hardly necessary to travel all over Latin America to find the revolutionary leaders. Just go to Monsignor Illich's place in Cuernavaca and you'll find them. But these revolutionaries are people who come and go, who appear and disappear. Sometimes you can't get to meet them. In any case, just go to see Monsignor Illich, who is the most revolutionary of them all."

As it turned out, at Cuernavaca I was to meet: Julião, the leader of the peasant leagues in northeast Brazil, who had just gotten out of prison; Miss Olivieri, the friend of Camilo Torres, who had followed his adventure in the guerrillas to the very end and had almost been killed; some priests who looked like priests and others who did not; and men who were not priests at all.

The "seminary" is established in a large, sunshine-flooded house built in the American colonial style. White colonnades, a pool, gardens, large airy rooms opening onto magnificent landscapes, and flowers everywhere. But inside the house the typewriters crackle, and the basement is crammed with files, mimeograph machines, and photocopiers. Publications are issued in every language. There are dossiers on every country and on every man—those who want to bring about the revolution and those who want to prevent it.

"The Vatican's Latin American *barbudos*," said one of my friends somewhat irritatedly. "But the priests of Cuernavaca are better organized and better informed. They have an agent in power in every Latin American village: the local priest. They know all the mysteries of these countries, but if so many secrets are confided to them it's because they are known to be discreet.

"The CIA serves the U.S.A., but the priests serve the last international in the world to survive with its dogma and hierarchy intact: the Church, with its post-Council 'new look.' All over Latin America, the other Church, the one belonging to the communists, has split into I don't know how many different tendencies. Everywhere in South America even among the guerrillas, people are insulting, fighting, betraying, and slaughtering one another. But not the priests.

"If I were a revolutionary, I would join the priests, if only for safety's sake. In spite of this I can hardly bear them, since I'm the son of a teacher and therefore deeply anticlerical."

In this large house there are neither crosses nor holy pictures, but photographs of the revolutionaries: Camilo Torres, Fidel Castro, and Che Guevara. After a few hours in this strange monastery I would not have been surprised to meet the mysterious vagabond of the revolution in one of the corridors.

I met with Monsignor Illich two or three times. He was an extremely intelligent man and made the most of his charm and culture. A mixture of Yugoslav and New York Jew, he had the Slavic charm and winningness of the one and the sarcastic humor of the other. He had a big nose, a wide mouth, heavy eyelids, a smile, and a warm, generous voice, all of which were irresistible. He still belonged to the New York diocese of Cardinal Spellman, a prelate who seemed to have had little sympathy with anything revolutionary.

By thirty, Iván Illich held a natural science doctorate from an Italian university, a doctorate in history from a German university, and a degree in philosophy and theology; he had already been the vicar of a New York slum made up of Puerto Ricans and Irish. For five years he was the vice rector of the Catholic University of Puerto Rico. He was driven from the university by his colleagues, the other bishops, for having opposed the founding of a Catholic party that wanted to vote against both Kennedy and contraceptives. A brilliant career was predicted for him in those mysterious Vatican bureaus where the Church's political policy is formed, but he himself destroyed this career. How old is he now? Forty, forty-five? He speaks with an inimitable accent that betrays the dozen languages he knows and uses. Dressed in light-colored clothes, he wears no ring on his finger. He is simplicity itself. His mind is busy with too many large projects to spend much time on the usual conventions. After the publication of an article on the "super-charitables" in the January 21, 1967, issue of *America*, Iván Illich was in serious trouble with the United States episcopacy. I will only cite some of the essential passages:

Five years ago, U.S. Catholics undertook a peculiar alliance for the progress of the Latin American Church. By 1970, ten per cent of the more than 225,000 priests, brothers and sisters would volunteer to be shipped south of the border. In the meantime, the combined U.S. male and female "clergy" in South America has increased by only 1,622. Halfway is a good time to examine whether a program launched is still sailing on course and, more importantly, if its destination still seems worth-while. Numerically, the program was certainly a flop. Should this be a source of disappointment or of relief?

The project relied on an impulse supported by uncritical imagination and sentimental judgment. A pointed finger and a "call for 20,000" convinced many that "Latin America needs YOU." Nobody dared state clearly why.

A campaign for more funds is now being proposed. This is the moment, therefore, at which the call for 20,000 persons and the need for millions of dollars should be reexamined. Both appeals must be submitted to a public debate among U.S. Catholics, from bishop to widow, since they are the ones asked to supply the personnel and pay the bill. Critical thinking must prevail. Fancy and colorful campaign slogans for another collection, with their appeal to emotion, will only cloud the real issues. Let us coldly examine the American Church's outburst of charitable frenzy which resulted in the creation of "papal" volunteers, student "mission crusades," the annual CICOP (Catholic Inter-American Cooperation Program) mass assemblies, numerous diocesan missions and new religious communities. . . .

Men and money sent with missionary motivation carry a foreign

Christian image, a foreign pastoral approach and a foreign political message. They also bear the mark of North American capitalism of the 1950's. Why not, for once, consider the shady side of charity; weigh the inevitable burdens foreign help imposes on the South American Church; taste the bitterness of the damage done by our sacrifices?

During the past five years, the cost of operating the Church in Latin America has multiplied many times. There is no precedent for a similar rate of increase in Church expenses on a continental scale. Today, one Catholic university, mission society or radio chain may cost more to operate than the whole country's Church a decade ago. Most of the funds for this kind of growth came from outside. . . .

This kind of foreign generosity has enticed the Latin American Church into becoming a satellite to North Atlantic cultural phenomena and policy. Increased apostolic resources intensified the need for their continued flow and created islands of apostolic well-being, each day farther beyond the capacity of local support. The Latin American Church flowers anew by returning to what the Conquest stamped her: a colonial plant that blooms because of foreign cultivation. Instead of learning either how to get along with less money or close up shop, bishops are being trapped into needing more money now and bequeathing an institution impossible to run in the future. Education, the one type of investment that could give long-range returns, is conceived mostly as training for bureaucrats who will maintain the existing apparatus.

In his statements to me, Monsignor Illich went considerably further. "The country of the Great Society, the United States, is now engaged in a triple war: a war against what menaces this society from the exterior—Vietnam; a war against what hampers it—Cuba, disorder, guerrillas, everything that is not productive and that hinders production in Guatemala, Venezuela, Colombia, and Peru; and a war against the interior threats—the black slums of Harlem and of Watts.

"In this triple war, the United States uses bombing and napalm in Vietnam, and in Latin-American countries it uses armored cars, national armies, and police forces . . . but it also makes use of the Peace Corps, and Catholic or Protestant missionaries whose job it is to explain that these wars are being carried on for the good of the people. For this reason, every missionary who comes to South America from the United States is looked upon with suspicion because he is in an ambiguous situation. Doesn't he represent, whether or not he wants to, that form of repression whose goal is the integration of this continent into the economic system of the United States? Because of this, we no longer want American priests but only those from Germany, France, Canada and Italy.

"Believe me, there are far too many priests in Latin America, even though it is said that we do not have enough—too many at least of the kind of priest who is merely an employee of the Church. In the future, ten or twenty years from now, the Christian community will be formed around a deacon who will be married, who will have children, and who after twenty years of secular life will be ordained a priest and say Mass. He will live off his own labors and he will be steeped in the people. The Council has set us on this road.

"The Latin-American Church must become poor, very poor. It must do so quickly in order to bring about a social change; if not, it will be a victim of this change. The only way in which to have a poor Church is for it to welcome wholeheartedly the progressive socialization of this continent. For this reason, I hope the Church will have fewer and fewer employees, less money, fewer institutions—even institutions of primary, secondary, and higher educations—and fewer possibilities of becoming involved as a Church in basic literacy and education.

"It is extremely difficult for the Church to remain in the service of social change if it continues to use its own institutions to control this social change—change which it can only distort, render suspect, or mark with its imprint.

"Instead of this, the aid brought to the Church from outside makes it too rich by wanting to make it too powerful.

"There is another danger: the use that people want to make of the Church, this new Church in favor of social change. Only five years ago, any intelligent man who wanted to work for the social reform of society would have found it unthinkable to identify himself with a Church that was a reactionary Church and in the service of immobilism.

"Today that same man moves toward the Church because it has ceased to be immobile and reactionary. The result is that all those who want to maintain the old structures in Latin America have only one thought in mind: to buy the Church, to make use of her to slow this evolution or revolution. But if the Church permits this, it can only lose the fruits of its own internal revolution and the success with which it has met everywhere on the continent. The function of the Church is not to do 'business,' to manage wealth; its first duty is to preach the Gospel. This means making everybody understand the glory, the happiness, in participating more and more joyously in any social, economic, or psychological change or development in the community."

I asked this unusual prelate, "Do you believe, Monsignor"—it's almost embarrassing to call such a man Monsignor, to imagine him robed in purple and with a miter on his head—"do you believe that in order to bring about this social change a priest like Camilo Torres had the right to go so far as to join the guerrilla bands?"

He sidestepped the trap. "I believe the function of the Church is to participate knowingly and joyously in all forms of change, in no matter what form of change, even the progressive socialization of a country. It is the task given us by Christ. Today we want a Church whose principal function is the celebration of change."

His smile was marvelous, a smile that could bring an old agnostic like myself back into the bosom of the Church of his childhood.

At this same "documentation center" in Cuernavaca, I also

met a very different kind of man—Father del Corro of the Society of Jesus. He is a small Argentine with graying hair. He too has a beautiful smile. He is an excellent handyman. Using a few odds and ends, he repaired our broken tape recorder. He knows about radio. People say that in Argentina he once took over a broadcasting station in order to call on the *descamisados* to rebel; he was able to make the broadcasting equipment work even though it had been sabotaged.

Where hasn't he been? What hasn't he done? For example, he spent two weeks in a Guatemalan guerrilla band with César Montes.

On first arriving in Guatemala City, he had made the rounds of the bars, where he met a member of the resistance. He did not hide the fact that he was a priest, and moreover a Jesuit. The resistance man began by insulting him, but Father del Corro spent the night drinking with him, and a few days later the priest was with the guerrillas.

What did César Montes tell him?

He smiled when asked, but made no reply. He has established associations, or rather unions, of ragpickers and scrap-iron collectors all over Latin America. He must have been in many areas which the army can only penetrate with machine guns and mortars. One of the top directors of the Creole Petroleum Company, a subsidiary of Standard Oil, told me in Caracas that he had had a "disturbing" interview with him. After leaving this man, Father del Corro may very likely have gone off to meet with Douglas Bravo in his guerrilla band, or to join his compatriot, Che Guevara, in Argentina, assuming the latter was there. Anything is possible with this timid, effacing, and at times stubborn little man, this Jesuit who believes so much in the poor and so little in the value of the charities set up to help them. Christian Socialist leaders everywhere—Reinaldo Teiffel, in Nicaragua, René de Leon Schlotter in Guatemala, Rafael Calderas in Venezuela—repeated his ideas about violence and the dynamics of poverty.

During the course of several meetings, Father del Corro was to say to me, "Christians are taken for rich people in the world today. This worries them and it worries the Church, the Council. "The material poverty in Latin America is due only to cultural and structural faults. It is a poverty undergoing rapid change. The closed sectors where poverty is chronic and endemic—as in certain Indian or peasant groups or among the inhabitants of the belts of misery around the big cities—now know, thanks to the radio and the press, of the advantages of civilization, culture, technique, and comfort that are enjoyed by the rich. They know that these advantages are in sharp contrast with their own dispossession and permanent dissatisfaction.

"The formerly unaware poor are now beginning to think about ways in which they can satisfy their fundamental, normal civic needs in the midst of the society in which they live. Chronic misery and poverty are rapidly being transformed into a resentful poverty, a poverty in crisis, an aware poverty that is trying to find in the cultural, social, and economic order some way out that does not lead back to the former situation of unconscious poverty.

"Poverty's own awareness of itself is widespread in Latin America. Thinking poverty is the most powerful explosive for a fundamental upheaval.

"It is important, it is urgent, to make Latin-American poverty think, to accelerate its awareness. Neither the 'myths of poverty,' nor the 'virtue of poverty,' nor the 'Church of the poor' presented in the confused manner and in the forms heretofore suggested are now of any more use.

"The Indians rebelling in Peru, the miners in Bolivia, the inhabitants of the shantytowns in Brazil (favelados) or Chile (callamperos), the proletarian colonies of Mexico, the downtrodden of Argentina, the guerrillas of Colombia, the exploited peasants and artisans, the beggars and the ragpickers of all the big cities—none of these can any longer be spoken to in the language that we, the non-poor Christians of today, still use.

There is poverty and misery in Latin America, but there are no abject creatures—in other words no people whose spirit has been broken by poverty and misery. There are no more poor—in other words no people willing to accept poverty. There is a constantly growing reaction and awareness. No mystique of poverty interests them, which is why they will not take advantage of the many institutions 'for the poor.' These poor know no poor in their religion, their lives, or their preoccupations. To the poor, the poor are comrades in the struggle against poverty.

"There is no hate in the poor. It is almost nonexistent; it has not taken, in spite of the efforts made to have it do so. The poor of Latin America are a socially healthy element prepared for change.

"National organizations of inhabitants of urban areas now exist in every country, and two years ago they were already talking of the first Latin-American Congress of the Homeless.

"Today's poor think differently: they are no longer people sunk in misery, but people scrambling out of it, people on the march toward a normal, economic, and humane incorporation into present society.

"Materially, they still live in their shantytowns, beg in the streets, or rummage through garbage, but psychologically they have left all that behind. They left it behind a long time ago. The poor are on the march: that is Latin America's most powerful and consoling reality. Their recently-begun march cannot be resisted, they cannot be stopped with gifts or soothing measures. Fortunately, they can no longer be contained or cheated. This march now underway will be irreversible.

"Are we ready to receive our poor people on the march and to begin the dialogue with them, or is our only response to help them accept their present situation?

"The poor no longer want charity whose secret goal is to maintain them in that poverty. What a horror that sort of charity is! These poor want no charitable institutions for the poor, no painting or music for the poor, no shops for the poor. They demand their due place in society. Latin America has a kind of 'pornography' of poverty. That is what these charitable institutions can be called. Consciously or unconsciously they are organizations designed to ameliorate and conserve poverty.

"What do our words, our organizations, our lives, tell the poor? That they are poor, that poverty is beatitude, that the poor will inherit the Kingdom of God, that Christ was poor, that He loved the poor, and, finally, that the Church is the Church of the poor.

"These good tidings are sad tidings to the poor. They have a derisive ring to them.

"Certain violent reactions of the poor are usually interpreted as externalizations and manifestations of hate. Generally speaking, they relate to a search for justice, a search carried on in their own way and with the means at their disposal."

"Like the guerrilla bands?" I asked.

"Latin America is experiencing violence due to the oppression, the poverty in which the people are kept. The reactions to this situation are normal, as is guerrilla activity.

"Let me say again, the poor are not those who are stagnating in misery, they are those who have already spiritually left it— even if they continue to rummage through the garbage heaps of the shantytowns. But if attempts are made to shove them back into misery by force, or by charity, then . . ."

"Then?"

"They will take the only path remaining open to them—violence, revolution. It will be bloody, and it will destroy everything. It is already almost too late to prevent it."

Before leaving Father del Corro, I asked him, "You have been separated from your order, but what tie with it do you still maintain?"

"Every month I report to my provincial."

Anybody who knows the Jesuits—that private and disciplined army of the Pope, that army whose members often take on the guise of independent agents—knows that they are at all times under the complete control of their superiors.

It was the answer I was looking for. The Catholic Church was present, even active, behind this revolution on the entire continent. It might even be about to take the lead.

The Church on this continent had been dying, crouching amidst its riches, limited to liturgical rites and scapularies, and now it was springing to life, revolutionary and all-conquering.

The Church was rich in Latin America. It was even one of the biggest landowners. For example, in Mexico, before the revolution, the clergy controlled 65 percent of the land. It should not be forgotten that the monks came with the conquistadors in the same galleons and that they had been given large domains. At the time of independence they not only retained them, but increased them.

Suddenly, in Colombia, Venezuela, Peru, Brazil, and Chile, bishops are distributing the lands of their dioceses. The Church is voluntarily impoverishing itself in order to be able to reassemble the poor and finally be heard by them.

Monsignor Fragosa, a Brazilian bishop, recently wrote this pastoral letter:

I see Latin America as a great oppressed people. There is no need to analyze all the forms of oppression. They are obvious to those who have their eyes open. It must opt for liberation. And this is why the entire people wants to effect a radical rupture with economic, political, and cultural imperialism. The peasants, the workers, the students, all the oppressed, are called to take the responsibility for their own liberation. In what direction will Latin America go next? It is not my duty to fix in advance the paths of our development. . . . In awakening its critical sense and its capacity for self-determination, Latin America will shake off the yoke of all oppressions and define its own physiognomy. The courage of the little island of Cuba can be taken for a symbol and a call. As the Latin-American people free themselves from injustice and the alienating effects of imperialism, the threat of Communism will be conquered.

The Church suddenly wanted to beat the revolutionary materialists on their own home grounds by making itself as revolutionary as they were. However, it has taken its time about it. But now it has found its first revolutionary martyr. In spite of the fact that the Santander guerrilla band was rebaptized the Camilo Torres Front, the Duchess' dead son was returning to his own, to the bosom of the Church.

As for that other great revolutionary, Che Guevara, he was already escaping the grasp of Cuba.

Green Berets, Guerrillas, and *Caudillos* 4

"What a job I had finding a maid! Finally, I got my hands on a 'gem'—a gem who doesn't know how to do a thing and for whom I have to buy everything, even her clothes. And in spite of that, she wants $150 a month in addition to room and board. The situation has become just impossible!"

The scene is not New York or Paris, but Caracas, the capital of Venezuela and one of the most expensive cities in the world. The maid in question is an Indian who has just come from the *llanos*—the country, that is—and though she is as strong as a mule, she is evidently just as close-minded and stubborn. The woman who is telling us about her domestic tragedies belongs to this rich, uneasy, and turbulent business class.

The sole source of Venezuela's prosperity is oil, 15 percent of world production. Between 120 and 160 million tons are pumped out annually, and the reserve supply is set at 2½ billion tons. But oil is a poisoned gift, dependent upon chance and geology. It's not something you deserve, and it's not something men can do anything about. Both the best and the worst can come from it, and generally it's the worst.

With its 7,000,000 inhabitants, its 352,000 square miles— almost double that of France—and its per capita income of $1,200, the highest in Latin America, Venezuela is considered multimillionaire country. Caracas is about three thousand feet above sea level and is connected to the port of La Guaira by a winding highway whose ten-mile length passes through a series of tunnels, one of them about two miles long. Just a few years ago there was only a dirt road with four hundred hairpin turns at which the truckdrivers of an Italian gang would shove their competitors into the ravine.

One drives through uninteresting countryside and comes to slopes of red earth crowned with unbelievable shacks of wood, tin, and tarpaper—the *ranchitos*, the shantytowns. Then you are in Caracas, where Simón Bolívar was born.

In the Venezuelan capital and its suburbs there are more buildings, more highways, more underpasses, more big roads that are piled on top of one another and pass over and above one another, than in all of France. People there work as hard as in New York or Paris. They are obsessed with the idea of making money quickly, at any price and by any means. It is a city of parvenus, and of course all these parvenus are snobs. The newspapers are full of social events: dances, charity balls, marriages, cocktail parties, and receptions. All of these items are avidly read by the Negroes and mestizos huddled in the shade on a bench in Plaza Bolívar. Expensive abstract canvases are bought by people who know nothing about painting; concerts are attended by people who want to be seen; and books, preferably bound ones, are bought by people who want to create a warm and intimate atmosphere for dens and offices. As for reading them. . . !

The Venezuelan woman is often a useless creature who resembles one of those *pájaros* of the islands. Like them she has beautiful feathers and spends her time smoothing them; her sole activity is ordering other "feathers" from shops on the Rue de la Paix. As in Mexico, the men keep mistresses, as the best way of showing off. They frequent the innumerable brothels as another way of demonstrating their virility.

The Church, unlike that in Colombia, has failed to maintain its hold over the population. Religious devotions are confined to a few folk celebrations and some superstitions.

The things that count in Venezuela are oil and the big companies that exploit it. The latter are almost all American—like Creole, the Standard Oil subsidiary whose floating derricks encumber Lake Maracaibo.

Then come the extremely well-organized oil unions, in which the communist influence, thanks to the large number of immigrants, is much like that of the French Communist party on the CGT.

Next come the army and its officers' clubs. It is one of the richest, most solid, and best established armies in the entire Caribbean area. It was flattered and showered with gold by all the *caudillos* in succession—from Guzmán Blanco, the creole whose son-in-law was the Duke de Morny and who led a high life in Paris; to Juan Vicente Gómez, who was brutal and intelligent; to Marcos Pérez Jiménez, a megalomaniacal dwarf, potbellied and booted to the hips, who made it the arbiter of the country's political life.

Then there is the university, and it is here that most of the revolts begin. Thanks to a law professor, Edgar Sanabria, who was president of the republic for a few months and who wanted to increase his popularity, the university received a magnificent and poisoned gift: its complete autonomy and the right to administer itself.

Then there is nothing. Oh yes, an immense, negative, and disorganized force—the *ranchitos*, the shantytowns that cover all the little hills around Caracas. They are made of wood, tin, cardboard, and sometimes even a few bricks. They are crawling with naked children, emaciated dogs, and flies. Every skin color is represented. Little girls of twelve sell themselves after having first been sexually initiated by their brothers or their fathers. More than forty thousand children live in organized bands of delinquents, sleeping wherever they can, ready to do anything to survive. The daily income of a *ranchito* inhabitant is never more than two bolivars—less than forty cents, in a country where the cost of living is higher than it is in France.

Every year eighty thousand peasants leave the dying *llanos* and come to swell the *ranchitos* around the cities.

These *ranchitos* spring up at the very foot of big buildings or, thanks to a custom declaring the banks of a waterway to be federal property, alongside a stream which is sometimes little more than a trickle of water. They grow like mushrooms after a shower, proliferating beside the splendid glass and steel constructions, living symbols of the most horrible poverty next to the most provocative wealth.

From time to time an army of bulldozers assaults the *ranchitos* and clears the hillside. Then attempts are made to resettle the inhabitants in abominable concrete cubes, which they flee, either because they don't like them or because they cannot pay the rent. Overnight, in just a few hours, another *ranchito* miraculously springs up a little farther off.

There are scarcely any industries. Industry demands too much patience, too much technique, and big investments on which there is no immediate return. People prefer to go into importing things such as refrigerators, cars, and television sets. Credit is freely available, and since no down payment is required, the credit system is even more widespread than in the United States.

Since winning its independence, Venezuela has had twenty-four constitutions, one hundred governments, and nobody knows how many *caudillos*. One of these was called Cipriano Castro. Like all dictators of the Andes he was a rough, violent man who mindlessly indulged in all sorts of extravagances and borrowed money from abroad. When ambassadors dared to dun him, he threw them into prison.

One day Western battleships intervened; he had to surrender, pay up, and go off.

On November 24, 1908, Castro was replaced by a former Andean peon, Juan Vicente Gómez, who had become a general and who had supported him with his troops when he was in trouble.

Gómez admired strong men: Kaiser Wilhelm II, Theodore Roosevelt, Napoleon, and Bolívar—especially Bolívar, with whom he tried to identify by all possible means. He even went so far as to lie about his birthday so that it would be the same as that of the *libertador*. The country has him to thank for some hundred massive and ugly statues of Bolívar. He also loved land, money, and women, for whom he had an insatiable appetite. He liked them young, like that Dolores Amelia who was less than sixteen when he set her up in the Presidential Palace. The fruit of his various conquests was ninety-seven bastards. But it was not this that was held against him. What people didn't like was that he showed up everywhere with his women, at theaters and at public ceremonies. The result was that he was thought of as an uneducated man—in other words, lacking in hypocrisy.

But because he had a good police force, all the innumerable plots against him failed. This police force was directed by his brother Eustaquio, a man whose skillful use of torture loosened many tongues. Gómez died peacefully in his bed after having dominated the country for twenty-eight years. The population of Caracas was so terrorized by him that it took three days for them to believe the news of his death.

Under "Gregorio el Bagre"—Gregory the Ogre, the nickname given to Gómez—Venezuela, where oil had just been discovered, was rich and well-managed, like a model *estancia*. Order reigned, but the prisons were full. The university revolted in 1928; the dictator closed it and sent thousands of students to construct roads in the most unhealthy regions. Many died there. Thousands of prisoners with chains on their feet died in the citadels of Puerto Cabello and San Marcos, where at high tide the sea flooded the cells.

Until then oil had been used only by the Indians to make torches or by the Lake Maracaibo pirates to lubricate their rifles. Then it became a lamp fuel, and finally it was used in internal combustion engines. Gómez distributed concessions and invited in the large foreign corporations like Shell. But he would never allow petroleum to be refined on the spot, for he was unwilling to see large working-class centers susceptible to the blandishments of communist propaganda spring up near Maracaibo or Caracas.

By 1929, oil was already contributing to 20 percent of the state's outlay. Gómez built factories, roads, and big buildings, but he did nothing for agriculture, whose decline dates from this period; nor did he do anything for public education; nor did he do anything for public health—except to improve the hygiene of the zones where black gold was being discovered.

Gómez died on December 17, 1935. After some difficulties, several military men, who like himself came from the Andes, took power with Generals Eleázar López Contreras and Isaías Medina Angarita. But they had to cope with the strong opposition that had developed around Rómulo Betancourt's Democratic Action party (Acción Democrática).

With the help of some discontented military men, the Democratic Action party took over power in 1945, and Betancourt became the leader of a revolutionary junta. In 1947, another Democratic Action man, Rómulo Gallegos, was elected president. (He was also one of South America's greatest writers and the author of *Doña Bárbara*.)

But the wealthy class, an oligarchy composed not only of the Creole *terratenientes*, but of oil-rich parvenus and big importers, complained of Betancourt's demagogy, of the increase in workers' salaries (67 percent), of "revolutionary" education laws, and of agrarian reform schemes.

On November 24, 1948, a coup d'etat mounted by three colonels, Delgado Chalbaud, Marcos Pérez Jiménez, and Luis Felipe Llovera Paez, overthrew the Betancourt regime and sent Rómulo Gallegos into exile. Soon only Pérez Jiménez was in power—after the assassination of Delgado Chalbaud, which was attributed to him, and the elimination of Paez, in which he had a hand.

Pérez Jiménez decided to "get rid of" the dependence on oil. He launched the most elaborate, outrageous, modernistic, and useless sorts of constructions, such as the Orinoco ironworks. He was especially interested in things that would make a splash and said as much to anybody who would listen. On all these projects he pocketed big percentages, as did the officers and functionaries of his group.

When he eventually fled to the United States, a reporter at the airport asked him what his plans were.

"I have enough to live on. I have put aside two hundred million in this country."

"Two hundred million bolivars?"

"No, dollars."

It had taken a military uprising, twenty-three days of street fighting in Caracas, the desertion of the navy, and a refusal by the air force to bomb the fleet to get rid of Pérez Jiménez in 1958.

The imprudent revelation of his resources caused Pérez Jiménez a bit of trouble. When Betancourt returned to power, he demanded the extradition of the refugee *caudillo*. Surprisingly enough, possibly because the U.S. State Department wanted to conciliate the new regime, this extradition was granted. Instead of living high on the hog in Palm Springs or Miami, as did many of his South American colleagues, he was shipped back to

Caracas, where he was held as a common criminal. (He is now in Spain.)

Rear Admiral Wolfgang Larrazábal, a playboy with a radiant smile, adored by the *ranchito* inhabitants, was interim president. He ceded the place to Rómulo Betancourt, who was elected president of the republic thanks to the union of the three big parties: Democratic Action, the Christian Democrats of the COPEI (Partido Social Cristiano), and the Democratic Republican Union. At the same time, on the other side of the Caribbean, events were underway that could not fail to arouse enthusiasm in a country which had just been relieved of a dictatorship: in Cuba, Fidel Castro's guerrillas and the people of Havana were ousting a dictator who was at least as well hated as Pérez Jiménez: Batista.

If two countries should ever have been linked in friendship at this time, they were Cuba and Venezuela. The Venezuelans had done everything possible to aid Castro during the difficult days in the Sierra Maestra. Six weeks after his election, Betancourt welcomed Castro at the Caracas airport. The *abrazos* over, Castro gave a speech from the gangway of his plane, and then rode through the streets of a wildly delirious capital. The two chiefs of state announced they had established a mutual assistance project.

The honeymoon was not to last long. Even though Betancourt had been a member of the Communist party in his youth, he was in no way inclined to approve the extremist evolution of Cuban politics. The difference in age between the two leaders was also to play a role. In his youth Betancourt had been as extremist and radical a revolutionary as Castro after his victory. Age and events had made a liberal reformist of him. The same thing may yet happen to Castro.

Betancourt had to face a problem considerably more delicate than the Cuban sugar problem: the problem of oil. In a few years, Venezuela had become the world's second-largest exporter, and the royalties paid by the big companies were sufficient to provide a good-sized pension for each Venezuelan family—if, of course, these hundreds of millions of dollars had been equitably distributed. This shower of dollars had transformed Caracas into the most modern city in the world, even though it was surrounded by the world's most poverty-stricken shantytowns. The enormous interests at stake forbade any kind of nationalization. Betancourt thought that by negotiation he could obtain an increase of these royalties, an increase that could, for example, finance his agrarian reform program.

It was in this way that he little by little became the darling of the U.S. State Department, which was pleased to be finally dealing with a moderate democratic regime at a time when Castro was becoming its *bête noire*. But this prudent policy was far removed from what Betancourt had promised during the elections. He had to rely more and more on the moderate elements of the parties that had brought him to power.

Some veteran Democratic Action militants who had fought a difficult struggle saw their disgusted children turn communist. An important segment of Betancourt's party split off to become in 1960 the MIR (Movimiento Izquierdista Revolucionario), which was further to the left than the Communist party and from whose ranks the cadres of the subversive movement were to be recruited. The MIR openly acclaimed Fidel Castro.

The Venezuelan government, which had formerly been revolutionary, was turning middle class, and extreme leftist agitation was breaking out again. A demonstration in June, 1959, led to twenty-five deaths; in another in August four died and three hundred were wounded. There were other skirmishes in April, 1960. Finally, in November of the same year, the first resolutely Castroite riots broke out.

At the same time several attempts at coups d'etat, a military insurrection, and some ten plots added touches to the picture.

The more Betancourt became the man of the United States, the worse his relations with Cuba grew. A violent propaganda campaign originating in Havana called for "a new Sierra Maestra in the Andes." Venezuela broke off diplomatic relations with Havana. In response, Fidel Castro shipped arms to the guerrilla bands that were forming. Betancourt replied by asking for OAS sanctions against Cuba. For the past five years relations have continued to worsen.

In anticipation of an agrarian reform law too long in coming, a group of peasants in the state of Aragua occupied some lands that were not under cultivation. La Guardia Nacional brutally repressed this movement and more people were killed. The police charged into another demonstration and completed the unification of the workers and students. The demonstration had been planned to show the solidarity of the Venezuelan people with the Cuban Revolution.

"Under these conditions," affirmed Douglas Bravo, now the uncontested leader of FALN (Fuerzas Armadas de Liberación Nacional), "the most progressive elements of the Venezuelan people no longer had any choice but to organize the resistance—in the form of self-defense groups—against the attacks of the army, of DIGEPOL (Dirección General de Policía), and all the repressive forces. An organized, violent, revolutionary force had to be opposed to the aggressive violence of the enemy."

These demonstrations, even though they left victims in the streets each time, would not have been enough to unleash a guerrilla movement. Other favorable conditions existed. First of all, there was the example of neighboring countries: the success of the Cuban Revolution, the guerrilla successes in Guatemala, the victories of the "independent republics" in Colombia against a halfhearted army. In addition, the extreme left, which had joined with the principal liberal parties to oust Pérez Jiménez, found that it had merely been used to pull other people's chestnuts out of the fire. Under the dictatorships of Gómez and Pérez Jiménez, it had acquired excellent training in clandestine activities. Finally, the members of the people's militias, which had victoriously confronted the police forces of the dictator and then disbanded, once more felt ready to take up arms, this time to bring to a definitive conclusion a revolution that had been whisked from under their noses.

However, the determining factor was the closer and closer alliance between Betancourt's government and the United States. The American oil industry that had been established with the complicity of the two "Yankee" *caudillos* was the object of the same execration. It was to get rid of both the *caudillos* and the American petroleum industry that the revolution had been undertaken. And now the same big financial and industrial corporations accused of every sort of evil were still in place, negotiating with the government and more powerful than ever. What was more, the U.S. State Department was sending planeloads of "technical advisers" who were establishing themselves in every ministry. Their mission was to organize and perfect the administrative machine eaten away by the dictatorship.

Among these technical advisers in mufti were some who had temporarily put their uniforms into storage. Venezuela timidly entered into the big military movement struggling against the insurgency springing up in one after another of the countries in Latin America. Groups of Venezuelan officers began leaving for the School of the Americas in Panama, or for Fort Benning.

And so, little by little, different guerrilla movements with varying political and social orientations were born. There was the one led by Alfredo Maneiro in the Julita mountains, the one led by Juan Vicente Cabezas in El Charral, and the one led by Lunar Marquez in Lara. Luben Petkoff joined with the peasant leader Ramírez to form a guerrilla band in the mountains of Aroa; Salazar set up his band in the Turiquimire mountains; and Douglas Bravo in Falcón.

Gradually the structural outlines came into relief. Four basic groups, each with its own tactics, permitted the guerrilla movement to enter into an almost organized period of struggle. The first to go into action were the rural guerrillas, then the more solidly established mountain guerrillas. The peasants dominated the first groups and the students the others. It was the latter groups, operating far from inhabited areas, that were to become the pivot of Castroite resistance. The city was the scene of operations for urban guerrilla bands, essentially made up of UTCs (tactical combat units) whose job was sabotage or street fighting. The final and last pillar of this structure was made of sympathetic army officers, political cadres who had escaped arrest, and above all the university.

The University of Caracas not only claims the autonomy which is the rule in the principal South American countries, it demands veritable extraterritoriality. In 1960, students who had been demonstrating in the streets and been pursued by the police, sought shelter behind its gates and prepared for a siege. Eventually, tanks took up positions, and the government obtained the surrender of the besieged.

But during the entire time during which constitutional liberties were suspended, during which parties of the extreme left were prohibited, during which skirmishes between the army and the guerrillas became more and more serious in the provinces, the university was becoming the real headquarters of the subversive movement. Communists and underground MIR members used it as an arms depot and as a propaganda and recruiting center. They held meetings, posted communiqués from the various fighting fronts, and even took up collections. Plainclothesmen making discreet investigations within the university grounds were arrested by student patrols, frisked, locked up, and finally expelled by the university administration. A few even disappeared and were said to have been buried in the cellars.

UTC activities were helped by the sprawling size of the suburban shantytowns. The city could not control the constant immigration that flowed from the *llanos* or the mountains. Entire sections were lacking in electricity, water, and sewers—actual no-man's-lands in which the police dared not set foot after dark.

All during the Betancourt regime, the urban resistance undertook a series of spectacular actions. In a single year, fifty police were killed; banks were attacked one after another; bombs exploded on newspaper premises; a guerrilla band seized a cargo ship; pipelines were dynamited; a large American store was pillaged; a celebrated bullfighter and a soccer player were kidnapped. When Maurice Chevalier was in the country, he had special bodyguards, because his kidnapping had been announced. The U.S. Embassy was attacked; five French paintings on loan for an exhibition were stolen and then returned, as were the bullfighter and the soccer player. Two high-ranking members of a U.S. military mission were kidnapped. It was proposed that they be exchanged for Nguyen Van Troi, the young Vietnamese who had tried to assassinate McNamara in Saigon. But though Troi was shot, the Americans were nevertheless freed. The combat units' main purpose was to arouse talk.

Though all these events had no definite political goal, they did succeed in embarrassing Betancourt, while the guerrilla bands continued to grow. They were active in eight provinces, especially in Falcón, and became almost as important as those in Colombia. More than nine thousand soldiers were put into the field under the orders of officers returning from training in Panama or Texas. The first "technical advisers" of the American army appeared on the scene, advance guard of the Green Berets.

Because of its oil, Venezuela was essential to the American economy, but it was just as vital for Fidel Castro. If Cuba had oil it could cease being a Soviet satellite; the fate of the revolution depended on its independence from the Russians.

On February 2, 1963, the representatives of various organizations and revolutionary fronts met somewhere in Venezuela and created the FALN. Among the participants of this meeting were the Movement of June 2nd, the Movement of May 4th, the Civic Military Union, the José Leonardo Chirnios Front, the Guerrillero Libertador Front, and the Comando Nacional Guerrillero.

The Sierra San Luis, between Maracaibo and Caracas; the

west of the central cordillera; the *llanos*; the coastal cordillera south of Caracas; and the eastern cordillera west of the mouth of the Orinoco became the principal operation zones of guerrilla bands that identified themselves more and more with the FALN. Its program included five points: to bring about respect for national sovereignty and independence; to defend the national patrimony and wealth; to support the authorities set up by the revolution; to protect the interests of the people; and to establish a revolutionary, national, and democratic government.

Three of these goals are obviously oriented against economic and political meddling by the United States, as the FALN spokesman at the time emphasized in his communiqué.

All training of officer candidates and officers, as well as that of sailors, is supervised by officers of the American military missions imposed by the Pentagon. All the programs of the various war colleges are established by the American mission, and the material used is American. The American mission has a hand in everything concerning the formation and training of antiguerrilla units. This takeover is supplemented by propaganda aimed at eliminating the Venezuelan characteristics of our army, to make it more and more resemble that of Puerto Rico, almost entirely under the control of the Pentagon.

The FALN was too inclined to optimism. In the beginning of 1963, frigate captain Medina Silva, its leader, announced, "Our detachments of guerrillas are every day gaining more and more of the confidence of the peasant masses, who see in them the instrument of their liberation from the exploitation to which they have been subjected. The repeated failures of the police forces against the fronts in Falcón, Oriente, and El Charral are proof of the valor of our movement's combatants."

It was in that same year in which the guerrilla movement seemed well organized, strongly supported, and near its objectives, that it began to suffer the most severe reverses. The antiguerrilla military machine set up by the Southern Command was effective. Defections multiplied in the guerrilla ranks. The civilian populations wearied of four years of bloody instability.

But other factors also worked against the insurgents, especially the absence of initial political unity—the mixture of various forces whose goals were sometimes in opposition. Everybody fought against the government and American imperialism, but nobody offered any concrete solution in case of victory. It was a romantic and idealistic élan. Only passion could maintain it—passion or a coldly calculated technique and a seamless technical organization. The passions have cooled now, and as for the organization—it never existed.

According to Douglas Bravo, the guerrilla forces were infected by "immediatism." "The goal of the guerrillas was to multiply military actions, to multiply their bands, then to reunite them into more powerful forces that would join in a final attack. We did not prepare with the strategic realities in mind; we had only one idea—to overthrow the government immediately."

The very victories of the FALN were the cause of their defeat. Instead of solidly organizing for future struggles, they had exhausted their troops to affirm their force and existence. Put into the field too quickly, the best elements were in prison, and that at a time when strongly organized repression had scarcely got underway.

Betancourt's term of office was almost over and the elections were near. The parties in power had carefully prepared for them. In a new error, the partisans of Fidel Castro, under unfavorable circumstances, forbade the population of Caracas to participate in the voting. Ninety percent of the electors voted nevertheless. The bell had just tolled for the Castroite insurgence.

As always happens in such cases, the coming to power of a new president, Raúl Leoni, revived hopes of a truce, a peace, a new political orientation. The truce came into effect in the city, where UTC's received orders to become dormant.

But the struggle continued in the countryside. This time the army was determined to finish with the guerrillas. The El Bachiller Front was attacked, and those guerrillas captured were immediately shot. Peasants who sympathized with the FALN were hunted down. The José Leonardo Chirnios Front to which Douglas Bravo belonged was bombarded by aircraft and artillery. Eighty *campesinos* were shot. In Portuguesa, the José Antonio Paez Front was encircled and destroyed. These repeated blows merely emphasized the crisis in the heart of the insurgent movement.

For the FALN 1966 was to be a year of "agonizing reappraisal." While under constant pressure from the army they had to prepare for a "long war," like the guerrillas in Colombia and Guatemala. In any case, instant revolution had failed.

"Revolutions," said Douglas Bravo bitterly, "not only fail because the social conditions favorable to revolution are lacking but also because of special circumstances such as a faulty manner of fighting, the errors and the weaknesses of the leadership." And he added: "We call this year 'the period of relative guerrilla weakness.' We may suspend operations in order to prepare new operations. We may beat a retreat, but that does not mean that the struggle has been given up. This period calls for the application of new lines of conduct, imposes special rules of development, action, and tactics. When the guerrilla forces are strong again, as strong as the regular army, they will take up the struggle once more, and perhaps the struggle will no longer be one of guerrilla warfare."

It was in this difficult period that the FALN was to suffer its hardest blow: the split between the Castroites and the Venezuelan Communist party.

I arrived in Caracas during March, 1967. The echoes of dissension between the Venezuelan Communist party and the Castroites of MIR had already reached me in Mexico, in Guatemala, and in Colombia. But I attached no particular importance to them. Splits and dissensions were the facts of life in all the regimes and in all the parties.

The pretext for this rupture was the assassination of the brother of the Minister of Foreign Affairs, Dr. Iribareu. Appointed head of Social Security, this man had plunged his paw deep into the till. His bound and riddled body was found in a suburb of the city. His assassins apparently belonged to a Castroite MIR group which had broken the undeclared truce decided on by the Communists.

With the remarkable verbal indiscretion for which he is known, Fidel Castro exalted this murder as the brilliant work of his partisans. The Communist party immediately and violently denounced this "savage assassination."

To meet up with revolutionaries, all you have to do is go to the University of Caracas, with its ultramodern buildings, enormous patios decorated with ceramic frescoes, eight-story libraries whose elevators are never out of order, and laboratories where equipment is never lacking. The sun shines on dazzling white walls.

The students had just fought with the army, and several classrooms had been completely devastated, their furnishings reduced to kindling.

I met several people "in charge"; people such as Boulgar, a member of the Communist party's Central Committee and president of student associations; his wife, daughter of the old communist leader Machado, whom Fidel Castro contemptuously called "Machado the Millionaire"; professors such as Hector Mujica, spokesman for the Venezuelan Communist party and one of the most important members of the Central Committee.

Hector Mujica is small and dumpy. He speaks French well and can cite French poets. He is a western communist who wouldn't be at all out of place at communist headquarters in Paris. Seated in the garden of his small house, he explained the party's official stance to me.

"We feel that though Fidel Castro may be an authentic revolutionary, he has no Marxist education and is committing a grave error in letting himself be carried away by caudillist, militarist, and adventurist tendencies. The guerrilla fronts are no end in themselves, and just because a man knows how to hold a machine gun doesn't mean that he is capable of governing a country or directing an administration.

"Armed struggle may be necessary in certain cases. It is no longer necessary in Venezuela, where we are not subjected to the power of a narrowminded dictator and where the political evolution of the people makes a legal struggle out in the open possible."

"And Douglas Bravo?"

"Douglas Bravo follows Fidel Castro and is making the same mistake that he is. He once belonged to our Central Committee, but he was expelled . . . for his deviations."

"The same you hold against Castro?"

"Yes, the same. Fidel's trouble is that he thinks he is the only one to know the truth. His egoism is unbounded. I, I, and I.

"He smears our Communist party with insults even though we have been fighting for thirty-five years. We helped and supported him when he was in difficulties, but he doesn't seem to remember that. He wants to be the unique, the top man . . . the *líder máximo.*"

"Do you and the Russians agree on these matters?"

"Yes, just as we are in agreement with all the other Communist parties in Latin America. For the moment, the time for guerrilla activities is over, and that goes for terrorism too. This is why we have strongly condemned the assassination of Iribareu.

"Each country has to carry out its revolution as it sees it, by taking into account the conditions special to that country. Fidel Castro is a dangerous madman who is compromising the entire future of the revolution in Latin America. He's an adventurer."

Hector Mujica caught himself. "However, we will always continue to support and aid the Cuban revolution."

At the university, the few students I got to know during the course of a meeting spoke pretty much the same way. However, I got the feeling that they had been especially selected by the Communist party. They more or less said, "We have no intention of taking orders from a foreigner. Let him tend to his own business."

"But isn't that nationalism?" I asked.

"Yes," replied one of them.

Another remained silent. It was only after his comrades had left that he said, "You might just as well understand that many of us still believe in and follow Fidel. If you see him in Cuba, tell him so."

Then events speeded up. The communist guerrillas did not lay down their arms but limited their action to propaganda tours. Just one more step and they would return to legal activities.

Douglas Bravo and his Falcón guerrilla front were isolated. His former communist friends had decided upon his undoing and he knew it. The instructors sent to him from Cuba with arms and money were caught. His sources of supply at the university began to dry up.

Six months later, the Bolivian communists abandoned Che Guevara.

The Andean area, especially in Peru, has always been the home of centers of social agitation caused by political and economic circumstances—famines, pillaging, confiscation of lands, suppression of fundamental liberties—and often this agitation was transformed into brutal and bloody local revolts. But after a brief flare-up, the revolts were smothered by ferocious repression— mass executions, that forced the poverty-stricken populations back into their passivity and their time-honored state of bondage. This phenomenon was accentuated by the fact that the majority of these sporadic revolts were of Indian origin. The Indians seemed incapable of extending their revolt beyond the problems of the community in which they lived, or to find in defeat the energy necessary to continue the struggle with other methods.

What are now called "guerrilla" activities are of an entirely different nature. From the very beginning, the guerrillas assumed a national stance. Their goal is not to obtain reforms, or a change of government that would make such reforms possible, but to destroy the current political system—which is either in the hands of an oligarchy, a military junta, or a combination of the two— and to replace it by a socialistic people's regime. The guerrillas are either Castroites, or communists of the Russian, Chinese, or Trotskyite variety. Their essential propaganda theme is the fight against "imperialism," and their goal is to rid the country in which they operate of American economic control, though they are far from precise about how this can be done, or how they intend to fill the vacuum.

In spite of the colossal military apparatus brought to bear against the guerrillas, three insurgent groups have been able to survive these last years—the guerrilla bands in Guatemala, Colombia, and Venezuela. Often reduced to a few handfuls of men deep in the heart of the mountains, they try to establish common cause with the peasant masses. The very fact that these guerrillas still exist proves that they have found some kind of modus vivendi with the *campesinos* among whom they live.

The "permanent" guerrilla bands are all situated on the periphery of the Caribbean Sea, only a few hundred miles from Cuba. Their contacts with Castroism are frequent, if not permanent. On the other hand, the countries in which they operate are those in Latin America most influenced by Western ideas. None of the three Caribbean guerrilla fronts would have survived without communist organization and aid.

In Colombia, where the resistance has a longer history, the peasants turned *bandoleros* would never have formed "independent republics" if party members had not come from Bogotá or other cities to help them organize. In Venezuela, until the FALN was formed, the cadres of the urban and rural insurgent groups were for the most part communists. Even now, more than 80 percent of the men fighting under Douglas Bravo still consider themselves communists.

None of the guerrilla fronts could have survived without outside help. The peasants were too poor or too leery; the bulk of the guerrillas' money and supplies always came from the cities, thanks to the organizations set up by the Communist party. Therefore their being "dropped" by the communists may lead to their final collapse. There are of course guerrilla bands that are purely Castroite; Castroism not associated with communism may have some romantic meaning for the guerrilla, but it has none for the peasant. And if the guerrilla is cut off from the cities, he can survive only with the help of the peasants.

In his diary, Che Guevara constantly repeats that "the Bolivian peasants are difficult, almost impossible people. They are as impenetrable as stones, and in the depths of their eyes you can see that they don't believe you."

It was peasants who betrayed him for fifty thousand pesos.

In the meantime, the orthodox communists and the Trotskyite miners had already abandoned him.

In his article "Castroism, the Great March of Latin America," which was published in *Les Temps Modernes* after his first trip to Latin America, Régis Debray listed and analyzed fifteen defeats of the subversive war. Of these fifteen defeats suffered before 1965, ten were in the heart of the continent, along the cordillera, in Paraguay and in Brazil.

Most of the leaders and cadres of these guerrilla groups have been arrested or killed, but there are still others who have not given up the struggle. The legal and clandestine political organizations that have supported them have not ceased activities. The universities of Lima, Quito, or La Paz still have the same percentage of elements who see radical revolution as the only solution to their country's problems.

Despite these general similarities, there are enough differences from one country to another to make no single country representative. The one country that seems free of armed subversive action is Chile, whose population, with the exception of a few

Quechua in the north and a handful of Araucanians near Temuco, is entirely white. The country is open to immigration and has the largest Communist party on the continent: 25 percent of the voters. It almost became communist in regular elections in 1963, when only a coalition around the Christian-Democrats was able to prevent Chile's peaceable transformation into a people's republic.

However, Argentina, another country composed entirely of immigrants and strongly Europeanized, had problems with guerrilla activity. Brazil's protection against the guerrillas is almost entirely its vast size. A few handfuls of armed men could work no miracles in the vast Mato Grosso region or in the Amazon Basin.

Politics in the three big Andean republics—Ecuador, Peru, and Bolivia—are dominated by the Indian problem. Peru, because of its political and economic evolution as well as its geographic situation, would seem to run the least risk of armed insurrection; however, it was here that insurrection was so violent that several years ago effective and ferocious repression put an end to the last guerrilla movement. But the struggle shows signs of springing up again with increased intensity along the Peruvian cordillera.

The economic development of Peru has emphasized rather than bridged the distance between the sons of the conquistadors and the descendants of the Incas. The coast contains all the wealth of the country; some 1,200 miles of narrow desert at the foot of the Cordillera Occidental and rocks that millions of birds cover with guano. In places the desert is cut by rivers that descend from the mountain. In those areas the valleys surrounding the river are luxuriously tropical, with fertile plantations of cotton, sugarcane, and citrus fruits. In the cities modern buildings surround old colonial homes and elaborately baroque cathedrals and palaces.

Almost all the industry in Peru is concentrated in these oases along the coastal fringe—especially in Lima, the jewel of the Pacific coast and the historic city of viceroys; in Miraflores, a combination of Palm Beach and Acapulco; and in Callao. In fifteen years, Peru, which had only a few fishing vessels, has become a great exporter of fish products. Every day, immense factories transform hundreds of tons into fertilizer. Industrialists, bankers, big landowners, businessmen, and their American associates meet at the Yacht Club or the Golf Club.

The inhabitant of Lima admires this coastal area of four million whites and mestizos proud of their Hispanic origin. To the east, in the sierra that begins almost at the outskirts of the city and whose summits are lost in the clouds, live five million Indians who weigh on the future of the country like an enormous, inert load. All decisions taken in Lima—the social laws and the agrarian reforms—leave them untouched.

More than half of them live in serfdom, in the hands of the *gamonalistas*, the big landowners who in their Miraflores villas seem as far off as the ancestral gods. The Indians are always hungry and bound to the property they are attached to. The rest of the arable land in the sierra belongs to agricultural collectives —the *áyllus* anterior to the Spanish Conquest—or to small landowners, the *comuneros*. Both these groups have to defend their rights against the greedy oligarchy.

The Indians often try to occupy peaceably the lands they have been deprived of. Usually the army then intervenes at the request of the *gamonalistas*. There are arrests, executions, and the Indians are returned to their communities. Rebellion leads only to massacre and defeat, and to the roads that lead to the capital, to the big coastal cities, or to the mines. The Indians become ignorant and easily exploited laborers of limited efficiency. In a Huayas *callejón*, an Indian working on the construction of an electric power station was earning ten soles a day, just the price of a meal at the canteen. At night, after twelve hours of work, wrapped in his poncho, he would sleep within the construction area. When I asked one of them why he had left his village, he replied, "At least here I get one meal a day."

Tuberculosis, silicosis, malaria, and typhus cause havoc among them, and the infant mortality rate is one of the highest in the world.

There is a third zone in Peru parallel to the two others and stretching down into the Amazon Basin on the other side of the Cordillera Occidental. It is all but uninhabited. The vegetation there is luxuriant and the lands on the hillsides are extremely fertile. Its development was undertaken by opening a road that went along the mountain from north to south, overhanging impenetrable virgin forests. It is *la carretera marginal de la selva,* built with U.S. aid. This development venture was accompanied by an agrarian reform, the most tangible result of which to date has been the allocation of some 1.5 million acres of land to an American company named Leturneau.

Another U.S. company in the sierra is the Cerro de Pasco Corporation, a mining company that has been allocated huge prospecting zones in the regions of the *áyllus.* For all practical purposes the Indians have been dispossessed. Generally speaking, about 3 percent of the landowners in the sierra control about 93 percent of the arable land.

On the coast, these figures are 10 percent and 89 percent respectively. Everywhere U.S. interests are closely allied with those of the Peruvian oligarchy, permitting them access to the political and economic life of the country. Almost all production is destined for export, and only a small portion of the capital is reinvested in the area. The parties of the right and center are controlled by this U.S.-oligarchy association, as are the most important newspapers. Two banking systems, the Caja de Depósitos y Consignación and El Banco Central de Reserva, are entirely in the hands of private banks—in other words, of Americans.

The unskilled labor supply seems inexhaustible. Every day more Indians come down from the mountains to settle on the outskirts of the cities. Lima alone has 160 of these settlements in which Indians, after having cut off their hair and dressed themselves in European castoff clothing, think themselves not unlike the mestizo. Though unable to meet the demands of this influx, municipal authorities try, with good will rare on this continent, to arrange for water and electricity supplies. They also distribute bricks and cement and leave the new arrivals to build their own houses under the supervision of a few technicians.

Despite conditions superficially ideal for the development of subversive activity, communism has failed to penetrate Indian life. The Indian is a mystery; the greatest efforts have been made to adapt him to our ways of living and thinking, but nothing has been done to adapt these ways to him. Only a few specialists know anything about his culture or psychology: The *áyllus* (an evolved collective system) and the *servicacuy* (trial marriage) are indicative of the mores that nonetheless shape the life of the country, since more than half the population is involved in them. For the Quechua, the political leader in Lima remains a stranger similar to his traditional oppressors, and as such he is blanketed in suspicion.

But to admit past failures is not to say that insurgency is impossible. To transform the Andes into an immense Sierra Maestra, some link must be forged between Western ideology and the Indian soul. Perhaps some university-educated Indian leader will discover how this may be done.

The political life of the former viceroyalty that developed outside the Cordillera Occidental has had a history, like the neighboring countries, of coups d'etat and of *pronunciamientos* that concerned only the Creole world and its interests. Twenty-four of Peru's thirty-four attempted coups d'etat since the beginning of the century were by the military; seven succeeded. Most of the uprisings were bloody affairs, as was the one in Trujillo in 1932 led by Haya de la Torre, popular leader and chief of the APRA (American Popular Revolutionary Alliance). Thousands of demonstrators took over the prefecture, the police stations, and the

army barracks. The defenders of the establishment were massacred. The army intervened, crushed the revolt, and shot four
thousand men. Other Aprista uprisings in the years that followed
widened the gulf between Haya de la Torre and the army, which
would never permit him the reins of power in spite of his popularity and his successes at the polls. He was to spend many years
in exile or in prison, and six years in the Colombian Embassy,
where he had gone for asylum.

At the time of Fidel Castro's takeover in Cuba, Dr. Manuel
Prado was in power in Peru and peacefully left office at the
expiration of his term in 1962. The elections confirming the success of Haya de la Torre failed to find favor with the army, and
a military junta took power. Under pressure from the U.S. government, the junta agreed to new elections. An architect, Fernando Belaunde Terry, was elected with, it was said, the help of
the communists. He was supported by his party, Acción Popular,
and by the Christian-Democrats. The opposition linked two
former enemies, Haya de la Torre and a former military dictator,
General Manuel A. Odría.

Communism had not been consistently popular since its arrival
in Peru in 1928. When it tried to create a popular front, its partisans were stolen by Haya de la Torre, who had taken control of
the unions. In 1962 it managed to get forty-four thousand votes
for its two candidates for the legislature.

The divisions among world Communist parties had a truly
shattering effect in Peru. Today there are nine parties, movements, or fronts of the extreme left: Trotskyite, pro-Chinese,
pro-Russian, Leninist, progressive, and socialist, to say nothing
of the Castroite group born of an APRA split, which here as in
Venezuela was to play a determining role in guerrilla history.

It wasn't until 1960 that there was talk of a Castroite subversive movement in the Andes. The Ovins Stockbreeders Association and the American-owned Cerro de Pasco Corporation
complained that Indians had invaded and occupied their legally

acquired lands, and Cuba was accused of being behind the movement.

For some time now the *comuneros* or the *áyllus* had been trying to reconquer their domains, which were shrinking daily as the result of transactions worked out in shady legal offices in Lima and confirmed by easily bribed judges. Indian commandos, led by some among them who had served in the army, took over the lands. They had everything but weapons. When they were driven off, they would steadfastly return.

In 1959, the Rancas Community had already opposed the Cerro de Pasco Corporation and been driven off by the intervention of the police. This time it was the turn of the Yerus Yacan Áyllu, which on the basis of property rights that went back to 1619 continued to pasture its herds on land that the American company claimed to have legally acquired. The Indians undertook court action, but the judges were, as usual, unenthusiastic about Indian claims. Bands hired by the company burned the pasturelands, destroyed the houses, and penetrated farther and farther into *áyllu* territory.

The leaders of the community decided to occupy the lands. Lima newspapers warned of subversion, and the army chased the Indians away. However, once the army retired, the Indians returned and the problem remained unsolved.

In Lima, the extreme-left groups thought that the moment had come to participate in the struggle, but once more they were unable to decide on any joint action. Some groups united and formed the FIR (Frente Izquierdista Revolucionario) a Trotskyist-oriented group which included the Quechua-speaking Hugo Blanco, a natural leader. The FIR had ties with the Trotskyist International and was visited by theoreticians and tacticians from Mexico and Bolivia.

During this time another Trotskyist organization, the POR, decided to move into immediate action in Jauja. On his own initiative, a Lieutenant Vallejo, a member of the Republican

Guard, contacted the peasant leaders who had agreed to launch an armed insurrection. He planned to get arms from the garrison, money from the banks, and then withdraw to the eastern slopes of the cordillera to organize a guerrilla force—the same sort of plan that had worked so well in the Sierra Maestra. A group of high-school students joined the conspirators.

On the date that had been set, in May, 1962, the only ones to show up at the rendezvous were the organizers of the plot, two peasant leaders, and the students. Together they seized control of the prison and the police stations; then, after robbing a bank, they left for the mountains. The army set off in hot pursuit, and after a few hours of fighting, the insurgents were defeated. Lieutenant Vallejo and one of the peasant leaders were killed, and the students dispersed. Some were captured and others arrested when they returned home.

During this time the FIR finally finished its preparations. Taking for its own the old Indian watchword "Land or Death," they threw the valleys of Concepción and Lares into permanent turmoil and started strikes in which the Indians took part. Terrified, the large landowners fled to Lima.

In the capital, two banks were taken by assault, but nobody could agree on how the money was to be used, what military tactics were to be employed, or what political line was to be followed. The leader of one militant group, which had attacked a bank on its own initiative, was condemned to death and executed by the "politicians." The military cadres sent to Cuzco grew impatient and were nabbed by the police. Before the insurrection even got off the ground, the government had all the time it needed to arrest the Lima revolutionaries.

In the valleys the peasants were still waiting for their cadres and their arms. What came was the police. Countermeasures were taken. Peasants were massacred by the dozens; the leaders of the front were hunted down and arrested one after another. Hugo Blanco, exhausted and sick, fell into the hands of the authorities and was thrown into prison. Decimated, the Indians gave up the struggle and took refuge in their ancestral passivity, more suspicious than ever of anything the white men could do to help them.

During this time, a group of some fifty "independents," men who belonged to no movement, decided to come to the aid of Hugo Blanco and his partisans. But it was too late. They got weapons in Bolivia, started out to join the rebellious peasants, went through almost two hundred miles of forest in the cordillera, and finally arrived in the area of Puerto Maldonado to the southeast of Cuzco. They were exhausted, sick, wracked by malaria and dysentery.

A detachment was sent into the city to make contact with sympathizers. It ran into a police group that was waiting for it. The guerrillas had been denounced by the Indians. There was a skirmish and then flight. The landowners in the region took part in the manhunt, an unexpected distraction in their boring lives.

The MIR took two more years to prepare for action, but after that it took six months, the massive intervention of the army, the total support of the Pentagon, and the arrival of modern U.S. equipment to put them down.

Despite the severity of the repression, despite the neglect of the various political movements that had abandoned them after having shaken them out of their torpor, the Indian masses had started to move.

"In July, 1963," wrote Amerigo Pumaruna in *Partisan*, "the occupation of lands by the Indians became a widespread phenomenon. It affected three thousand haciendas and mobilized half a million peasants."

While the parties of the extreme left, divided and dismantled, were looking for a political solution to the problem, the MIR prepared for the struggle. It affirmed itself resolutely Castroite. Its existence was a direct consequence of the Cuban Revolution. Its leaders were the former cadres of the left wing of the APRA who had been expelled from the party for having opposed Haya de la Torre's alliance with the Prado government in 1959. With the young lawyer Luis de la Puente Uceda, they formed the "rebel APRA," then in 1962 the MIR. Luis de la Puente came from Cuba, and he was a personal friend of Fidel Castro.

After 1963, some groups took to the mountains to prepare for the organization of guerrilla activity. In the beginning of 1964, Luis de la Puente publicly announced at a meeting held in the principal square in Lima that his organization was leaving the capital to establish itself in the cordillera. The MIR brusquely separated itself from the other leftist parties and decided to continue the struggle unilaterally.

After the beginning of 1965, the Peruvian press was inundated with communiqués and photographs announcing that the struggle had begun under the leadership of Luis de la Puente Uceda. Other reports followed, specifying that the guerrilla front, called Pachacutec, was operating in the Concepción Valley region. The government could hardly say it had been taken by surprise. The army itself went to investigate the area. On its return it affirmed that there were no guerrillas in the locality indicated by the MIR.

On June 8, 1965, sixty men in olive-drab uniforms and armed with automatic rifles and revolvers, seized an hacienda in the region of Concepción. They stole supplies and a radio transmitter-receiver and systematically wrecked the place. Six of them went on horseback to attack the Santa Rosa Mine and made off with forty cases of dynamite. After stealing a truck to transport their booty, they blew up two bridges on the Concepción-Satipo road. They pillaged another hacienda and distributed part of the food supplies to the Indians, telling them, "You are our brothers. What we have taken from your bosses belongs to you."

Continuing up the valley, they disappeared into the mountain. An infantry battalion and two hundred civil guards were sent after them; they continued to steal livestock, food supplies, arms, and explosives, and held public meetings in the villages through which they traveled, all the while distributing part of their goods. In the city of Andamarca, they pillaged the storehouse of an hacienda, captured a police station, and peacefully spent the night there.

The next day, in the first skirmish, the forces sent out against them suffered some losses, but the guerrillas seemed to fade away like smoke. Reports reaching Lima gave the impression that the entire region had been invaded by guerrillas who had suddenly sprung from the forest. Another group, baptized "Tumuc Amaru" after a legendary Indian hero, was indeed operating in the same area, also under the control of Luis de la Puente, but its commander, Guillermo Lobatón, was considerably more cautious. (About thirty years old, he had studied at the Sorbonne and spoke four languages. He had been seen in Algeria, in Vietnam, in Moscow, and in Peking.)

After June 12, four hundred members of the police and one hundred rangers fruitlessly patrolled the region. On June 27, a police patrol ran into an ambush and lost thirty men. The guerrillas disappeared, taking pack animals loaded with arms and munitions. On July 6, in the course of another encounter, seven members of the police were killed and ten others wounded.

In Lima bombs were set off in attacks on the bourgeoisie. The extreme left had finally awakened. Its life and its goods threatened, the oligarchy forced Belaunde Terry to institute repressive measures.

This explosion of violence worried the United States, which in turn worried the army. This was especially true because the MIR, which seemed much too publicity-minded, announced the coming opening of new guerrilla fronts in five provinces, including Puno and Cajamarca—in other words, from the north to the south, all along the cordillera.

On July 14, the leaders of the combined armed forces gave the president an ultimatum. Either the army was to be allowed to take over and assume entire responsibility for the fight against the guerrillas, or the government would be overthrown. Belaunde Terry gave way. A state of siege was declared in Lima. Capital punishment was decreed for all those who helped the guerrillas. Though peasants and workers were victims of the struggle being carried on in their name, they took no part in it. It was carried on by student-formed subversive groups. On the other hand, the U.S. military advisers were everywhere, in the field of operations as well as at staff headquarters.

While bombs sporadically continued to explode in luxury hotels or in clubs frequented by the bourgeoisie, the Armed Forces combed the guerrilla zones. Their planes bombed the forests with napalm; others, equipped with loudspeakers, flew over the villages and made announcements in Quechua urging the Indians not to aid the guerrillas. On their transistors, however, the Indians heard another tune, a regularly repeated MIR call to rebellion.

Once again police and army columns were attacked, posts in population centers were taken by assault, and haciendas were stripped. All these operations were combined with active propaganda and the distribution of tracts detailing the political program of the guerrillas. Rumors of summary executions and machine-gunnings reached Lima and were immediately denied by the army. The students went on strike. According to the representative of a big French bank, who happened to be in the region, thousands of peasants were the victims of this blind repression. One night he saw a convoy of military trucks loaded with corpses move along the street on which his hotel was located. Little by little the advantage passed to the army. Initially, some guerrillas surrendered individually, then in groups. Others were taken prisoner. Interrogated according to methods that have proven successful in every country in the world, they gave information that permitted the army to form some idea of the insurgent organization. Though other guerrilla *focos* sprang up, it was too late.

In the Cuzco region, the army used every means at its disposal: planes, helicopters, five-hundred-pound bombs, and parachutists. Gradually surrounded by airborne troops, the guerrillas were forced to withdraw to the high mountainous plateau called the Mesa Pelada. They held out for another two months.

The plan of General Maldonado, who had been given the responsibility for the repression, had borne fruit. His goal had been to drive the insurgents far from their supplies and caches. Some of the captured groups were without ammunition and dying of hunger. The aerial bombardments by light aircraft and helicopters continued. Parachutists were dropped to cut off escape from the plateau to the mountains.

On October 10, Luis de la Puente's group underwent a final attack and the Mesa Pelada fell into army hands. Fifty-four guerrillas were killed and twenty-five were taken prisoner. The army and the police had also suffered heavy losses. But Luis de la Puente and his staff managed to slip through the net.

Several days later, the MIR leader and seven men were killed by an army patrol while attempting to resupply themselves at a hacienda. The army and the press cried victory, but Lobatón continued the struggle, and the clandestine radio station, The Revolutionary Voice of the Andes, continued its broadcasts.

The upheaval caused by the guerrillas seemed destined to spread a veritable fever over the country. On November 4, for some pointless reason, Juliaca, a city not far from Lake Titicaca, rebelled: general strike, barricades, and a blockaded airport. The army and the police intervened. The inhabitants of the city defended themselves with stones, Molotov cocktails, and sticks of dynamite. It took the forces of law and order three days to reconquer Juliaca, street by street, with cannon and machine gun.

On December 4, another guerrilla leader, Máximo Velando, was captured near Satipo. On the 18th, the army announced the death of Guillermo Lobatón, and this news was to be confirmed in January. Finally, on the 24th, Belaunde Terry announced that the guerrilla fronts had been definitively crushed and their men scattered throughout the jungle. On that same day an arms ship-ment was seized less than three hundred miles north of Lima, and fighting broke out again between Lima and Cuzco, near the Ecuador frontier.

In the meantime, the Federation of Peruvian Students met in Lima and elected Luis de la Puente honorary president. Then these students sought for ways to unite the extreme left in order to prepare for new struggles. But the congress they finally man-aged to set together only accentuated the divisions between the various groups. The students separated without having managed to reach agreement.

While other bombs were exploding in Lima, an MIR repre-sentative, García Urrutia, outlined the situation at Havana's Tri-continental Congress and drew the same conclusions that other Latin-American guerrillas had drawn: "We must intensify and reinforce both the fighting and the political education in areas inhabited by peasant masses and in cities with a heavy proletarian population."

In October, 1966, the surviving cadres of the MIR met to reorganize the movement with a new central committee. That same year the latter announced, "The blows suffered by our movement have been severe, but they have not been able to check revolutionary progress." The Peruvian Minister of War, in a publication entitled "The Guerrilla Fronts in Peru and Their Repression," admitted that "the armed struggle could begin again at any time and in any place."

In his article, "Revolution, Insurrection, and Guerrilla Fronts in Peru," Amerigo Pumaruna analyzed the MIR failure and explained it by a too systematic and too rigid interpretation of Castroism, which he called *foquismo*. Che Guevara had written in *Guerrilla Warfare* that it was not necessary for all conditions to be present before beginning the struggle because the guerrilla *foco* could create these conditions in action. *Foquismo* consists in attributing to the guerrilla *focos* too important a role in the revolutionary struggle.

Because of this, the creation of a mass movement is neglected during the struggle, the combatants' vision being clouded by the Cuban example in which a dozen men in the mountains, directed by a leader of exceptional character, Fidel Castro, were able to bring about a revolution. Luis de la Puente had been the victim of the incessant repetition by Havana that "the Cuban revolution carried out by Castro was in no way exceptional and could be undertaken everywhere with more or less the same means."

"Because of this," concluded Pumaruna, "the Peruvian revolutionists unleashed their insurrection thinking that they were in a situation analogous to that of Fidel Castro and his men in 1958. The Andean Sierra seemed to them as good as the Sierra Maestra and they themselves seemed to have the same personal and military value as Fidel, Che, Camilio Cienfuegos, and Raúl Castro—which was not the case." But above all they had had to deal with the Indians.

Foquismo had also played a part in most of the other guerrilla fronts formed in Latin America during the past ten years. In most cases their existence was short-lived.

The Ecuadorian guerrilla front beat all records in this matter of duration. It lasted only forty-eight hours. Near Santo Domingo de los Colorados, a region between the tropical coast and the high Andean plateaus, some forty young people were encircled and captured by parachutists in March, 1962.

In Argentina, the "Uturuncos," tiger-men of Peronist orientation, operating in the Tucumán region toward the end of 1959, dispersed as mysteriously as they had come together. In 1964, the failure of the EGP (Ejército Guerrillero del Pueblo) was considerably more serious. On March 4, 1964, in a forest region north of Salta, a sugar-growing area largely populated by Indians, an Argentine police patrol uncovered a guerrilla training camp near the Bolivian border and made several arrests. The rapidly organized repression brought to light some other camps and revealed the existence of arms smuggling from Bolivia.

For six months the group had been preparing for armed combat. After several skirmishes, some of the guerrillas were killed while others fled and died of hunger in the barren sierra. Of the fourteen who were arrested and brought to trial, two were condemned and executed. The survivors are still serving prison terms in Salta.

In July of the same year, another arms cache was discovered in the Formosa region, and several Castroite groups composed of students were arrested. On August 4, the police uncovered an even larger cache in Buenos Aires, where, according to the police, the members of the entire subversive movement had been meeting. Among those arrested were some young people who had just had several months of training in Cuba.

Various well-known communists were apprehended, but it seemed that the Communist party as such was not involved. It was busy forming union cells through which it hoped to regain some part of the large Peronist following.

Régis Debray mentions the ephemeral existence in Paraguay in 1959 of a group of eighty guerrillas composed of young militants, *febreristas*, and liberals, of whom only a dozen or so managed to escape to Argentina. A year and a half later, the guerrillas of the FULNA (Frente Unificado de Liberación Nacional) were also abandoned by the Communist party and vanquished by the army.

In Brazil, military training groups tied to the agricultural union movement of Francisco Julião were established in the northeast. They disappeared when the union failed to give them promised support. The peasant leagues split up during the course of 1962 and ceased to be a national political movement. After the military came to power, Julião was arrested, as was Governor Arraiz, who had supported him. Since then the Church and the Social Christians have tried to reconstitute the union solidarity of the *caboclos*.

In 1964, the same military coup d'etat provoked the formation of guerrilla fronts in the south of the country near Iguazu, at the Argentine border. This region was the political fief of Leonel Brizola, the brother-in-law of the deposed President Goulart. He was accused by the military junta of having tried to form "groups of eleven" in an attempt to establish Castroism in Brazil.

Since then, the net thrown by the army over the entire country has prevented any major insurgent action. Though Brazil has played a negligible role in the Castroite subversive movement in South America, it is nevertheless a country in which feelings of revolt and frustration are prevalent. Some forty years ago, it was the scene of an extraordinary guerrilla operation.

The man who may well be called the ancestor of the guerrillas was a young rebel lieutenant, Luis Carlos Prestes, who is today head of the Brazilian Communist party. With eight hundred men who were constantly pursued but never caught by the army, he swept through Brazil for three years, was in fifty-six battles, signed treaties with the Indians, and set up in those states through which he passed cadres ready to take power upon signal. From the Uruguayan border to the Amazon Basin, from Mato Grosso to Baía, he continued on his way. Then, when the "Prestes column" reached the Bolivian border, it was disbanded and its men passed into Bolivia. Luis Carlos Prestes had met with not one defeat.

Panama is a city of contrasts. On the one hand there is the abject poverty, the tropical filth, the markets ringing with cries and redolent of strong odors, the mountains of green watermelons, the shackled iguanas. On the other hand there is the Canal Zone, American territory in which fifty thousand U.S. citizens, soldiers and civilians, live in a manner not unlike that of their compatriots in Florida or California.

The pretext for this American presence is the canal, which is now too small, for the big tankers and ships like the *France* cannot pass through it. This canal is extremely difficult to defend in the context of modern strategy.

"We are here not only to defend the canal," Colonel Church-ville, spokesman for the Southern Command, told me. "That's actually a secondary mission for us. Our real work is to fight against Castroite subversion. You are in the anti-Cuba."

At least I knew where I was.

General Porter nodded in agreement. He had four stars on his cap. He is responsible for all of Latin America, from the Rio Grande to the Tierra del Fuego. Short-cropped hair, a business-man's head, a warm handshake belied by his much too light and immobile eyes, and a much too strong jaw that is hidden by no beard. Physically too he is anti-Castro.

The briefings took place in large, well-lit rooms furnished with chairs that have writing surfaces on one side, like those in univer-sities. I saw schematic charts and movies given with a running commentary by a commander or a colonel who recited his lesson with all the warmth of a parrot.

At no time did I feel they were suspicious of me. I had simply been authorized to see and know certain things after having received I am not sure just what classification. As some American reporters before me had done, I might very well then contact a guerrilla group in Guatemala or go off to see the May Day parade in Cuba. It made no difference to the directors of the Southern Command. They were convinced of the value and the justification of their methods and made no effort to hide it.

I visited the jungle school with its zoo of fish and animals—poisonous, dangerous, or edible—that are found in the Panama jungles. On this little stretch of land could be found all the forms of vegetation that exist in Latin America or in Vietnam. In the survival schools pilots are trained in what to do if their planes are shot down and they have to bail out; the same training is also given to special agents or small commando groups that are to be dropped into the jungle. They learn how to live there for days or weeks on roots and wild berries. They are taught how to build shelter, how to fish with rudimentary equipment, what fish are edible, how to make contact with the native population, how to find their direction with or without a compass, how to eliminate their tracks. "Training for Vietnam," I was told.

The Green Berets go through the training cycle along with Latin-American officers of the OAS countries. Teams of two, three, or four men are parachuted deep into the Darién swamps, sometimes at night. All they have with them is a pocketful of concentrated food (to be used only as a last resort), a compass, a carbine, and a knife. For a week they fend off mosquitoes and leeches, roast lizards over wood fires, and chew on plants that are chosen carefully, for some of the plant life is poisonous. Covered with scabs and mud, they must find their own way back to the base.

The first time the American army was in Panama was in 1851, when the Secretary of War sent California's 10th Infantry Regiment to the Panamanian isthmus during the Gold Rush. The journey was made by train as far as Chagres and then along the Las Cruces trail. Eighty solders died of cholera.

In 1911, the U.S. Marines returned to defend the canal. In 1913, they were joined by a detachment of coast artillery. They were based at Camp Empire.

At the time the defense system was limited to strong fortifications at either end of the canal and a mobile force based in the center and ready to intervene on one side or the other to meet a land attack.

Then an area stretching from Balboa to Fort Randolph was turned over to the American troops. The Pacific garrisons established themselves in Fort Amador and Fort Grant, while the Atlantic units were in Fort Sherman and Fort Randolph.

After World War I, the number of troops stationed there was reduced; then, because of international tension, the number rose from ten thousand in 1933 to sixty-seven thousand in 1942. The Caribbean Defense Command was created in 1941.

The assignment given Caribbean staff headquarters was as follows: land defense of the Panama Canal; military support of the policy and the treaties signed between the United States and Latin-American countries.

This second function included logistic support, help in case of emergencies, supervision of the military missions program, special training for Latin-American officers, and technical cartographic assistance.

On July 1, 1963, the Caribbean Command became the Southern Command.

The cornerstone of the entire strategy of U.S. policy in Latin America is La Escuela de las Américas, which is an integral part of the Southern Command.

La Escuela de las Américas was founded in 1949 by General Porter. Courses were initially given in Spanish only at the request of South American countries, some of whose officers went through the training cycle. Because of the popularity of these courses, they grew in number until the school revamped its organization.

In 1956, all teaching in English was eliminated and only Spanish was used. While in 1949 the school had given diplomas to 743 North Americans and 195 South Americans, in 1962 there were only 120 North American graduates to 1,200 Latin Americans. The North Americans mostly belong to Puerto Rico's National Guard or to the advisory missions in Latin America.

Today, Spanish is the official language of the school. All the instructors speak it perfectly; they are even forbidden to speak English among themselves.

Almost all the instructors belong to the Special Forces and wear the green beret; they have attended courses in the big universities and have received some training in ethnography and sociology, and they are well acquainted with the history and geography of Latin America. Often they have been taught Indian dialects. They have been taught to be discreet and to respect Latin-American national pride.

In large private-enterprise firms they were taught to build roads and to direct construction crews. Veteran FBI men have taught them how to conduct a police investigation and CIA specialists have taught them how to make use of men for special undertakings.

Since its foundation in 1949, the school has had 23,000 students who belong to all the regular armies of the Western Hemisphere. At the present time it turns out three thousand men a year. Some of these, such as Yon Sosa in Guatemala, join the guerrillas, but most of them work for their governments.

The training cycle sometimes lasts for forty weeks. The courses are divided into two groups. Of these the most important is the one labeled "Internal Security," which includes lessons on the creation of an antisubversive operational center, intelligence, police, jungle operations and airborne operations, counterinsurgent operations, paramilitary forces, political forces, sociological forces, psychological forces.

The other part of the program is devoted to courses in military and civic action designed to develop the economy and create an economic, psychological, and social atmosphere in which guerrilla forces can no longer develop.

The first objective is the training of officers for fighting against subversion. Its secondary objective is to make these men technicians who after leaving the army will be able to develop the economic life of the country and open the market to American industry.

The most promising students often are given scholarships to Fort Benning or Fort Bragg.

The Southern Command, of which La Escuela de las Américas is only a part, can at any time and at any place furnish countries menaced by subversion with teams of Green Berets grouped in sticks of seven men ready to go into action in a few hours.

They were present in Guatemala in the Sierra de las Minas when the Guatemalan army began its offensive against the guerrilla forces of César Montes' FAR. They were in Colombia when the Colombian army broke up the last "independent republics" and attacked Santander's Castroite guerrillas. They arrived in Bolivia when Régis Debray was made prisoner. They were with the Ranger battalion that wounded and took prisoner Comandante Ramón—in other words, Che Guevara.

One of these Green Berets was in Vallegrande, near the body of Che Guevara. When somebody questioned him in English, he replied, *"No entiendo."* Another Green Beret, this time a doctor, embalmed Che's corpse before it was shown to the press.

All or almost all of these Green Berets have seen service in Vietnam, but only as advisers sent to train minorities like the Mois of the high plateaus.

In Panama I met a number of men I had known in Vietnam as part of Cabot Lodge's entourage. Officially they had been reduced to subaltern ranks to follow South American politics discreetly. They had immense resources and a considerable number of agents hidden in the U.S. Information Services, the Peace Corps, and other similar organizations, but also in the big commercial companies and in the big oil corporations. They were often professors and university people who, like Régis Debray, had caught the contagion of direct action. They were no longer the agents ridiculed by Graham Greene in *Our Man in Havana*. But just what did they have to offer, aside from talk about American-style well-being? It was a lack on their part, and they knew it.

However, credit is due them for a number of daring operations:

—The Cuban Embassy in Lima is burgled by Cuban exiles from Miami. The documents that were captured, or presented as such, cause Peru to break off diplomatic relations with Havana.

—A mysterious plane crashes in the Brazilian sierra. Everything is carbonized and even the metal framework melts. But an American helicopter gets to the scene first and its crew salvages a mysterious leather briefcase: relations are broken off between Brazil and Cuba.

—The same thing happens with another, equally mysterious plane that crashes in the Chilean cordillera in a spot accessible only to another American helicopter. Some documents are found intact that lead Chile to break with Cuba.

Two years ago the American government had to choose between the policies of Roosevelt and Kennedy, who set up civilian governments everywhere, and support for military regimes.

In 1945, Latin America had twelve *caudillos* who had sprung from the army. In 1961, there was only one left. All the democratic regimes showed a tendency to veer to the extreme left, perhaps because the Communist parties, though small in memberships, were the only ones to have organization, methods of action, and a program. Other parties, like that of the Goulart regime in Brazil, tended to be provisional assemblies of joint interests.

Castro's seizure of power in Cuba, his decision to join the communist camp, the failure of the Alliance for Progress, the growing interest of China and Russia in the South American Third World, impressed upon the U.S. State Department the need to check the wave of revolution. General Porter, overall commander of the Southern Command, was given wide-ranging powers.

The Pentagon landed Marines in Santo Domingo, supported *caudillos*—Somoza in Nicaragua or Stroessner in Paraguay— and infiltrated, by means of La Escuela de las Américas, all the national armies.

In 1957, as a result of this short-term policy of meeting the most immediate danger, the military *caudillos* or the regimes more or less controlled by the army were once again in the majority: Argentina, Brazil, Ecuador, Bolivia, Guatemala, Paraguay, Peru, Colombia, Honduras, the Dominican Republic, El Salvador, and Nicaragua. The only exceptions were Uruguay, Mexico, and Chile.

In 1829, Bolívar was saying, "The United States seems destined by Providence to impose poverty on America in the name of liberty." But today, the United States finds it in its interest to eliminate poverty in order to open new markets. The more guerrilla activity increases the disorder and the poverty, the more the intervention of the United States, because of its superior economic power, is seen to be the only way out.

The Castroite guerrilla fronts, even when they are victorious, seem incapable of creating anything but disorder. To this extent the analysis of the orthodox Communist parties seems to be right.

The United States itself initially needs guerrillas to liquidate profitless feudal structures such as the oligarchy. In the next stage, Latin America will find itself unable to do without the United States in order to rebuild the continent on a new and healthier basis. Russia, the only competitor of the United States, still cannot afford a higher standard of life at home and the support of revolutions as wasteful and formless as those in South America. This may be the reason that Fidel Castro stands condemned today.

The situation is regrettable for the Latin American and for his heroic, romantic, humanistic vision of existence—a vision he is one of the last to maintain.

Che's death will prevent the unification into a great crusade of all those who still dreamed of this disorderly conquest of Don Quixote's sepulcher. The evolution of the modern world rejects such a crusade.

But Americans must not forget that the greatest empires have died, that the tempo of history is continually increasing, and that peoples sunk in despair can, like the Vietnamese, resist them indefinitely.

In 1962, the great Mexican writer Carlos Fuentes addressed the following plea to Americans:

I beg you, Americans, to look beyond the intellectual provincialism of the cold war. Take note of where we want to go, we men of the underdeveloped, hungry, and revolutionary world. . . . We are different from you. Do not be provincial! Try to understand the diversity of the world. . . . We want to coexist with you as loyal friends, not as badly treated, badly fed, and ignorant slaves. . . .

And we want to free you from a fate worse than that of the slave: that of the master.

Understand this—Latin America does not intend to be a suburb of your country. We are going to make our entry into the world. . . . The first act of cooperation incumbent upon you is to know how to respect the revolutionary transformations that are the work of our peoples. . . . Latin America knows which is its path. Nothing, my North American friends, will stop the march of these 200,000,000 men.

The attempt by the United States to maintain the status quo until the war in Vietnam is over has often had catastrophic results. Let us take as an example Nicaragua, where the Pentagon in order to avoid disorder, gave its support to the detested Somoza regime, instead of taking advantage of an opportunity to get rid of it.

Nicaragua is virtually a U.S. economic colony par excellence. Some figures: 90 percent of its exports and 75 percent of its imports are tied to North America.

In 1961, a single timber company, N.I.P.C.O., exported eighty million dollars' worth of timber, on which it paid only a 3 percent tax; gold mines paid scarcely $100,000 for eight million dollars of ore. In both cases, however, the Somozas own shares in the companies. Nicaragua also defends the approach to Panama, and the Somozas have always lent their territory to the CIA for its operations.

Pentagon support for the Somozas resulted in new guerrilla violence in Nicaragua at a time when guerrilla activity in the rest of Latin America was decreasing. To complete the portrait of this little "tropical paradise" let us note that 70 percent of the population is illiterate, that only 2 percent of the population has direct access to drinking water, and that 50 percent of the children die before the age of five.

The capital of Nicaragua, Managua, is situated on the edge of the lake of the same name, a gray stretch of dirty water that smells of mud and rot. This lake communicates with the large Lake Nicaragua, which is the only fresh-water body to have sharks living in it.

On the other side of Lake Managua is a volcano named Momotombo. Earthquakes have often destroyed the Nicaraguan capital, and as a result Managua has neither monuments nor churches of any particular distinction.

For the last thirty-five years, Nicaragua has been governed by the Somoza dynasty. In 1855, Nicaragua was taken over by the last of the modern-day filibusters, William Walker, with the help of his "American phalanx," adventurers of all types and nationalities. Walker looked less like his picturesque followers than like a clergyman. Successively a lawyer and a reporter, after having tried to be a priest and a doctor, he became a vigorous defender of slavery. Walker and his phalanx met scarcely any resistance. He seized the country, had himself elected president of the republic, reestablished slavery, and confiscated the property of Vanderbilt, with whom he had had some harsh words. But Vanderbilt already had the money to furnish Walker's enemies with arms. The last of the filibusters died in front of a firing squad.

With startling originality for a country with a high illiteracy rate, Colombia has nevertheless chosen as its reigning national hero a poet, Rubén Darío. Long unknown to his compatriots while he was admired all over the world, this lover of Paris cafes and Madrid's avenues, this man who used French symbolist technique to reshape Spanish poetry, this genial, drunk, and generous madman who died at fifty because of his excesses, owed the honor to an unusual combination of circumstances. Normally the place would have gone to Augusto César Sandino, hero of the entire Latin-American continent and a man much more in keeping with Nicaragua's style. He had been a real sage rider, a *pistolero* of considerable class who had both the dimensions and the temperament of a true *libertador*.

He was the first to have fought the Marines, and he managed

to keep them in check for seven years (from 1926 to 1932) after they landed in Nicaragua to protect the lives and property of U.S. nationals. It was really a matter of protecting the investments of certain large banks, of certain big corporations, and of preserving strong positions against that day in which a transatlantic canal paralleling that at Panama would be put through. With a small group of *campesinos* and young students, Sandino set up a guerrilla front in the northern mountains. Aerial bombardments were unable to dislodge him. "Mosquito bites," said the American newspapers, but General Logan Feland told one of his friends: "I would need fifty thousand men to get rid of him." At the time, Nicaragua lived under a truly colonial regime. Presidential elections were held at bayonet point. Only the candidate who had the support of the general commanding the U.S. troops could be elected. Afterward, this president merely had to obey orders, fill his pockets, and distribute to his family and friends posts and prebends that he invented as he went along. For example, a President Emiliano Chamorro created for his nephew a post—Exhaust-Tank Inspector—that was both well remunerated and included the right to an official car.

In the countryside, Sandino blew up roads and bridges, and attacked small U.S. garrisons. "A foreign army is on our soil," he said. "Our first duty is to get rid of it." Sandino, a rich landowner, an Indian mestizo, a man of incredible, inexhaustible energy despite his small size, had decided that he would not put down his arms until the last U.S. Marine rifleman had left Nicaragua, and he kept his word.

The principles that guided his guerrilla front made it practically invincible. It is an example well worth the pondering by all those who currently dream of armed revolution.

—To begin with, it was national, and its goals were limited to getting rid of the occupying power and to promoting great or social justice.

—It sprang from neither a foreign leader nor a still more foreign ideology such as Marxism.

—It was revolutionary without in any way wanting to over-throw the country's basic structures—small property ownership, the family, the customs and the way of life—in one swoop.

—It was not made up of representatives of a single class who lived outside the country, as did the Guatemalan students and young officers, but included in its ranks peasants, Indians, and mestizos.

—It called upon a feeling common to the entire population, a mixture of wounded pride and nationalism provoked by the presence of foreign troops. You couldn't be against Sandino without feeling like a traitor.

(In Bolivia and in Argentina, it is quite easy to be anti-Castro without feeling in any way uneasy about it and while still remaining a partisan of revolution.)

When Franklin Roosevelt recalled his Marines, Sandino kept his word and disbanded his guerrillas. But he had made some incautious speeches in the mountains. He had spoken to his comrades of agrarian reform. It was clearly necessary in this country in which half the land remained uncultivated and in which 360 landowners controlled almost all that was arable, a country in which, according to established tradition, agricultural workers were not paid a salary but were merely permitted to farm a patch of land and build a hut.

Eager to repair the harm done by his predecessors, Roosevelt was ready to help Sandino constitute a truly democratic government and make those reforms necessitated by the feudal organization of the country. But Nicaragua was in the hands of several large Creole families who did not see things this way. As in Colombia, they belonged to two clans, the conservatives in the city of Granada, and the liberals in León. They joined forces in order to ask jovial "Tacho" Somoza, commander of the National Guard, to get rid of Sandino as quickly as possible. Tacho was everybody's friend. He had studied "business" in the United States. Since he spoke English well, he had no trouble seducing the wife of the U.S. ambassador, who prevailed upon her aging husband to give good old Tacho a command for which he had no preparation, and the rank of general. Just a few months earlier, Tacho had been selling automobiles.

Disguised as a general, Tacho did no worse than others. The work of the National Guard was not to fight, but to maintain order and make itself some money. Just another business venture. Tacho therefore agreed that in return for cash he would rid the country of Sandino. He invited him to a big banquet and had him assassinated as he left. In Managua I was shown the spot where little César fell. I was not shown the assassins. Tacho Somoza, with a commendable concern for discretion, had seen to it that they disappeared.

Obviously, after that it would have been difficult to ask Sandino's assassin or his sons to make a national hero of the man who had won fame fighting against the United States protectors of the clan. However, unless it wanted to be laughed at, Nicaragua couldn't go on without a national hero. Since Spain had granted the Central American countries independence without there having been any fighting, there was just no *libertador* to be found, and so people fell back on Rubén Darió.

The present General Somoza, the son of Tacho and familiarly known as "Tachito," a man who had himself named president of the republic as the result of some vague electoral consultation, was able to say to me without irony, "Just see what a democratic country Nicaragua is. Our national hero is a poet, and out of 1,400,000 inhabitants we have 872,000 voters, all of whom voted." He seems unaware that this percentage of voters is the highest in the world, that an American journalist was able to have himself inscribed on three or four electoral lists without showing any identification (there is no *carte d'identité* in Nicaragua), and that more than half the population lives in the distant countryside and knew nothing about the elections.

General Somoza—the father, Tacho—governed the country by means of straw men until 1936. Then he had himself elected president of the Liberal party because he came from León and had let himself be seduced by the Sacazas, an important liberal family. Several months later he became president of the republic, and he held that office for twenty years. He would probably still have it if he had not been assassinated at a celebration while the orchestra was playing and the firecrackers were going off. His eldest son, Luis, succeeded him.

Old man Somoza loved the soil, so by using any available means he appropriated for himself more than a third of the arable land in Nicaragua. His former friends, the rich conservative landowners who had financed the assassination of Sandino, missed the little guerrilla. At least he had only talked of sharing the land; General Somoza was robbing them. Tacho also liked mines, so he took them—but subtly, by having shares quietly turned over to him. Then he would turn around and sell big American and Canadian companies the right to exploit these mines. He went so far as to free these companies from the obligation to pay customs duties—in exchange, of course, for healthy royalties paid directly into a bank in New York or Switzerland.

Since forests were a good source of profit, he couldn't resist taking them over. He was interested in aviation, so he became the owner of several airlines; he was interested in boats, so he built his own port—Puerto Somoza—in which customs duties were dispensed with. At his death he left his sons, Luis and Tachito, more than five hundred million in cash alone. Having had some little experience as a soldier, General Somoza was somewhat suspicious of his army. He gave it the old rusty weapons and kept the good ones locked in his cellars. On the other hand he established a praetorian guard of some twelve hundred men. It was called the Somoza Battalion and had the most modern equipment. He also created a sort of *tontonmacoutes* corps, the AMROKS, which was well-armed and dressed in coveralls and canvas shoes. During the 1967 elections, their number rose from three thousand to ten thousand. One of the Somoza bastards who had been made a colonel was given command of them.

Tacho Somoza established himself on the Loma, a midcity hill whose cleared sides provided slopes for machine-gun fire. Most of the members of the opposition disappeared or went into exile in Costa Rica, leaving behind their goods—which became the property of the Somozas. Several of them unfortunately fell into a small volcanic crater filled with black water at the foot of the Loma.

On the death of Anastasio "Tacho" Somoza, Nicaragua became the Somoza *finca*, the Somoza farm. In October, 1956, thanks to the support of the United States, and especially of the Pentagon and the CIA, his eldest son, Luis, succeeded him. Luis' brother, Tachito, who had just graduated from West Point and spoke English better than Spanish, took over command of the National Guard. He married one of his cousins, who had French ancestors and a U.S. passport.

Nicaragua was the U.S. military's surest bastion. It was in Nicaragua, in Puerto Cabezas, on the property of the Somozas, that the ill-fated Bay of Pigs invasion was prepared, just as was the previous and successful invasion that overthrew the Arbenz regime in Guatemala. Such precious and discreet allies well deserved to be forgiven for the way in which they made order reign in Nicaragua.

Luis therefore ruled peacefully for six years. But there was too much talk of this dynasty of *caudillos*; it had even become one of Castro's favorite propaganda themes. In addition, President Kennedy couldn't bear the Somozas. The U.S. advisers of the family asked the two brothers to make some sort of democratic gesture; so it was therefore decided to vote in a new constitution, one that forbade members of the family to succeed one another as president without there being an intervening legislative period.

Luis Somoza chose a straw man, René Schick, to replace him until his brother Tachito could in four years take over the spot that had been kept warm. There couldn't have been a better choice than Schick. He owed everything to the Somozas. He was something straight out of a Dostoevsky novel. Nobody knew for sure who his father was; maybe he had been one of the Sacazas—the big family allied to the Somozas—in whose home Schick's mother had been a servant. A Swiss adopted him when he married his mother, whom he quickly abandoned along with her child.

Schick had been a bootblack, a newsboy, and a general local errand boy. He evidently managed reasonably well since he was able to get his law degree. He became one of these drunken, unkempt, scruffy lawyers whose pockets bulge with newspapers and books and who mumble incoherently in neighborhood bars until they are found dead-drunk in the gutters.

René Schick found his true path in the hospital to which he had been brought after an attack of delirium tremens. He was converted, gave up drinking, became very pious, and married a rich widow who had a daughter from a previous marriage. Though he avoided bars, he still loved company, and so he decided to launch himself into politics. He began by swearing allegiance to the Somozas. Soon he was made an embassy adviser, then an ambassador, and then a minister. He knew how to be flexible, humble, and grateful—particularly appreciated qualities. And suddenly he became president of the republic.

Of course, the Somozas kept a close watch on him—and an even closer one when he showed signs of wanting to mix into education and agrarian reform. He was brusquely put in his place. In the meantime, Schick's stepdaughter had grown into an extremely attractive young lady. Weary of saying his beads and having no particular role to play as president, Schick made her his mistress. A few weeks before the end of his term of office, he decided to flee abroad with her. He made secret contact with members of the opposition, who agreed to help him on condition that he publicly denounce the Somoza regime. In the course of a Liberal party convention, on August 1, 1966, Schick gave the opposition proof of his sincerity. He came out against holding elections before a population census was taken and an identity card system established.

Once more the Somozas called him to order. Schick fainted as he left the convention. After that there was much talk of his heart trouble. Schick felt threatened. According to the story, he left a valise containing $200,000 dollars in cash and two plane tickets—one for him and another for his stepdaughter—in a room at the Grand Hotel of Managua. Neither the valise nor the money nor the tickets were ever found. The Somozas were warned by their efficient police service. The next day, when Schick's personal physician came to see his by now completely recovered patient, he was refused entrance into the president's room. So were Schick's wife and confessor. Without consulting anyone, a doctor sent by the Somozas decided on a blood transfusion. René Schick died two hours later. Nobody had been present but the male nurse.

A vice president nobody had ever heard about completed his term of office, and General Tachito Somoza, completely disgusted with straw men, officially presented himself as a candidate for office.

To confront him, the opposition finally decided to rally around a single candidate, Dr. Fernando Agüero Rocha. But the strong man of the opposition remained Chamorro, the editor of the newspaper *Presencia*, who had some personal and family scores to settle with the Somozas. He belonged to the important Granada family that ruled over the conservatives.

Only the Somozas were authorized to propagandize. The opposition's radio broadcasts were suspended "in order not to excite the people." Nevertheless, some of the students were organizing passive resistance demonstrations three or four times a week. Finally, on January 22, the opposition received permission to parade down Avenida Roosevelt from 9 A.M. until 4 P.M.

There were approximately forty thousand people in the streets.

The National Guard was deployed. Taking advantage of the absence of the Somozas, who were in León, Dr. Agüero tried to meet with the general staff of the National Guard to ask that it join him in studying "a modification of the electoral process in an effort to avoid bloodshed"—tantamount to an invitation to join his party in its stand against the Somozas.

The U.S. Embassy hesitated. It was certain that in a country so closely controlled by the United States, Agüero would not have taken such a risk without having obtained some guarantees. The influence of the American instructors at La Escuela de las Américas on their former students is well known, and many of the Nicaraguan officers had gone through training cycles there.

The opposition had arrived at some agreements among the National Guard, even if only with Lieutenant Sixto Pinédo, a jet pilot who was now rigged out with a fire hose in order to contain the crowd. He was standing well in front of his comrades. Suddenly a shot rang out. Wounded in the head by a rifle bullet, Lieutenant Pinédo tumbled from his fire engine, dead. (Later it would be discovered that the bullet had been fired from behind, from a group of soldiers in the Somoza Battalion.) The National Guard, using the death of the officer as an excuse, fired into the crowd. Everybody understood.

The Pentagon had chosen General Somoza in spite of the fact that the Embassy had a weakness for Dr. Agüero.

The avenue was covered with the dead and the dying. The demonstrators either obtained arms or had some with them. Soldiers were fired on from the roofs. The demonstration leaders and some of their faithful took refuge in the Grand Hotel and were besieged there by the National Guard. Sixty foreigners, the majority of whom were Americans, were kept as hostages. The demonstrators had pistols, a few carbines, and two or three automatic weapons. The hotel was bombarded by the guns of old armored cars that had been through the African campaign, then been sold to the Israelis and finally resold to Somoza.

The goal of the besieged forces was to hold out in the hotel as long as possible in order to move international opinion and give the United States an attack of bad conscience; the goal of the Somozas was to end it quickly in order to discourage scandal. Colonel Francisco, one of the key men in the American secret services, proposed, or rather imposed, his mediation. The members of the besieged force, who had run out of ammunition after the first night, were authorized to leave the hotel. The leaders were arrested, but the candidate for the office of president of the republic, Agüero, was released the same night. On the other hand, Chamorro, who was considered more dangerous and who was accused of plotting, collusion with the Castroites, and many other things, was kept in prison.

When I arrived in Managua several days later, I learned that there were about 200 dead in all—150 demonstrators and 50 members of the National Guard. There had been no burials in any of the cemeteries. What had happened to the corpses? To save embarrassment, the Somozas shipped them off during the night—National Guardsmen and members of the opposition all heaped together. A priest was asked to bless the bodies, and the story got out that the bodies were buried near a lagoon on Somoza land.

Finally the election took place, with doctored voting lists, armed AMROKS at the polling places, transparent ballots so that those who voted against the Somozas could be spotted, armored patrols of "electoral police," ballot boxes that were filled before the voting began. Moreover, when the polls closed, Luis Somoza had the ballot boxes taken to his house and locked himself in with them for the next six days while he decided what percentage of voters he would give to the opposition.

The U.S. Embassy had told him to make it look democratic, and wanted Dr. Agüero to receive 40 percent of the vote.

"No," said Luis, "Agüero is too vain already."

After some dickering they decided on 32 percent. General

Anastasio "Tachito" Somoza was elected president of the republic with 68 percent of the vote.

Soon afterward, Luis died of cancer, a blow for the new president, for Luis had been the skillful politician, whereas Tachito was violent and hot-tempered.

After these strange elections, I met some members of the opposition—all conservatives, Catholics, generally rich, far from the revolutionary type, and all of them pro-American. They said, "It was a great victory for the communists and for Castro. We now have only one resort against the Somozas: rifles and machine guns. Don't the Americans understand that in letting the Somozas behave this way they are sacrificing their reputation once and for all?"

Robert Kennedy spoke out publicly against the scandal of the elections and the massacres in Managua. It did no good. The Somozas have hated the Kennedys since President John Kennedy refused to let the U.S. Air Force come to the aid of the exiled Cubans during the Bay of Pigs fiasco. The invasion of Cuba was something dear to the hearts of the Somozas. They were so involved in it that General Tachito Somoza himself had inspected the exiles before they loaded onto the tubs he had furnished.

Robert Kennedy was called a communist, and while they were at it they reminded everyone that his brother had been one too.

Shortly afterward, I visited one of those gold mines from which ingots go directly to the United States without any tax being paid on them. In the truck that was taking us to the red pits from which copper and gold ore were being ripped, a young Nicaraguan engineer told us: "Don't think that we will let them get away with it. There will soon be guerrilla fronts right here among these mountains and in these forests."

It has already happened. Sandinoist guerrillas of Castroite inspiration have already fought in the mining region, as well as somewhat farther north in the Pouzacou mountains. In one ambush, the National Guard lost twenty-eight men. Many students

236 / THE GUERRILLAS

have disappeared from their homes and are thought to have joined the guerrillas.

In Costa Rica—an oasis of democracy, a sort of Switzerland anchored in the Middle Ages—I saw that amazing person "Don Pepe" Figueres, a lively and paradoxical Catalán. He created the Caribbean Legion to fight against the dictatorships, and fought alongside Father Núñez, a priest with something of the democratic Templar about him, against Somoza's mercenaries.

His program can be summed up as follows: "We've had enough of dictatorships and don't want anything more to do with them, whether they come from the left or the right. They all lean on the military."

All of which makes for the fact that Don Pepe is anti-Castro as well as anti-Somoza. He said to me, "It is a catastrophe. The Americans committed a great error in letting the Somozas behave like highway bandits again."

But when I asked him if he would go so far as to send arms to the anti-Somozaists, he gently shook his head, "No, it's too late for that."

Does that mean it's up to the Americans to settle these problems?

What an abdication!

It also means that guerrillas of no matter what label will continue to be born as long as there are Somozas, as long as there are injustices and crimes engendered by such regimes, and as long as there are, fortunately, men unwilling to put up with them.

A Sepulcher
for Che Guevara 5

On May 3, 1967, I was awakened by a telephone call from *Paris-Match*. I was asked to leave Mexico City and get to La Paz as quickly as possible. Régis Debray had been taken prisoner in Muyupampa, Bolivia, on April 20, and was in danger of being executed even before he was sentenced.

It was the same Régis Debray I had heard so much about in Cuba—that brilliant theoretician of guerrilla activity. He had been picked up on a village street in the company of two other journalists.

So I went speeding down from the dry heights of Mexico City to the humid depths of Panama, and I went back up the Bolivian *altiplano* to a height of almost fourteen thousand feet into a

237

rarified, luminous, and cold atmosphere that has its equal only in Nepal and in Tibet.

Régis Debray had been captured unarmed by the civil police. He had not been with the guerrillas pursued by the army, but in a group of "three civilians." Although the death penalty was nonexistent in Bolivia, and the maximum he could get was thirty years, Bolivian soldiers often took such matters into their own hands. The army had been dissolved after the 1952 revolution, but the new government had fabricated another army out of the victorious revolutionary forces that had fought against machine guns with sticks of dynamite wrapped in steel bolts strung on wire. Despite the efforts of American advisers, it was an undisciplined band. And the president of the republic, Air Force General René Barrientos Ortuño, half Quechua Indian on his mother's side, was a man whose reactions were unpredictable.

From El Alto Airport, one descends by a winding road into a sort of funnel around which La Paz has been built in concentric levels, like the coils in a snail shell. The houses begin at about thirteen thousand feet and end at about eleven thousand feet. The Spanish conquerors who established themselves in this mad site thought only of their most immediate needs and were mainly interested in sheltering themselves from the violent *altiplano* winds.

The residential quarters are at the bottom of the funnel. Apparently it's easier to breathe a few hundred yards farther down. There I met the French Ambassador, Dominique Pontchardier ("Pompon"), a small, round, stocky man who always wears sunglasses because the harsh Bolivian light stings his eyes. With him was his wife, whom he addressed familiarly as "Tounet." He seemed as nice and gentle as a big cat. He is a mixture of hardness and gentleness, of stolidity and flexibility, of brutality and kindness. He speaks with a *stéphanois* accent, which becomes heavier when he is furious. Such was the case at the moment.

He rhetorically asked me, "Whatever gave those nincompoops the idea of coming to this country to set up a guerrilla front? Bolivia has just gotten over a revolution, and it was no laughing matter. In 1952, there were fifteen hundred corpses on the streets of La Paz. The miners and their sticks of dynamite went into action against the army, as did the workers' militias with their old popguns. There was a little lieutenant named René Barrientos in these militias. Today he is the president of the republic, and the French newspapers are calling him a fascist and a bloody tyrant. That kind of thing is out of style! All the land has been divided up, all the mines have been nationalized. The money disappeared abroad with the members of the oligarchy, known here as *la rosca*. There are no more big land holdings. Some holdings, like the Zabra one, have gone from 275,000 acres to 50 acres. There are no more large fortunes or even any small ones. Barrientos was elected with tremendous popular support. He can even make speeches in Quechua, and the *altiplano* Indians are all for him.

"What did Régis Debray expect to accomplish? He was sent on a suicide mission. It's insane. But that's no reason to shoot him down. He never bore arms—I know that and the Bolivian army has admitted it. He deserves a kick in the ass more than anything else. The trouble is he didn't give a damn about what the Bolivians would think. Do you at least know anything about the history of this country? We're in an Indian world here—80 percent of the Bolivians are Aymara or Quechua. And there's no way of knowing what goes on in their heads."

I saw these Indians trotting around the El Alto Airport, barrel-chested, their earflap helmets over sienna-color, squashed faces that had been baked and rebaked by the sun and the wind. They chew on coca leaves to relieve their hunger or forget their misery. They are dirty and silent. They can live without heat in mud and reed huts, even though the strong glacial winds around Lake Titicaca often bring the temperature down to zero.

Bolivia has had 186 revolutions in the last 150 years. Twelve presidents of the republic have been assassinated. The last one, Gualberto Villarroel, was defenestrated in 1946 and then, with his aides-de-camp, hung naked by his feet from a lamppost on Plaza Murillo under the windows of the palace. Three diplomats, including the papal nuncio, went under the cover of darkness to cut down the president's swaying body. They wrapped it in a sheet and took it to a secret burial place. The revolution ended as brutally as it had begun. The only ones to remember it are the children who still play "hanged men." Here the people are used to death and treat it casually.

Debray was lucky to have had for his defense a man of character who was willing, when necessary, to go beyond the diplomatic routine. Pontchardier desired death for no one—especially not for Régis Debray, who was the same age one of his sons had been when he was killed, and almost the same age as the other, who has never recovered from his wounds.

Régis Debray's guards had agreed to let the comrades of three officers recently killed by the guerrillas visit him. At the last minute, arrangements were made to change the guards. The next day, a killer, posing as an investigator for the police, was arrested at the door of the prison. In the course of the transfer between Muyupampa and Camiri, the so-called *ley de fuga*, "law of escape," was to be applied to Régis Debray. It was to be announced that he had been shot while trying to escape. Once more the assassination attempt was thwarted. A helicopter came to take the prisoner to Camiri, the petroleum area.

Régis Debray was alive, but by no means out of trouble. The day I arrived in La Paz, the walls were plastered with photographs of the officers "assassinated by the Castro-communist adventurers and the foreign mercenaries." A military tribunal consisting of three sergeants and a captain could easily have been set up to try Debray and to execute him against an adobe wall.

It was also rumored that this guerrilla band, said to be operated by remote control from Cuba, could be under the command of Che Guevara himself.

It was both easy and difficult to get information in La Paz. Mysterious individuals visited you; they either knew many things or knew nothing. They wanted to use Régis Debray as a political springboard or else to involve him even further. Nor were the U.S. secret services inactive. From Panama, the great antiguerrilla center, helicopters flew in not only arms, and Green Berets assigned to provide on-the-spot "advice" for combat troops, but also CIA specialists.

You had to be able to pick your way through this tangle in which you never knew where you were treading.

Lawyers volunteered for the defense of Régis under their party banners. I went to mysterious night rendezvous, I was switched from car to car, I was driven along deserted roads.

I was told that the Bolivian communists were opposed to Régis Debray's Castroite theses on the guerrillas. Nevertheless a number of communists had joined the insurgents along with some Trotskyite miners. At their head was Coco Peredo, a former cab driver—a communist in good standing who had nevertheless spent a long time in Cuba, as had his brother Inti.

The soldiers fared badly in their first encounters with the guerrillas. The army recruits came partly from the Bolivian *altiplano*, as had those other Indians who during the Gran Chaco War had left their bones to rot in the warm and humid lowlands. They were taken prisoner, chased like pitiful animals exhausted by a climate not their own. Perry Anderson described this army in the *Nouvel Observateur* as "a sorry-looking collection of soldiers badly trained and badly equipped, without traditions, understaffed, and of more than uncertain morale." However, there was another Bolivian army, a few battalions at most, that had not yet gone into action—and that one was in no way sorry-looking.

In August, 1966, the Peredo brothers bought an abandoned

finca in the oil region of Camiri. The Casa de Calamina, in a spot known as Monte Agüedo on the edge of the Río Ñancahuazú, was to become an agricultural cooperative, and it is said that they even obtained a government loan to provide agricultural training for a number of unemployed miners.

Ten thousand out of more than twenty-five thousand miners had been paid off by the mines after a drop in the price of tin. Bolivian tin prices had not been competitive with those of Malaysia and Indonesia since the nationalization of the mines.

In Camiri, Coco Peredo often appeared in a restaurant owned by a big, jovial Italian woman, Doña Marietta. A fast talker and a handsome tipper, he soon became known to everybody there, even the officers and functionaries. Here, as in other Latin-American countries touching on the Amazon, people ask few questions about a man's past or about his business if he pays for what he buys. Nobody knew exactly what Coco Peredo was dealing in or whether he really came, as he sometimes said, from the El Beni region. He might be producing cocaine to smuggle into the United States or he might be a "philanthropist" appointed, as he said, by the government to teach the miners of the cold *altiplano* how to farm the lowlands. Anything was possible.

At this same time it was reported that a number of miners, all known as agitators who belonged to Juan Lechín's Trotskyite groups, had disappeared from the *altiplano* in the regions of Oruro and Potosí, the glacial mountains from which tin is drawn, leaving their families about a hundred dollars in Bolivian pesos to live on. Members and even leaders of the workers' militias, they were skillful with rifles and dynamite.

In February, 1967, an antimalaria team working on the border between Bolivia and Brazil, near the Rincón del Tigre ranch, ran into a group of some twenty armed men wearing olive drab who spoke Spanish with a strange accent. They could have been Europeans, but they could also have been Cubans, Argentines, or Peruvians.

Were these men commanded by Che Guevara himself? They were the same ones that had been seen by Father Pelegrini on the other side of the border, and he had definitely recognized Che among them. This group was on the way to Casa de Calamina, where Coco Peredo, the Trotskyite miners, some students from the Santa Cruz region, and some members of the La Paz Communist party were waiting for them. They told the members of the antimalaria team they belonged to a geological mission more or less financed by an international organization, hence their different nationalities, and that they were armed because geologists often spent weeks in dangerous regions and they had to hunt for food.

The two groups met again two days later before a little clump of huts and straw shacks known as Bambarrán. Two of the "geologists" were busy transmitting over an excellent radio, the antennas of which were spread. They were speaking Spanish, but when they saw the employees of the Ministry of Health, they continued their transmission in English. Later, the official services of the Bolivian army claimed that Che and his men were communicating directly with Havana.

The "geologists" folded up their equipment and disappeared into the mountains. The next day the same health officials found on their path the bodies of five Anorroes Indians who had been guides across the *selva* for the strange "geologists."

That was the beginning of Operation Bolívar, which under the command of Che Guevara was designed to bring about revolution in Bolivia, Paraguay, Argentina, and Brazil. This Pan-American guerrilla front would be the first of the three or four Vietnams which Che, using Castro as an intermediary, had asked for, first at the Tricontinental Congress and then at the OLAS.

The antimalaria team thought it its duty to warn the military authorities at Camiri. But the latter, members of the 4th Division, were not impressed. It is likely that they had received orders "to keep hands off." No doubt these orders had come from General

Barrientos or from General Alfredo Ovando, commander in chief of the army, who were passing on the instructions of their American advisers.

A few days later, on the frontier between Bolivia and Paraguay, two Red Cross doctors ran into another group of some twenty armed men wearing olive drab. These men said they were "zoologists," but they showed interest in what the inhabitants of the Santa Cruz region thought of the political situation. Like the first group, this one was mostly composed of foreigners—Argentines or Cubans. Everybody moved off in the direction of Casa de Calamina. The doctors in turn informed the authorities—with no results. When all the groups were to meet in the mountains above Río Ñancahuazú, the guerrilla force would have about 120 men, never more.

In Camiri, people began to wonder about Coco Peredo's many guests; so the army announced, well in advance, that it would search Casa de Calamina. Of course, it turned up nothing.

One day a man called Vargas came to see Colonel Rocha, who was in charge of the zone. Vargas was a petroleum worker in Lagunillas, but he also grew vegetables on the banks of the Río Ñancahuazú at a spot where the river ran into the mountain and had worn out a narrow gorge. For some time now, small groups of armed men had regularly been coming down from the mountain to buy his produce. He was put off less by their weapons than by their foreign accents; like most Indians, he tended to xenophobia.

Colonel Rocha was forced to investigate; there was much talk in the region, and the presence of some hundred men willing to pay two or three times the going price for supplies they needed was beginning to strain the local economy. The petroleum workers in Camiri lived among themselves; they had their own stores and their own canteens. The colonel sent a patrol, guided by Vargas, to the entrance of the gorge from which the men generally came. They fell into an ambush; Vargas and an officer were killed. The ambush was so smoothly executed it might have been rehearsed many times. After their weapons and boots were taken from them, the wounded soldiers were well treated and taken care of.

That was on March 9, 1967. Coco Peredo suddenly disappeared from Camiri, but the Bolivian authorities took their time reacting.

Two weeks later, on March 23, an all but unarmed detachment repairing a path in the Iripití region was surprised by guerrillas. A captain and two lieutenants were killed, but the survivors were all treated well. Among them were two high-ranking officers of the engineering corps. One of them, Major Sánchez, declared afterward that all the guerrillas they had come into contact with were foreigners, a sort of "international brigade." An experienced doctor took excellent care of their wounds. During the two days they were with the guerrillas there was no lack of propaganda sessions. The enlisted men were told that no harm was intended them, that on the contrary the guerrillas had come to free them; the officers were told that they ought to join the guerrillas and help free the country from American imperialism. Major Sánchez was to show himself properly grateful. He later visited Régis Debray in his cell and not only prevented the civilians from lynching him, but intervened to prevent more of the harsh treatment to which Debray had been exposed.

Surprised by this unexpected appearance of the army—an appearance that may not have been desired either in La Paz or by the Southern Command—the guerrillas installed in the Camirina *finca* or in neighboring camps had to move out. Formed into two columns, they tried to reach the shelter of the forest as quickly as possible and without running into government troops. It was another stroke of bad luck that led them to tangle with the detachment including the three Bolivian officers. The soldiers of the 4th Division were now put on the alert, but they had no heart for this difficult war of jungle terrain, gorges, poisonous spiders, snakes, oozing water, and sticky mud.

The Ranger units specially trained for this jungle warfare by the experts in Panama were not to intervene until much later. Obviously the Bolivian government, and especially the U.S. secret services, had for some time known what was going on at the *finca*. (The name of one of their spies is already known.) They followed the affair from Cuba, from Argentina, and from Brazil. They let the abscess grow, and it drew into this triangle of forest all the Latin-American revolutionaries who had come to enlist under Che's banner.

Now that operations had begun, American "advisers" were present in the Santa Cruz area of Bolivia. After the first skirmish on March 9, the guerrillas were left in peace in an attempt to reassure them. But it was too late. The guerrillas knew that now that they were discovered, flight was their only recourse.

When the Bolivian army occupied the *finca*, only a short distance away they found a well-camouflaged guerrilla encampment. Reporters were invited to inspect it. There were some wooden barracks of basic but solid construction, a vegetable garden, an oven for baking bread, and even a kind of small amphitheater—like those of the Vietcong—for courses in political indoctrination and sessions of autocriticism. The army also found uniforms that seemed to have been made in Havana, and propaganda material—tracts that included translations of speeches by General Giap. There were also piles of photos of Che Guevara, some of them dating back to the days in which he was in the Sierra Maestra with Fidel Castro. It was these photos that the Bolivians were to present to the OAS in Washington as proof that Che was in Bolivia.

The fighting continued sporadically. According to reports, the guerrillas had formed into two columns, one of which was headed toward Muyupampa, the other toward Iripití. In the course of new skirmishes, several of the guerrillas were killed. They had worn the olive-drab uniform of the Castroites and had been armed with rifles and automatic weapons of Soviet and Czech origin.

On Thursday, April 20, about five miles from Muyupampa,

some forty guerrillas appeared. Getting in touch with the priest, the doctor, and the subprefect of the region, they promised not to attack the village if they were given food and medicine. After three hours of discussion, an agreement was reached. But the peasants warned the army, and planes came to strafe the area that had been fixed as a rendezvous. At this point the police found three unarmed foreigners, who said they were journalists, wandering near the village of Muyupampa. They were the Argentine Fructuoso, really Bustos; the Englishman George Roth; and Régis Debray, who had on him a French passport, $2,600, and a driver's license. All three were locked in the local prison, but were not mistreated. Then a complete blackout followed.

Che Guevara's diary shows that he was always suspicious of the population. He reported his lack of confidence in his namesake, Moisés Guevara, and in the miners he had brought with him. These miners were soon to abandon him, as did the few communists, who were now deprived of their leader: Coco Peredo had recently been killed.

On October 12, Régis Debray declared in Camiri, "I had asked Guevara to let me join the guerrillas but he had refused, saying that my duty was to reveal the existence of the revolution and to spread revolutionary ideas. I had wanted to be treated as a guerrilla; I did many of the things they did, I had gone hunting, I had been on guard duty both inside and outside the camp. I had also asked to be assigned a number, as the others had been—a number used to check on those going in and out of the camp—but I had not participated in any fighting. If I had been a guerrilla, I would never have left them without arms and been arrested at Muyupampa. But even though I never fought, I fully share the ideas of Che and the guerrillas."

For three weeks, from March 23, 1967, until their capture, Régis Debray and Bustos followed the guerrillas, who had abandoned their encampment and gone into the *selva*. They marched continuously; the painter and the philosopher, neither of whom had had any training or had ever held a weapon, fell behind. In reference to Régis Debray, Che Guevara noted, "I have assigned him a mission for the guerrillas,"—a gentle army technique for getting rid of a willing soldier who can't keep up.

George Roth, a photographer and journalist who had often worked for *Life*, then appeared on the scene. He had first followed the operations from the army side; then to complete his reporting job he had joined the guerrillas. For a few pesos, a peasant agreed to guide him to the guerrilla camp. This was somewhat unsettling because the same peasant might just as easily have guided an army detachment. Ten hours after the journalist's arrival, Che Guevara expelled him along with Debray and Bustos. Captured in the company of a press correspondent well known to the army, Debray and Bustos might with some luck have been able to pass for journalists and get away with it. But that was forgetting—as Régis Debray had forgotten in his book, as Fidel Castro and Guevara had forgotten in their plans—that the adversary they faced was the United States, its army, its secret services—American organization and efficiency. In addition, the entire apparatus of the orthodox Communist parties was to be brought into play against them.

The day after my arrival in La Paz it was announced that Régis Debray had been transported to Camiri, the military headquarters of the antiguerrilla zone. He was still with the Englishman and the Argentine. But the authorities refused any sort of authorization to enter that zone. The next day at ten o'clock, Ambassador Dominique Ponchardier, the correspondent of Agence France-Presse, Bianchi, and myself were to be received by Chief of State Barrientos. We wanted to ask him for authorization to see the prisoner. Normally such authorization would have been granted, but after we had waited half an hour in the chilly palace, the general sent his excuses and put off our meeting until four o'clock that afternoon. Finally the meeting was canceled *sine die*.

To understand what had happened, we will have to know something about René Barrientos* and the motives that led him to behave in what was often a disconcerting manner. It would be a mistake to take the Bolivian chief of state for one of those blood-thirsty narrow-minded, and pitiless *caudillos* that have long symbolized Latin America for the rest of the world. Brought to power by intrigue and violence, the latter exploited their countries as though these lands were private property—before they were overthrown, exiled, shot, or hanged from a lamppost. Bolivia had had about a hundred dictators of that sort. The race has now almost entirely disappeared. Trujillo and Batista were among the last. Only one still anachronistically survives, Nicaragua's Tachito Somoza.

Barrientos belonged to another breed. Rather tall, thin, large-shouldered, regular-featured, with an almost childishly soft skin stretched over high cheekbones that showed the Indian influence of his mother's side of the family, a clear-eyed gaze capable of suddenly growing hard, short hair with a few unruly locks, always dressed in an immaculate air force officer's uniform, he appeared to have sprung full grown from the imagination of a Hollywood scriptwriter.

I saw him once as he got out of a plane on his return from the guerrilla zone. He had a silk scarf around his neck, and his aides-de-camp were young and casual. One of them had a small pantherlike animal on a leash. Barrientos was both sensitive and passionate. In his native Cochabamba, during the election campaign, he made speeches in Quechua which aroused Indians known for their passivity and resignation. In the subsequent tumult of drums and flutes, covered with confetti, he was lifted

---

* He was killed in a helicopter crash in April, 1969.

onto their shoulders. He was so moved that tears rolled down his cheeks as he waved his hands in greeting. In five years he escaped seven or eight assassination attempts. One man fired point-blank into his chest, shattering a pilot's insignia that diverted the bullet, but several of the splinters lodged in his chest. Barrientos made it a point of honor to personally test the fighter planes bought from the United States on long-term credit. During the training cycle of a parachutist unit, two men plummeted to the ground when their chutes failed to open. There was talk of negligence or sabotage. Barrientos took the first handy parachute, went up in a plane, and jumped.

René Barrientos saw himself as having a mission. During his childhood in a Franciscan orphanage, he dreamed of going into the Church. He went into the army and directed his peasant leagues with the same faith. He often reminded people of one of his predecessors, Germán Busch—the angel-faced dictator torn between a thirst for purity and a taste for pleasure and drink—who committed suicide in 1939, disillusioned by his own failure and by his responsibility for the corruption that surrounded him.

Barrientos had been proud to see his country spared guerrilla activity at a time when the Peruvian army was pitilessly hunting the guerrillas in the sierra, when Argentina was trying those arrested at Salta, when the political emissaries were trying to organize the *bandoleros* of the *violencia* in Colombia, when the troops of Douglas Bravo were operating in several provinces of Venezuela, and when César Montes was taking over from Turcios as head of the Fuerzas Armadas Revolucionarias in the Sierra de las Minas in Guatemala. He felt he had nothing to learn about revolution from Castroism or communism. He had been one of the first militants of the National Revolutionary Movement (MNR), a heteroclite group with a revolutionary program for the nationalization of the mines and the confiscation and division of large landholdings. He had fought alongside miners armed only with sticks of dynamite. He had gone to find Víctor Paz Estenssoro, the leader of the movement, in his Argentine exile, and brought him back to La Paz aboard his plane, flying at more than thirteen thousand feet after passing through an antiaircraft barrage. He had then traveled for three years in the United States and in Europe—to undergo psychiatric treatment, say his enemies; to learn his business as a soldier and a politician, say his friends.

He returned to help in the creation of a new army composed entirely of revolutionary elements. Having no faith in the political demagogy of Paz Estenssoro, he had become vice president to help the revolution keep its dynamism. The president's unwillingness to have Barrientos alongside him was overruled by the popular enthusiasm intensified by the first assassination attempt against him.

In his post as vice president, powerless to modify Paz Estenssoro's policy, Barrientos—with the approbation, it is said, of the mysterious American Colonel Fox, itinerant South American agent of the Pentagon and the CIA—prepared the coup d'etat that overthrew the president. While Barrientos was trying to win the support of his army comrades in Cochabamba, and while mobs demonstrated in the streets and fought with the police, General Alfredo Ovando Candia, the chief of staff, persuaded the president that all was lost and that he had just time enough to flee. The trick succeeded. General Ovando accompanied Paz Estenssoro to his plane, let him get in, and then slammed the door and went to join Barrientos, with whom he had plotted from the beginning.

Barrientos was given photocopies of the papers that Debray had been carrying. The political affair was becoming a personal matter, for the immediate family of the president was compromised by a letter of accreditation which his brother-in-law, Marcelo Galindo, had given to Régis Debray. Régis Debray had therefore taken personal advantage of Barrientos, and this was a serious matter. Régis Debray was officially declared a common law offender.

General de Gaulle himself wrote to General Barrientos to make sure that the prisoner would be judged by an ordinary military tribunal and not by a special one, automatically precluding a death sentence.

At the beginning of his trial, Régis Debray stood by his initial declarations. He had never participated in the guerrilla front; he was only a journalist who had come to investigate the situation. But under the seal of secrecy he told his lawyer that he had seen Che Guevara and that it had been Guevara whom he had come to interview. The lawyer lost no time in revealing this information to the world, probably to help Debray by emphasizing that his mission in Bolivia was only to write a sensational article.

In the dark laundry room that serves as a morgue for the Hospital of the Knights of Malta in Vallegrande, on a small cement washtub covered with a board, lay the half-nude, formaldehyde-stinking body of a man riddled with bullets.

There were no windows, and an ominous light came from the half-open door. The long-haired, bearded corpse, dressed only in a pair of olive-drab pants of the type worn by all the guerrillas, was that of a certain Comandante Ramón who strangely resembled Ernesto Che Guevara.

The hands and feet of the corpse were unusually well cared for, which was surprising in a man who had just spent several months in the *selva*, and who had never been known for personal cleanliness. Even though there now seems to be no doubt that Comandante Ramón and Che Guevara are one and the same, there are a certain number of troubling facts.

His friends sometimes used to call him Pithecanthropus Erectus. His teeth are in perfect state even though they were always known to be very bad.

On Sunday, October 9, at five o'clock the body had been tied to the skids of a helicopter and brought from La Higuera, where Che is supposed to have died. It was embalmed in the presence of army chief General Ovando and a hospital nun by a bald-headed American doctor belonging to the Green Berets. A liter of formaldehyde had been injected into the jugular artery so that the body would be preserved for a month.

Two years previously he had disappeared and then reappeared everywhere while the Cuban propaganda apparatus was presenting him as the "coordinator" of revolution on a continental level.

In August he had even been elected "honorary" president of the OLAS, the Organization of Latin-American Solidarity, which under this cautious label hid its real goal: to win over all revolutionaries to the theses of Fidel Castro and make them accept as their sole commander the man who through many ups and downs had remained his faithful lieutenant—Che Guevara.

He lay there at the edge of this big colonial village of Vallegrande which was crushed under the heavy, humid heat of the nearby *selva*. On the ground were two other corpses, that of a Bolivian known as El Moro, and a Peruvian known as El Chino. Their bodies had not been as carefully "prepared" as that of their leader. They stank and were horrible to look at.

Driven more by curiosity than anything else, the entire local population had filed past the bodies. Except for those who had hunted him down, who—in this disinherited region—knew who Che was? His violent death neither surprised nor frightened any of them. Sometimes the army killed; more often they killed one another when they had drunk too much, or when life suddenly seemed unbearable.

Nevertheless, a peasant crossed himself and said as he looked at the three corpses, "God forgive me, but he looks like Christ between the two thieves."

Then came the reporters with their notebooks and old photographs of Che, with their cameras and their flash equipment. They had been flown in from La Paz aboard an old army Dakota. They could not believe they were looking at Che, the man who had been killed and come back to life so often, that "vagabond of the revolution" who had become a symbol, a myth, a legend, and

254 / THE GUERRILLAS

who had ended his turbulent career so stupidly, so wretchedly, a few miles from this small town in a canyon of the Churo. They were all heartsick as they listened to these officers who had carefully dressed and shaved for the occasion, and who now eloquently explained in great detail why there was no doubt that it really was Che Guevara. They seemed to be promoting the corpse as though it were a detergent. Alongside them stood a silent man whose uniform bore no rank or army insignia, but whose general appearance fooled no one: an American Green Beret from Panama. He too had come to make sure that the enemy was really dead, or maybe he had come to see what use his students would make of the corpse. When he was questioned in English, he pretended not to understand. *"No entiendo."* Then he left. But a Bolivian officer was to tell the reporters that the man was an American instructor from the school in Santa Cruz.

The reporters found this wretched and macabre display hard to take, and they felt the same way about the childish pleasure of these officers who had unconsciously destroyed a part of themselves, who had, in shooting Che, destroyed their own revolt against poverty, injustice, and United States control. But the reporters had to admit that it was really Ernesto Guevara. The correspondent of Agence France-Presse wrote, "An error in identification seems impossible."

The death of Che—like his entire life—nevertheless continued to be surrounded by mystery.

In this affair, as well as in the trial of Régis Debray and in the communiqués published on the progress of the antiguerrilla struggle, the officers and chiefs of the Bolivian army had always behaved in a disconcerting manner. Their notions of the usages and customs of justice seemed as strange as their notions of reporting information. They facilely contradicted one another, became hypnotized by points of detail, neglected the essentials, and at the same time seemed driven by motives completely foreign to the rest of us.

The reporters lost confidence in the Bolivian military men,

despite the latters' disordered and rather touching efforts to present their country, their regime, and their way of making war and rendering justice in a favorable light. They even began to be suspicious of this much-too-well-prepared corpse. For example, General Ovando, leader of the Bolivian army and right arm as well as brains of the president of the republic, told me while I was in Bolivia that there were at least four hundred guerrillas. Today, with the same assurance, he says that there had never been more than sixty, and that that's what he had always said. Actually, there were 120.

When he had announced in the beginning of October that a large Ranger force trained for antiguerrilla fighting by the Green Berets had encircled a group of guerrillas commanded by a man called Ramón, but who was really Che, nobody paid any particular attention. Che had already been "killed" two or three times. Hadn't Régis Debray declared that Guevara had left Bolivia after he had interviewed him in the Ñancahuazú area?

But two guerrillas had surrendered, and one of them, Antonio Domínguez Flores, gave the military quite a bit of detailed information. According to him, Che had been stricken by illness since September and could only get around astride a mule. He no longer cared about anything and showed complete contempt for his own security. He had no more than sixteen men with him.

Domínguez Flores indicated the precise area in which Che was. According to a special correspondent of *The New York Times* it was a kind of canyon, the Quebrada del Yuro. The interior and the borders were covered with very dense vegetation, but the upper part was bare, a factor that made it impossible to escape without being spotted. It was an area in which dust and insect bites turned all human skin into a cloak of misery. The hopelessly tangled vegetation, dry and thorn-covered, made it impossible to move anywhere except along the closely guarded paths and riverbeds. The eight hundred men of the 2nd Ranger Battalion had been sent here against Che.

This time the guerrillas were dealing with specialists in guerrilla warfare rather than *altiplano* Indians doing their military service nine thousand feet below their usual habitat and stupefied by this change of climate. The officers of the battalion had been trained in Panama, the men in Bolivia by the Green Berets, who accompanied the expedition and saw to its radio liaison, its supplies, and its contact with the air force.

The lead company of the battalion was commanded by a Captain Prado Salmón.

Che wrote in his diary:

October 6: Reconnaissance showed that we had a house nearby. . . . We went there and cooked all day under a big rock ledge that served as a roof. . . . Because supper was delayed, we determined to leave early in the morning for a tributary close to this little stream and then make a more exhaustive reconnaissance to determine the direction to take. . . . The Chilean radio gave a censored news report indicating that there were 1,800 men in the zone. . . .

October 7: Our guerrilla organization has lived eleven months without complications. . . . At 12:30 an old woman shepherding her goats came into the canyon in which we were camped and we had to hold her. The woman told us nothing we could believe about the soldiers, she just kept saying that she did not know anything and that she had not been there for a long time. She merely gave us information about the roads and from it it seems that we are about one league from Higuera, one league from Jagüey, and about six leagues from Pucará. At 5:30, Inti, Aniceto and Pablito went to the old woman's house where she had two daughters, one crippled and the other half-dwarfed. They gave her 50 pesos and asked that she keep quiet about this, but they put little faith in her promises. The 17 of us set out . . . leaving many traces in the canyon. There are no houses nearby but there are potato fields irrigated by the same stream. At 2 we stopped to rest since there was no point in going farther. . . .

The army put out strange information about 250 men in Serrano to contain those encircled. It said there were 37 of us. . . .

Although that old woman did not betray Che and his comrades, another peasant woman did.

Major Miguel Ayoroa, commander of the Ranger Battalion, told Franco Pierini, of Italy's *L'Europeo*:

> The commander of the division had ordered the area along the San Antonio River to be swept. We had been marching for two days, combing the terrain bit by bit. We had covered about ten miles in two days. On Sunday morning, a woman working in a field above the Quebrada del Yuro told a patrol that she had heard voices below in the gorge where the Churo spills into the San Antonio. Captain Prado then organized the operation and sent two platoons onto the mountain where the two rivers begin. Then at noon he started out with another platoon and went up the San Antonio. Between one and two o'clock, the platoon going up the river ran into the guerrillas.

It was Sunday, October 8, at approximately one-thirty in the afternoon. The following is the report of Captain Prado, commander of the company:

> . . . I heard the first burst at about one thirty. It was one of our own guns. I immediately heard other arms return fire and understood that we had established contact. They weren't going to escape. I was not at all worried because I had done everything to make them fall into the trap. I moved out in their direction. The first one we saw, and whom we afterward killed, was a man called Willy. He was a good shot; he'd shoot at us and then disappear. We were about 150 feet apart. The second man I saw was Guevara. We immediately began firing.
>
> *Pierini:* But you still didn't know it was Guevara?
>
> *Prado:* No, not yet. One of our bursts had gotten him in the leg. Willy tried to put him on his back and carry him up the mountain, but I had other men stationed higher up. The fight started again. One burst sent Che's beret flying into the air. Afterward we found out that he had again been wounded in the leg as well as in the chest. Willy set Guevara down on the ground. My men called to him to

surrender, but instead of answering, Willy picked up his weapon and started to fire. My men cut him down. He was stone dead. Guevara was in our hands. . . .

We continued to fight until nightfall. We had killed six of them, had taken Guevara alive, but ten had managed to escape. . . . Later, when it was all over, I spoke to Guevara. It was he who told me who he was. He knew that we were a special Ranger unit. He asked me if I had been trained in Panama with the American Marines. You could see that he was in great pain. He couldn't move. At first he tried to stand, but he couldn't manage it. We had to carry him in a blanket.

Pierini: Did you see a wound on Guevara's chest near his heart?

Prado: I didn't count his wounds. I know that people say we killed him, but it isn't true. We are soldiers, not judges. . . . When I captured him he was wounded.

Pierini: Mortally?

Prado: I don't know. I'm not a doctor. At first it didn't seem too serious to me. He talked about the guerrillas and I reminded him that since March he had killed about fifty soldiers and a good number of officers. He answered by talking about the miners who had been massacred.

The following is the testimony of Benito Giménez, a soldier who had been wounded in the fight. He was in the shed at La Higuera, where Che too had been brought.

It was Colonel Selnich [the Ranger commander] who spoke most with Che Guevara. We wounded soldiers and Guevara were all in the big shed. He was on a sort of stretcher at the other end and it was hard to understand what he was saying, but we could hear the colonel distinctly. He was shouting. Then he told Che that he was the leader of bandits, that he had killed a lieutenant whom he, the colonel, had loved like his own son. They talked about America. Colonel Selnich stayed with Che Guevara a long time. Two hours or more. They argued about something the colonel wanted to know and that Guevara refused to tell him. Then Guevara slapped him with his right hand. The colonel had been sitting on a chair and bending forward, and Guevara's slap caught him right in the mouth. After that the colonel got up and left.

Second Lieutenant Tomás Toty Aguilera said:

. . . I took care of his wounds when he was brought here. I'm not a doctor, but he is and he told me what to do. No, he had no heart wound. He had two near his shoulders, but none in the heart. I was ordered to take care of him until about ten in the evening, then in the morning I saw a helicopter take him away. Colonel Selnich stayed talking to Guevara quite a while, and there were also some intelligence officers. A lot of people were coming and going.

But it was a corpse that the helicopter carried off on the morning of October 9. During the night, orders had come from La Paz to execute Che Guevara.

Drs. Moisés Abraham Baptista and José Martínez Caso, who examined the corpse after it was brought to Vallegrande, declared, "He must have been dead some five hours, because the body was still warm."

We can more or less set the execution of Ernesto Che Guevara at between nine-thirty and ten o'clock on the morning of October 9.

It was the La Paz correspondent of *The New York Times* who raised the embarrassing question. A young Bolivian soldier belonging to the Ranger platoon that had skirmished with the guerrilla group told him that Captain Prado was the one who fired the bullet into his heart after a machine-pistol burst had wounded Che in the legs.

One of the noncommissioned officers in Prado's company said that after Che was wounded in the legs, "Willy managed to get Che out of the ravine while the other guerrillas continued the fight to cover the wounded man's retreat. Willy carried Guevara as far as the hill and then ran into four Rangers. Panting with effort, Willy carried his leader on his shoulders as far as the top of the hill. When he stopped to rest and tend to Che Guevara, the soldiers waiting in ambush ordered him to surrender. The guerrilla picked up his carbine, but he never got to fire. The soldiers riddled him with a burst of bullets. Then Che shouted to the soldiers, 'Don't kill me, I'm Che Guevara.' "

Willy has been identified as being Simón Cuba, the former leader of the Huanuni district. The soldiers who reached Che looked after him. His wounds were serious, and because of his asthma he couldn't breathe. After the fight was over and the bodies of the soldiers who had been killed were evacuated, Captain Prado ordered Che to be brought to a place where a helicopter could land and take him to Vallegrande. Che's condition was growing worse, and it was impossible to give him any immediate aid because the soldiers had no doctor with them. Lying in a blanket, Che was carried as far as La Higuera. He reached there as night fell, and the helicopter had already left for Vallegrande with the wounded and the bodies of the dead soldiers. "I'm in great pain. Please do something to dull the pain," Che asked the 2nd lieutenant who had given him some immediate first aid. The lieutenant did so under the direction of Guevara himself, who told him: "Here, on the chest, please. I'm in great pain."

In spite of this care, Che could not hold out. He spent all Sunday night moaning. He died Monday morning. Actually, he was helped to his death.

Time magazine reported that, informed of the capture of Guevara, the Bolivian authorities met in La Paz and asked themselves what was to be done with him. Since the death penalty did not exist in Bolivia, the worst that Che could get was prison, maybe after a long trial, loud propaganda from the entire communist world, and the possibility that other guerrillas might intervene in Bolivia. The next morning orders went out to La Higuera to execute Che.

In lieu of a funeral oration, General Ovando made the following statement: "The guerrilla adventure has ended just as any mad adventure must end. Its failure is due to the total absence of popular support and the aridity of the terrain chosen."

Killing Che or his ghost has not killed revolution in Latin America. In the course of a skirmish, a man, Dr. Ernesto Guevara de la Serna, got eight bullets in his chest, was taken prisoner, and was finished off the next morning with a bullet in the heart "to avoid complications." But the myth of Che is very much alive. Some day soon all the starving wretches and those who dream of change will affirm that he was never killed and that he never can be while they are alive.

On the other hand, what may very well have been killed, to the great joy of all orthodox communists in Latin America, is Castroism as a guerrilla technique and a political ideology.

It has been proven that the Sierra Maestra can never be recreated outside of Cuba, that the Cuban Revolution was an exceptional phenomenon which will never reappear in the same form, and—alas!—that revolution today can never succeed on the basis of romanticism and improvisation.

Chile's Foreign Minister, Gabriel Valdés, said to *L'Express* on the day Che's death was announced: "I do not understand how a man as talented, as brilliant, a man with so much experience in the guerrilla movement, only managed after two and a half years to form a small group of barely 120 guerrillas lost in the jungle. The undertaking did not measure up to the man."

Che should have directed his revolution from Cuba, by means of liaison agents and clandestine radios—as was done during the French Resistance—or even from a safe spot in a city in Argentina or Uruguay. He should have been made to do so, even if it went against his grain. But maybe Che could no longer remain in Cuba. He had been obliged to leave because he had become an undesirable. He was not a courtier or a government man, and all governments, even revolutionary ones, quickly become courts and nests of intrigue. This "vagabond anarchist" was too independent, too insolent, and too autocratic.

All these Cubans, these Peruvians, these Argentines, who tried to mount a model guerrilla front in Bolivia—a country that had barely gotten over a revolution—were supported by only a few students in La Paz and a few miners in Oruro. They established themselves in a zone where they were unknown, and where the only possible response of the local population was suspicion and hostility. They were "foreigners." It was a foolish waste of energy to behave this way, since in Latin America the feeling of nationalism is stronger than anything else. The peasants and the Indians gave information to the army. They were not even nationalists— they hadn't reached that stage; they were simply xenophobes. They hated change and all those who came to stir up their wretchedness. But still, they would get the twenty thousand-peso reward promised for Che's head.

Finally, and more seriously, Che as well as Fidel Castro—or Régis Debray, who was merely their spokesman—made a great mistake in underestimating the enemy. The United States has woven on this continent a spider web in which many flies will still be caught. It has reorganized, disciplined, and trained all the South American armies, and in a few years it has turned them from comic-opera armies into skilled anti-insurgent instruments trained in the techniques of psychological warfare.

The revolution will have more trouble triumphing than the revolutionary optimists in Cuba think. They cannot hope to accomplish their goal by methods that have more to do with adventure novels than with revolutionary realism. They will have to learn to be less self-satisfied and more serious if they do not want to disappear and leave the scene to their adversaries—the orthodox communists who without fanfare, and using methods perfected over half a century, do a considerably more efficient job.

Nevertheless, the revolution is not dead, for all the abuses Che fought against remain: injustice, poverty, unequal distribution of land, hunger, disease, illiteracy, the colonels, the oligarchies, the political bosses, the professional politicians, and all the rest.

It is impossible to have for so long taken an interest in a man like Che, to have gathered so much testimony about him from his friends and enemies, without ending by either detesting him or loving him.

Che, the man of flesh and blood, was killed in Vallegrande; but for me, the other man, the man who several years ago wrote to his parents: "Dear Folks, once more I feel Rosinante's ribs between my heels," is still alive. This Don Quixote who believed too much in the goodness of man and who was made use of by all those who doubted, remains for me, for men of my type and age, the symbol of our nostalgia for our lost illusions.

It was not only to the north of Vallegrande that Ernesto Che Guevara was killed by a Bolivian Ranger unit trained by Green Berets from Panama. In his letter to his parents he wrote: "I am like a cat, I have seven lives." Like a cat he was killed seven times.

He was killed first in Cuba, in obedience to the pragmatic demands of governing which leads a country to get rid of its authentic revolutionaries as soon as the revolution is over. The revolution then becomes a matter of speeches, pomp, parades, committees, parties, intrigues—but also of plans, administration, and bureaucracy. This sort of thing had no appeal for Che. He left Cuba because he had such an absolute and vast conception of revolution that he endangered the very existence of the country where revolution had just succeeded.

He attacked the Russians, those who were lending the money necessary to a country that could not survive unless it was supported by one of the great powers. He accused Russia of having become middle class, of having lost its ideals, of having ceased to believe in Communist Man, of trying only to become like North America, with the same faults, the same successes, and the same efficiency.

He attacked Cuba's old Communist party, which had collaborated with Batista and survived by all sorts of compromises.

He attacked Fidel Castro himself, who from a popular leader

and a revolutionary commander was turning into a *caudillo*, even if on occasion that *caudillo* continued to behave like a true revolutionary according to Che's lights—in other words, a utopian revolutionary who wanted to change not only institutions, but man himself.

Perhaps at his own request, Che was stripped of all the attributes of a successful revolutionary—his post as minister, his rank of *comandante*, his Cuban nationality—and once more went off astride Rosinante. But the man of the Sierra Maestra had been killed.

He was killed in Santo Domingo when the United States intervened under a phony pretext and landed its Marines with impunity. Nobody could stop it from, as it said, "cleaning house." Latin America clenched its fists in secret but dared not show them. Russia was silent, and so was the rest of the world. All they did was protest, which was just another way of remaining silent. There was no revolutionary floodtide, no revolt, and the sons of the conquistadores once more bent their backs before the Boston Bible merchants.

The United States knew that it could intervene with impunity at any point where the revolution desired by Che might spring up again as it had in Cuba.

Like Bolívar, Che had hoped to unite the Latin-America countries and free them from the American yoke. What had been needed was not a single uprising in Santo Domingo, but two, three, or four Vietnams simultaneously, so that the United States would have had to disperse its forces.

He failed in this too, and that was how he was killed a third time. Inside the very countries where guerrilla fronts had managed to survive, the antagonistic groups had been unable to reach agreement. How then could he unite them? In Guatemala, Yon Sosa's Trotskyites and César Montes' Castroite communists, exhausted after having sold out and betrayed one another, barely had the strength to draw together, perhaps only to grapple with one another and betray one another once more under the technically interested eye of the Southern Command's Panama specialists.

In Colombia, the communist FAR broke all contact with the Castroites, refused them the support of the oil unions, and forced them in order to survive to look to Cuba for arms and supplies.

In Venezuela the orthodox Communist party worked with the government to get rid of Castroism within the university as well as in Douglas Bravo's front. In Cuba it is said that the Communist party betrayed to the army that group of Cuban officers who one night landed on the coast to reinforce the guerrillas.

Machado's daughter, speaking in the name of her father, Old Machado, accused Fidel Castro of having liquidated Che Guevara. But hadn't Machado and his followers morally participated in the liquidation of the Argentine revolutionary?

Che was killed for a fourth time in Moscow, when the leaders of the U.S.S.R. decided that guerrilla tactics in South America had to be abandoned in favor of the parties' classic struggle to reenter legal activities. They found that Cuba was costing them too much. The tone the Cuban revolution was taking was not to their liking. For the time being, they were leaving the field free to the United States, once more sacrificing the idea of revolution to the idea of party.

Things had to return to order, so Che—who said that everything important happens in disorder, and who was so suspicious of party lines and tactics—had to be killed.

He was killed a fifth time in the air-conditioned buildings of Panama's Escuela de las Américas. The Latin-American armies under the baton of American instructors were preparing to join forces within the structure of a Pan-American force, something the revolutionaries had been unable to manage. They were being taught "tricks" of jungle warfare and psychological warfare that would enable them to finish off a guerrilla front. These "tricks"— and even more his despair when he realized that others working under the banner of American order, American peace, the American dollar, might well realize his dream of union—killed Che, for at the same time his compatriots were accepting the rule of a foreign government, a government from another planet, a government that offered as a paradise and hope only "an American way of life" which could not have been more at odds with the Hispanic soul and the Latin-American temperament.

Che was killed a sixth time in La Paz—not in Vallegrande—when the Bolivian Communist party, after having promised him help, after having been let in on the entire operation, and after having gingerly participated by means of the Peredo brothers, suddenly abandoned him. He was slowly killed during his retreat —and after every meeting he himself wrote as much in his diary—when he felt the hostility of the Bolivian peasants he had come to liberate.

It remained only for Che to die a seventh time at the hands of a little officer who pressed his pistol against Che's heart and fired because he had received orders to do so.

A certain type of revolution died with Che—the revolution of Don Quixote, of youth and romanticism, of indignation and madness.

Fidel Castro and his partisans have been eliminated, or will be soon. It is both too bad and necessary. Necessary, because a man doesn't have the right to play at being the sorcerer's apprentice when he doesn't know how to use his wand. Too bad, because the Castroite revolution had a warm and comforting side that had been missing in Marxist revolutions up to that time. All that remains now are three forces.

1. The Armies. Supported, equipped, and supplied with leadership by the United States, these armies are not just concerned with repression, but more and more with civilian tasks. Either they will remain faithful to their masters, or perhaps another revolution will spring from them.

2. The Church. Though it leans on the existing Christian-

Democrat parties, it is trying to win over a young, revolutionary following. The Church remains an unknown. But both the priest and the officer—if they remain too long in contact with poverty and injustice—are easily converted to revolution and toss their collars or their epaulettes into the ditch.

3. The Communist parties. With the death of Che they hope to have gotten rid of the Castroite heresy and to be able to return to "unified" action. But they forget that they will lack the new blood that comes from youth. As the result of an over-concern with tactics they have become compromised with the governments and the police. They are old and outmoded; they belong to another age. Most often they propose only antiquated ideas and empty words. They are no longer what the Latin-American continent needs. Actually, they have ceased to be revolutionary.

Luckily, this land still has hope and dreams in its corner.

Because he tried to assume the mantle of Bolívar in a bad time and with faulty methods, Che is now dead. Others will try and others will fail. Only one need succeed. . . .

About the Author

Jean Lartéguy was born in Paris and took his Master of Arts degree in history from the University of Toulouse. He served with Free French forces in World War II and with the French Battalion in Korea. Rising from lieutenant to captain, he was wounded on Air Break Ridge in Korea and thus concluded his active combat service.

He has served as a war correspondent in Korea, Indochina, the Far East, Middle East, and North Africa. Since 1952 he has been a correspondent with *Paris-Presse.*

Among his many works of fiction and nonfiction are *Sauveterre,* a novel, *The Bronze Drums,* and a recently completed study of the Arab-Israeli confrontation and the guerrilla movement there.